THE SOCIAL
PSYCHOLOGY OF INDUSTRY

HUMAN RELATIONS IN THE FACTORY

J. A. C. BROWN

PENGUIN BOOKS

Penguin Books Ltd, Harmondsworth, Middlesex, England
Penguin Books Inc., 7110 Ambassador Road, Baltimore, Maryland 21207, U.S.A.
Penguin Books Australia Ltd, Ringwood, Victoria, Australia
Penguin Books Canada Ltd, 41 Steelcase Road West, Markham, Ontario, Canada
Penguin Books (N.Z.) Ltd, 182–190 Wairau Road, Auckland 10, New Zealand

—

First published 1954
Reprinted 1956, 1958, 1961, 1962 (twice), 1963, 1965, 1967, 1969,
1970 (twice), 1971, 1972, 1973, 1975

—

Copyright © the Estate of J. A. C. Brown, 1954

—

Made and printed in Great Britain
by C. Nicholls & Company Ltd
Set in Monotype Times

CONTENTS

EDITORIAL FOREWORD

INDUSTRIAL psychology, in its early days, nearly captured from economics the right to the title of the most dismal of the sciences. It vied with economics in giving the impression that by diligent and conscientious work the scientist could reduce the romantic story of man's technological achievements to a compact mass of dry-as-dust statistics. The figures produced by the industrial psychologists proved beyond all doubt that accidents and fatigue could be reduced, that output and earnings could be augmented, by the simplest of devices. Much of this could be done merely by changes in lighting, heating, and ventilation. Still more could be effected by changes in factory layout, by the redesign of machines, by time-and-motion study, and by more ingenious 'incentives'. Men could be scientifically trained to produce more and more by doing less and less; and they could do all this the more cheerfully to an accompaniment of music while they worked. But when the figures were all added up they somehow left the impression that the ultimate goal of these endeavours was the creation of an ideal factory fashioned in the style (to use the words of the author of this book) of a 'model cow-house' – the milch cows of which were, of course, the industrial workers.

The patient and placid cows were not impressed. To them it seemed all too true to be good. It seemed, too, to miss something out. The industrial psychologists and the scientific managers had to think again. They *did* think again and they thought to good effect. What was missing, they discovered first of all, was an adequate conception of the individual worker as an ordinary human being. Hitherto they had thought of workers in the mass as a vast number of little 'economic men' – each impelled by an irresistible inner force to seek the maximum wage at a minimum effort. True, it had long been known that men in battle or in love are moved to great endeavours by other and more eccentric motives; but this had been supposed to be one of the curiosities of life outside the province proper to the scientist. Still, being honest scientists, they took another look at human nature and at actual human motives. They discovered the individual human being. In the course of doing this they made a second discovery. They hit on 'the working group'. This, too, it might be said, was but another spectacular rediscovery of the obvious; but, after the event, so many revolutionary findings take on this appearance. That 'man is a social animal' had been taken so much for granted in general that no one had stopped to think what this might mean in particular situations. A new chapter in the history of industrial psychology was opened when the scientist began to inquire what was implied by the sociability of man in the workshop situation. The fact of 'informal organization' and of its impact upon the motivation of the individual then came as a blinding revelation. Industrial Psychology ceased to be a minor branch of applied physiology or of 'industrial engineering' and became a major branch of social psychology.

The redirection of scientific interest towards social issues happily coincided with a trend in industry towards greater mutual understanding than had hitherto been displayed between the two 'sides'. Enlightened management can no longer be accused of treating the worker as the milch cow of the system; and organized labour can no longer be said to lack interest in the problems of management. On both sides, too, there is a greater disposition to look at the needs of an industry with some regard to the needs of the community as a whole, and to think of that industry, whether nationalized or not, as a public service. Practical good sense, serviced by this new industrial psychology, may yet accomplish in a quiet way an industrial revolution as momentous as any industrial revolution in the past.

This new chapter in industrial psychology is still being written. It is a chapter full of promise. The story of the emergence of a brighter prospect is told in this book. It is told by one who enjoys a unique combination of qualifications to write it: impressive erudition, relevant practical experience in industry, and that humane understanding which alone can breathe freshness and life into the desiccated figures of research reports.

C. A. MACE

INTRODUCTION

The title of this book adequately indicates its scope. It is concerned basically with the emotional aspects of human inter-relationships in industry, and lays no claim to be a study of industrial psychology as such. Nor does it set out specifically to give practical details of what might be done to improve conditions in industry. What I have tried to do is to put forward for the consideration of the factory manager, the personnel manager, the time and motion engineer, and the interested layman certain fundamental aspects of 'human nature' and social organization which must be taken into account by anyone attempting to re-organize factory life.

In a book which touches on such varied subjects as psychology, history, medicine, anthropology, economics, and the practice of management, much of what is said will appear painfully elementary to those with expert knowledge of one or other of these subjects. I can only hope that it does not also appear erroneous.

J.A.C.B.

I

HISTORICAL RETROSPECT

SCIENTIFIC concern with the manual worker and his problems is of fairly recent origin, although scattered references to the subject may be traced back to quite early times. From the standpoint of industrial medicine, Paracelsus' monograph on *Miners' Sickness and Other Miners' Diseases*, published in 1567, is an important landmark, but the earliest text-book seems to have been the *Diseases of Tradesmen* by Bernardino Ramazzini (1633–1714). The industrial psychologist, too, may claim to have been represented in the sixteenth century. A book by one John Huarte written in Spanish and translated into English as *The Tryal of Wits* was the first attempt to discuss what is now known as vocational guidance. Huarte recognized that people vary both in general intelligence and in special abilities and recommended that an attempt should be made to discover each individual's special bent in order that he might be given the sort of training for which he was most suited. Important studies on work, movement, and fatigue were carried out by the physiologists Coulomb in the eighteenth century and Marey in the nineteenth. But modern industrial psychology could not begin until general psychology had become an experimental science, an event which dates from 1879 when Wilhelm Wundt at the University of Leipzig opened the first laboratory to be devoted to the scientific study of human behaviour.* Prior to this date, in spite of the work of such men as Weber, Fechner, and Helmholtz, psychology had been regarded as a branch of philosophy, and such information as was available was based on arm-chair theorizing or was the

* Text-books of psychology almost invariably attach great significance to the part played by Wundt in establishing scientific and experimental psychology. This does less than justice to our own Francis Galton (1822–1911), who not only founded the science of eugenics but devised new statistical methods for measuring individual differences, studied the inheritance of talent, and investigated mental imagery and the senses of hearing and smell.

result of more or less shrewd observation and intuition. The rapid advances in the physical sciences from the seventeenth century onwards had distracted scientific attention from more specifically human problems, and it was not until the early twentieth century that attempts were made to apply the new experimental psychology to the problems of industry. One of the first workers in this field (although he was not a trained psychologist), was an American Quaker from Philadelphia, Frederick Winslow Taylor, known by his colleagues as 'Speedy' Taylor.

As a student in college, Taylor was an enthusiastic member of the baseball team and he studied the technique of the game with the curiosity and ruthlessness which became typical of all his later ventures. He soon discovered that the method of bowling underhand then in general use was inefficient and proceeded to substitute the overhand method which, as he pointed out, 'got results'. When other players protested that overhand pitching was not provided for in the rules of the game, he insisted that, if this were so, the rules should be changed – to such effect that Taylor's method finally became the universal one. In tennis, too, he devised his own racket (a spoon-shaped one) which, however efficient it may have been, has not yet come to be accepted by the hide-bound traditionalists who play that game. Had Taylor's health remained good, he might have continued as nothing more than a thorn in the side of his fellow-sportsmen, but, when still at college, he began to have trouble with his eyesight and was advised by his physician to give up all thought of an academic career and instead to learn some sort of manual work for the sake of his health. Some years later, after undergoing various courses of training in technical subjects and gaining some experience in different types of job, Taylor became chief engineer at the Midvale Iron Works. In this position he found once more that the traditional ways of doing things are often inefficient, and that in industry, unlike sport, inefficiency costs money. He also noted that, whereas the industrialist has a clear idea of how much work he is entitled to expect from a machine, he has no comparable knowledge of the limits of efficiency of his workers. Obviously, if it were possible to estimate how much work a really capable worker could produce in a given operation working 'all out', the employer would then have a useful standard by which he could assess the efficiency of other employees doing the same job. The road would then be open to increase the efficiency and output of each worker, and, if the work were scientifically organized, this might well be done without a proportionately increased expenditure of energy. With this aim in view, Taylor proceeded to work on three basic principles:

(1) To select the best men for the job.
(2) To instruct them in the most efficient methods, the most economical movements, to employ in their work.
(3) To give incentives in the form of higher wages to the best workers.

These principles were first tested out in a famous experiment at the Bethlehem Steel Company, to which Taylor had meanwhile got himself appointed as 'Consulting Engineer in Management', the first of many to bear that title. There he had found that seventy-five labourers were each loading into railway trucks an average of 12½ tons of pig-iron a day. After careful observation of the operation, Taylor decided that it should be possible to get a really efficient worker to handle between 47 and 48 tons a day. The management of the company, when asked for an opinion, refused to believe that any worker could deal with more than 18 to 25 tons per day under any ordinary circumstances. Taylor then set out to prove the validity of his beliefs.

He selected for his purpose a Dutch worker who had been noted to be strong, industrious, and thrifty with his wages and asked him whether he wished to earn more money. When the man said that he did, Taylor told him that if he did exactly as he was instructed he would be paid according to the amount of work done. There was to be no argument, no 'back-talk', no initiative, nothing but the bare carrying out to the minutest detail what he had been ordered to do. When he was told to lift, he was to lift; when he was told to walk, he was to walk; when he was told to put the iron down, he was to put it down; when he was told to rest, he was to rest. By the end of the day, this labourer had loaded 47½ tons of pig-iron, and for the three years he was under observation he continued to load this amount and was paid 60 per cent higher than his former wage. The other workers were later trained in the same way, but it was found that, although their productive capacity went up appreciably, only one man in eight of the gang of seventy-five was capable of the effort of loading 47½ tons a day. Taylor also used his methods to increase the efficiency of men doing shovelling at the plant. The men were instructed in the most effective way to work, the shape of the shovels was altered according to the material to be dealt with, and incentives were applied in the form of higher wages for raised output. In such ways as these, the first efficiency engineer was able to decrease the number of workers needed to load wagons at the steel company from 500 to 140, increase daily earnings by 60 per cent, and save the firm about 75,000 dollars a year.

But there was another side to this success story. Taylor, who stood with his stop-watch over the workers, timing their rest-pauses and their every movement, altering the layout of the plant, and changing the traditional ways of doing things, was not very popular. Years later he wrote of this period of his life: 'I was a young man in years but I give you my word I was a great deal older than I am now, what with the worry, meanness, and contemptibleness of the whole damn thing. It's a horrid life for any man to live not being able to look any workman in the face without seeing hostility there, and a feeling that every man around you is your virtual enemy.' The movement which, as it now appears, Taylor had hoped would increase not only industrial efficiency but also the standard of living and the health of the worker was to appear to many workers as a form of exploitation, a means of increasing output for the benefit of the owners. Since the success of his work was measured in part by the number of workers who could be discarded when the new methods were applied, and Taylor himself took the view that 'all employees should bear in mind that each shop exists first, last, and all the time, for the purpose of paying dividends to its owners', the attitude of the workers is hardly surprising. The researches of Taylor and his successor Frank B. Gilbreth came to form the basis of what is now known as Time and Motion Study, while the professional psychologists studied for the most part such problems as fatigue and conditions of work or the devising of selection tests for vocational guidance. One of the most prominent of the latter group was Hugo Münsterberg, a former pupil of Wundt, who became professor of psychology at Harvard and published his *Psychology and Industrial Efficiency* in 1913. With the First World War of 1914–18, industrial psychology became of increasing practical importance, and in 1920 the National Institute of Industrial Psychology, a privately supported organization, was founded in Britain by C. S. Myers, a former director of the psychological laboratory at Cambridge. A government-sponsored body, the Industrial Fatigue Research Board (later known as the Industrial Health Research Board) was founded here about the same time. As in the case of Taylor's Time and Motion work, these early researches were often resented by the workers who considered that the psychologist was on the side of the employers and was concerned with increasing production rather than the general well-being. Professor J. C. Flugel writes in his book *A Hundred Years of Psychology* that 'although many of these pioneer studies enjoyed some real success, the early investigators, as is now pretty generally admitted, took a too crudely mechanistic view of their problems, stressed the factor of output too exclusively, and thus antagonized many of the workers, who looked upon the new methods merely as devices of their employers to get more work done at less cost to themselves'.

What, to the modern student, is most striking about this early work is not so much its specific content as the assumptions upon which it is based. It is clear that the psychologists and efficiency experts of this period had accepted the attitudes of management which arose during the early stages of the Industrial Revolution and these tended to form the background to all their investigations. Behind each experiment there lies the tacit implication that human nature is possessed of certain fixed properties which decree that most men find work distasteful, are naturally lazy, solely motivated by fear or greed (a motive now described as 'the carrot or the stick'), and always do as little work as possible for the largest possible wage. Economic man – for that strange perversion of human nature devised by the Physiocrats is the origin of this picture – is a rational creature who uses his reason primarily to calculate exactly how much satisfaction he may obtain from the smallest amount of effort, or when necessary, how much discomfort he can avoid. 'Satisfaction' does not mean pride in one's job, the feeling of having accomplished something, or even the regard of others; it refers only to money. Similarly 'discomfort' refers, not to failing in one's task, or losing the respect of one's comrades, but solely to the fear of starvation. Economic man is naturally competitive, basically self-interested, and in the battle of life strives hard to outwit every other man; so far from helping the weak or the underdog, his sole concern is with his own survival. Adam Smith writes thus of 'self-love, the governing principle in the intercourse of human society': 'It is not from the benevolence of the butcher, the brewer, or the baker, that we expect our dinner, but from their regard to their own interest. We address ourselves not to their humanity but to their self-love, and never talk to them of our own necessities but of their advantages. Nobody but a beggar chooses to depend chiefly upon the benevolence of his fellow-citizens.' Finally, the hypothesis assumes that man is a machine, a mechanism with (to placate the orthodox) a shadowy entity of a mind somehow attached to it. But the mind of the worker was not the concern of the employer – nor, to all appearances, was it a matter of any serious concern to the early industrial psychologist. The latter's idea of a good factory was one which produced the goods with maximum efficiency and minimum effort, although with the passage of time, when the worker's bodily health came to be tied up with the concept of efficiency, his ideal factory came to bear a close resemblance to a model cow-house. When lighting, heating, ventilation, humidity, and every other conceivable factor in the physical environment was so perfect, what right had the worker to grumble?

In the rest of this chapter we shall attempt to trace the origins of this view of mankind in which every detail is almost completely fallacious. There is no such thing as a fixed human nature, either good or bad, which determines minutely how people shall behave. There is no evidence that men are naturally competitive or self-interested, and there are many things which are more important to the worker than his wages. Human beings are not machines in any significant sense of the word, nor does a good physical environment, in itself, make them happy. In fact, any truth the picture may contain relates solely to the peculiar conditions in certain highly industrialized countries during the nineteenth and early twentieth centuries. Yet it is probably quite safe to say that the management of most factories and even a good deal of industrial psychology at the present day is still based on these outmoded assumptions. In the main, the questions the industrial psychologist asks himself tend to take such forms as, how to devise tests to select the best man for a given job, how to find whether he is working at full efficiency, how far his performance is affected by the temperature, lighting, humidity, and noise in the workshop, what are the causes of fatigue and how may they be eliminated by suitable rest-pauses, what are the effects of boredom, doing repetitive work, and so on. It need hardly be said that such work is important and that such investigations as have been carried out often give useful and valid results – *other things being equal*. But 'other things' are *not* always equal, as Elton Mayo discovered in his investigations at the Hawthorne plant. The worker is not an isolated machine producing results which vary only with his internal state of health and good or bad conditions of the physical environment. He is a human being who is also a member of a team. There is, for example, little point in selecting by the most irreproachable technique the 'best man for the job', if he cannot get on with his workmates. Good lighting and heating arrangements are small consolation if the relationships between workers and management are unsatisfactory, and every observant factory manager or supervisor knows the absurdity of supposing that, if four men can each as individuals shovel 25 tons of material a day, the four working together can shovel 100 tons. It may be that they *can* – but will they? The emphasis in industrial psychology has shifted from studies of the isolated individual and the physical environment to the consideration of motivation and morale. It is now clear that the most important single factor in determining output is the emotional attitude of the worker towards his work and his workmates. 'No men can act with effect who do not act in concert; no men can act in concert who do not act with confidence; no men can act in confidence who are not bound together with common opinions, common affections and common interests.' These words of Edmund Burke, the eighteenth-century politician, contain the keynote on which all modern research in industrial psychology must be based.

When we turn to the field of management, we soon discover that attempts are still being made to base discipline on bribes and threats, the carrot or the stick. But it is becoming increasingly evident that these sanctions are no longer so effective as they once were. There are, after all, limits to what can be done with financial incentives, and if discipline is to be based on threats, it is apparent that only two threats are available:

(1) The fear of unemployment.
(2) Government legislation against indiscipline.

Now (1) is no longer practicable, firstly because it seems certain that any future government of this country will be compelled, so far as possible, to maintain full employment, and secondly, because it is degrading, to say the least of it, to maintain an army of unemployed in order that others may be compelled to work harder. The alternative (2) has been used, for example, in the Soviet Union, where, it would appear, industry is regarded as a para-military force with state-approved systems of awards and punishments. But few people would be willing to apply this method here. The main problem facing industry today is how to apply the carrot and stick theory in a situation where jobs are open to choice and dismissal merely means getting another job. More figuratively, how does one make the donkey work when carrots grow everywhere and no sticks are available? The modern factory manager is often genuinely perplexed at the apparent indiscipline, lack of interest, and even sabotage which appear to surround him; he has no doubt thought long and hard over these matters and asked himself innumerable questions. The only points he seldom or never queries are his fundamental assumptions, and if he fails to find the answers it is not because they are hard to discover, but because he is asking himself the wrong questions. If these assumptions were not distorting his outlook, he would see that the real problem, the real matter for surprise, is that his workers should not *want* to work, should not *want* to meet together at a collective task in his factory, and *should* want to sabotage his efforts. When the problem is looked on in this light, the reasonable question to ask is, 'What has happened to these people to make them act with such resentment or indifference'? Or, to put the matter from the negative point of view, as Dr R. F. Tredgold has done in his excellent little book *Human Relations in Modern Industry:* '"If only," it is said, "workers would work hard right up to the hooter instead of stopping a quarter of an hour early to wash, or to get their coats ready, or just to stop" – the details of this procedure vary only with the tolerance of the charge-hand – "that would be an increase of 3 per cent a day" – but somehow the workers won't. (Why should they?) "If only", it is said, "workers wouldn't stay away with vague pains in the back, when really there's nothing to worry about, we should put up our production by 5 per cent" – but somehow they do stay away. (Why shouldn't they?) These questions "Why should they"? and "Why shouldn't they"? are not rhetorical. They need an answer – and need it badly.'

Modern industrial psychology must seek for causes. If the factory manager finds that his workers are 'lazy', he must ask himself why this is so. He must note that, as individuals, they are far from lazy when digging their allotment on Sunday – why, then, should they be lazy in his factory? Furthermore, the quality of laziness can hardly be 'inside' each single worker. Some people, it is true, may be 'naturally' lazy, whether by reason of physical ill-health or neurosis, but most people are not, and it would be a strange coincidence if every 'naturally' lazy person in the area had simply happened to come to his factory. Some people are 'naturally' aggressive or suspicious, but, again, it would be strange if all of these had deliberately come together to plague him. It follows that the behaviour of which he complains must be a function of the situation he provides in the factory rather than a result of individual personality traits. If, in the army, we find a good platoon and a bad one within the same battalion the commander of the bad platoon would certainly not be allowed to excuse himself on the grounds that all the incompetents in the battalion had happened to be placed in his particular platoon. He would immediately, and quite rightly, be reminded that 'there are no bad soldiers, only bad officers'. It follows that, when groups of people misbehave, it is fruitless to seek the cause in individual peculiarities (except in the personality of their leader). We must ask ourselves: 'What is wrong with the conditions under which these people are acting'?

Industrial psychologists have, in the past, taken too much for granted. The whole structure of industry, its traditions and superstitions, have been accepted almost without question, and one had the uncomfortable impression that human beings were being made to adapt to industry rather than the reverse. Of course, the executive has a right to expect, and the nation requires, that the psychologist's work should help to increase production and general efficiency. But these are not enough. The industrial psychologist should, like the industrial physician, be on nobody's side, and he should certainly not be what the worker contemptuously describes as a 'bosses' man'. Increases in 'efficiency' carried out at the expense of health and happiness are neither efficient nor humane, for, as we shall try to show later, it is no longer a vague moral platitude to say that whatever harms others will harm society and ultimately ourselves. It is necessary, therefore, to consider industry in a wider perspective and primarily with a view to observing, not only its productive capacity, but also its social influence on those connected with it. Does it, or does it not, make them better members of society? This is not an academic problem – a democratic society cannot continue unless its members are critical, intelligent, and responsible. Does industry produce people of this type, or must we agree with Charles Péguy that 'there is no place of perdition better made, better ordered, and better provided with tools, so to speak; that there is no more fitting tool of perdition than the modern workroom'? Again, this problem has been so well expressed by Dr Tredgold, that we cannot do better than quote his words: 'There is . . . in some places an impression that the individual must adapt to his surroundings, and that if he does not conform to type – or perhaps more accurately, conform to the behests of his employer – he had better get out. Let us say at once, at this stage, that we are by no means suggesting that adaptability is not to be encouraged: obviously it is desirable and healthy that it should be. What is less desirable and less healthy, is that it should be expected to be one-sided. Perhaps we should say, that there was (before the war) a very general impression of this kind, but that is altering now, for the simple reason that labour is too short and conditions too severe to permit of sacking people. A cynical reason for suddenly starting to regard the worker as a human being, but there it is, and at this point we need not discuss the reasons. Still it is not really certain that our attitude has really swung the right way. Whether by "right" we are thinking of the rights of man, or the rights of productive efficiency, we have certainly swung into a position where we pay considerable lip-service to the individual's human rights – though we often have considerable mental reservations. But at the same time it happens in some firms that all that is done for the individual is to provide an excess of spoon-fed welfare (or so it appears to him) instead of making any attempt to study what he, as a human being, really needs – and what, from the angle of industrial efficiency, will make him do more work, or stay away from work less.'

It follows, then, that we must concern ourselves with the following questions:

(1) What is the nature of man as an individual, and what, if any, are his basic needs?

(2) What is the nature of man as a social animal, and how does he relate himself to society?

(3) What is the nature of industry, and how far does it fit in with what we know of man as a human being both socially and individually?

The first and second of these questions will be discussed in the following chapter, but, for the moment, we shall go on to consider how modern industry has evolved and how its assumptions relating to human nature arose.

For purposes of description it is useful to divide the history of the machine and machine civilization in the past thousand years into three successive but overlapping and interpenetrating phases – the Medieval phase, the phase of the Industrial Revolution, and the Modern phase. Although each of these phases corresponds roughly to a period of history, its main significance lies in the fact that it is characterized by a particular technological complex. Lewis Mumford, the American sociologist, in his book *Technics and Civilization* describes the technological complex characteristic of the Medieval period (which in varying degrees persisted right up to the middle of the eighteenth century), as 'eotechnic', and the technological complex of the period of the Industrial Revolution as 'paleotechnic'. The emerging modern phase which has not as yet developed its specific form and organization and has not yet completely displaced the paleo-technic complex, is described by Mumford as the 'neotechnic' complex. Of each of these technological complexes we may note that (1) it had its origin in certain definite regions, (2) it tended to employ its own typical resources and raw materials, (3) it had its typical means of utilizing and generating energy, (4) it brought into existence particular types of workers, trained them in particular ways, developed certain aptitudes and discouraged others, and organized them in a manner peculiar to itself. Thus the eotechnic phase, in terms of power and materials, was a water-power and wood complex; the paleotechnic phase was a coal and iron complex; the neotechnic phase is, or will be, an electricity and alloy (and probably an atomic energy) complex. A further characteristic of each phase, not mentioned by Mumford, is (5) that it formulated a specific ideology in order to explain or justify its social organization. Although most of what follows will doubtless be familiar to the reader, it may prove helpful to go over the historical background of industry, firstly, as a means of understanding how things came to be as they now are, and secondly as a salutary reminder of the fact that the outlook of the modern industrialist which he accepts as 'natural' and common-sense was not always thought to be so.

The eotechnic or medieval phase of industry stretches roughly from about A.D. 1000 to 1750. Throughout most of this period the main material used was wood and the main sources of power were wind and water. Animal power was also used in many operations The water-wheel was used for pumping water or grinding grain and, from the seventeenth century, for cutting iron and sawing wood, while windmills were used for draining the land. Metals were, of course, mined, but their main use was for weapons, armour, and ornamental objects. They were not used to any extent in technology. Machines, tools, ships, and houses were made mainly of wood, which was also the chief fuel. In the early part of the period in a Europe recovering from the impoverished conditions, both material and cultural, of the Dark Ages, the characteristic form of community was the manorial village dominated and protected by the castle of the feudal lord. But after about A.D. 1000, towns began to spring up as economic recovery brought into being a new merchant class which, although not without conflict, finally came to terms with the nobles on whose lands it began to settle. The easy and regular trading of the ancient world in the days of the Roman Empire had been destroyed when the Empire collapsed, and the merchants had become a nomadic class travelling about in ships and caravans. When improved conditions made it possible for the merchants to settle down in the feudal towns, they proceeded to form merchant-gilds in order to maintain their position in the struggle with the feudal lords who, on the one hand, welcomed them as sources of wealth and greater luxury, and, on the other, resented the refusal of the merchants to be treated like the unfree peasants who worked on the land. As the trading community increased in power and wealth, it often overflowed beyond the boundaries of the walled town and formed a faubourg or district of its own from which it claimed political independence of the local authorities. Gradually the rich merchants of the towns became a middle class beneath the barons, and peasants were attracted from their work on the land to new employment in the towns. The villeins, who under the Feudal System had been tied to their lord's land, cultivating it and paying in other services in return for his protection, slowly freed themselves as the custom arose of commuting these services for money payments. By 1300 about half of the peasants were free. The terrible depredations of the Black Death in 1349 merely served to hasten this process when it was already under way.

During the Dark Ages, what industry there was had never been able to do much more than supply local needs, but the enterprise of the merchants soon led to a flourishing export trade. In the early days of medieval economy it was the merchants rather than the artisans who led the way, but as conditions improved, the artisans and craftsmen began to assume greater importance. Craft-gilds were formed to protect the producers as opposed to the distributors. Whereas the merchant-gilds had been formed primarily in order to wrest liberties from the feudal nobles, the craft-gilds were formed to protect the interests of the craftsmen from the economic tyranny of the merchants upon whom they depended for their markets. But in addition to this function, the craft-gilds did a great deal for the organization of a common life – their regulations protected both producers and consumers, their members had many of the advantages of a modern friendly society, and some of the wealthier gilds even supported schools. Above all, they insisted on preserving the quality of the work done and the equality of those who did it. The apparatus used by medieval industry was very simple, and no elaborate or expensive machinery was necessary. The craft-gild was an association of craftsmen each owning his own tools and equipment and employing two distinct types of employees: apprentices and journeymen. An apprentice was a youth learning the craft, living with the master-craftsman, helping him in his workshop, and being taught in return. When this stage was past, he became a journeyman who was permitted to hire himself out for wages to other master-craftsmen within the craft. Ultimately he might hope, when enough money had been saved, to set up as a master-craftsman on his own. The small size of these early industrial units is indicated by Tawney in his *Religion and the Rise of Capitalism*, in which he points out that even in a great city like Paris at the end of the thirteenth century the 128 gilds included 5,000 masters who employed collectively not more than 6,000 to 7,000 journeymen. It is important, too, to remember that only a minority of medieval workers were ever members of a craft-gild; in England more than nine-tenths were peasants, among whom, although friendly societies called gilds were common, there was no question of craft organization. Even in the towns, Tawney believes, there must have been a considerable population of casual workers who were never organized. But at the height of its power the craft-gild was a successful instrument in the maintenance of economic justice. For the craftsman, hours of work were often long, but he was his own master, working when busy and taking a rest when he felt he needed it. He worked in his own home and was a respected member of the community, each member of which he knew by name and by whom he was, in turn, known. A unique member of society, he took a pride in his work and in its variety, adapted as it was to the needs of the individual customer.

The system of ideas or ideology which was used to explain or justify feudal social organization was a simple one. 'From the twelfth century to the sixteenth, from the work of Becket's secretary in 1159 to the work of Henry VIII's chaplain in 1537, the analogy by which society is described – an analogy at once fundamental and commonplace – is the same . . . It is that of the human body', writes Tawney in the book already mentioned. 'Society, like the human body, is an organism composed of different members. Each member has its own function, prayer, or defence, or merchandise, or tilling the soil. Each must receive the means suited to its station and must claim no more. Within classes there must be equality; if one takes into his hand the living of two, his neighbour will go short. Between classes there must be inequality; for otherwise a class cannot perform its function, or – a strange thought to us – enjoy its rights. Peasants must not encroach on those above them. Lords must not despoil peasants. Craftsmen and merchants must receive what will maintain them in their calling, and no more.' In medieval society there was no absolute division between the sphere of religion and the sphere of everyday life; it was supposed that every sphere of action was under the judgement of God. This view led to the two basic assumptions upon which medieval economic thought was based. These were, firstly, that all economic interests are subordinate to the real business of life which is salvation, and, secondly, that in economic as in personal conduct the rules of morality are binding. Usury was forbidden and profits were not to exceed the wages of the craftsman's labour. Riches, said St Antonino, exist for man, not man for riches. Hence the concept of the 'just price', a price based on the intrinsic value of the commodity and divorced from such factors as individual preference or material scarcity. In the medieval world, financial transactions, competition, social mobility, and large-scale organization played very little part.

The Middle Ages, it need hardly be said, were in no sense of the word ideal. Material conditions were in many respects like those in Asia today – the common people lived in miserable hovels, the country was swept by plagues, and cruelty and superstition were common elements of daily life. The moral concepts we have just been discussing were by no means always followed in practice, although, as Tawney says, it was perhaps not wholly without value that even lip-service should have been paid to the ideal. Within the great commercial centres there was often ferocious competition and class-wars between artisans and merchants were not uncommon, especially when in the later Middle Ages a capitalist class of the modern type – 'captains of industry' – began to arise. On the other hand, it seems likely that in the sphere of human relations conditions were often a great deal better and more satisfying than they have ever been since. Dr Gregory Zilboorg, the eminent historian of psychiatry, has shown in his *Mind, Medicine, and Man* the significance of the fact that medieval life was founded on the concept of the family. At the best, there was an affectionate and obedient attitude not only towards the real family but towards the father substitutes right up the hierarchy: the master of the gild, the lord of the manor, and finally the benevolent authority of the Church. 'There operated the principle of being loved and taught and protected and being grateful and loving and responsive in return for love and protection at the hands of the father. It was an almost ideal psychological constellation of adulthood, from the standard of the proper alignment of instinctual drives.'

Although a society in which status is fixed at birth may seem to have many drawbacks from the standpoint of the modern individual, it is likely to be forgotten that it also had its advantages. The anxiety and sense of insecurity which are inseparable from a competitive society with mobile status were avoided, everyone had a secure awareness of belonging, and, contrary to what might be supposed, social intercourse between those of different status was much more easy-going than it later became in industrial society. Dr Paul Halmos in his *Solitude and Privacy: a Study of Social Isolation* clearly demonstrates that this was the case in the Middle Ages (consider, for example, the pilgrims in Chaucer's *Canterbury Tales*), and of the eighteenth century C. S. Orwin writes: 'There was ... a freedom in the intercourse between classes in the country which is quite unknown today. Where social inequality was accepted without question on either side, fraternization was possible to an extent which has been impossible ever since the French Revolution exploded the idea of a predestined natural order. And so Parson Woodforde would dine with his tailor and both could enjoy it, while the Rev. Mr Porter ... could drink with the mercer and, later, pull him naked from his bed, in pursuit of "innocent mirth". Johnson's lifelong friend Dr Taylor, the "King" of Ashbourne, counted among his friends two retired innkeepers, a cheese factor, two tanners, and a gentleman farmer: these people were accustomed to meet at his mansion.' (*Johnson's England*, ed. by A. S. Turberville). Dr Halmos notes that ' ... this is not so extra-ordinary as it may appear at first. In a society in which status is rigidly defined and in which rising in the social scale is rare and never unobtrusive, snobbery cannot infect many individuals. Everybody "knows his place" and realizes the finality of his position; therefore there is less cause for pretence and ostentation, both of which are the faults of insecurity and social mobility.' Unfortunately, we have got into the habit of thinking in terms of purely material wellbeing – we seriously believe that an infinite supply of gadgets will sooner or later make everybody infinitely happy. No doubt material goods may often add to people's happiness, but they are not the foundation of happiness. A society cannot exist unless it satisfies certain psychological needs as well as the obvious material ones, and amongst the most important of the psychological needs is the need for status and function. That is to say, each member of a society, no matter at how lowly a level, must be able to feel that he has a well-defined status or position in his society and performs a function which, in however slight a way, furthers the ends for which his society exists. J. L. and Barbara Hammond comment in their book *The Bleak Age* on the contempt which the nineteenth-century radical felt towards any society which did not grant its members the right to vote; his sole criterion of progress was whether or not every adult man had a vote for Parliament, and in his eyes despotism, however kind its face, was still despotism. 'Yet', the Hammonds continue, 'as we look back over history we see that almost every sort of government has been made tolerable to human nature, and that men and women have lived with equanimity under political systems which left them not merely without political rights, but without any pretence of personal liberty. In such cases it is clear that in some way or by some device these excluded men and women were given a sense of sharing in the life of this society; their imagination and their emotions were satisfied, some would say deceived, by its dispositions or its illusions. *For if men and women are to be attached to a society, they must look on it as something in which they have a part; a world in which what we call the common mind finds in some degree, or by some means, scope, peace, comfort and self-respect; in which distinctions of class and fortune, however sternly and hardly drawn, do not forbid all ties of sympathy, all unity of sentiment.*' We are not, it need hardly be said, condoning or recommending despotism; we are simply pointing out that no society can long exist which does not give its members a sense of sharing in its life. Mere efficiency, material wealth, or theoretical beliefs count for nothing. As another writer, Peter Drucker, has said, ' . . . to think, as a great many social efficiency engineers think today, that functioning is all that matters in social life is a complete misunderstanding of the limits and the importance of sheer efficiency. In itself functional efficiency is nothing unless we know the answer to the question: efficiency to what purpose and at what price?' (*The Future of Industrial Man.*)

There can be no doubt that when the paleotechnic phase of industry, the stage of capitalism, arrived it brought with it many advantages. There was vast technological and scientific progress, and for the first time in human history it became theoretically possible to supply the basic needs of the whole population. In the long run, the standard of living of the whole population was raised. Personal freedom, too, was greatly increased, and it became possible to move up (and down) the social scale regardless of accidents of birth and hereditary power. The authority of the Catholic Church to interfere with freedom of thought and scientific investigation was taken away – although it is often forgotten that, in their early days, the Protestant Churches were even more tyrannical than the old order had ever been. But the greatest creation of the new way of life was a psychological one; the gain in individuality. In medieval times, as Jacob Burckhardt was the first to remark in his *Die Kultur der Renaissance in Italien,* 'man was conscious of himself only as a member of a race, people, party, family, or corporation – only through some general category.' Studies by von Martin (*The Sociology of the Renaissance*), and Dr Erich Fromm (*The Fear of Freedom*), have elaborated the same point. In psychological terminology, the 'basic personality structure' of Western European man began to change at some time in the middle of the seventeenth century. The rise of individualism in the social and cultural spheres developed parallel with that of the individualism of private enterprise in the economic sphere. Whereas, formerly, men had only existed as members of a social group or gild, they began to be simply themselves. In an early Renaissance play, the characters are primarily conditioned by their social rôle; they are first and foremost king, soldier, priest, or courtier. The later drama deals with real people. The novel, which as a mode of literary expression lends itself to the exploration of personal uniqueness, came to the fore.* Music, which had been largely conventional, an expression of social rather than personal attitudes, lost its formality and began to take a new shape which led up to the colossal individualism of Beethoven and his successors. In all fields of art, formalism gave way to the individual, the strange, the exotic, and finally, the purely subjective as we see it today. In the field of science, accurate measurement (which is of fundamental importance to the financier) began to assume its modern importance. All of this was good in its way, but somewhere a wrong turning was taken, and what subsequently happened was

* See also Leonard Woolf's *After the Deluge.*

very different from the early hopes of the humanists of the Renaissance.

A gradual rise in the standard of living due to new and expanding demands and new means of satisfying them finally led to the end of the eotechnic phase. Increasing wealth caused ideas of the 'just price' and social justice, as formerly defined, to disintegrate, and the gilds broke down as more and more capital outlay became necessary for elaborate machinery and equipment. New types of business-men arose, says Professor E. L. Woodward in his *History of England*, who were 'without scruple and without pity' – free men, but lacking in any sense of obligation to their fellow-men. If the defects of the eotechnic phase lay in its rigidity and lack of enterprise, the defects of the paleotechnic phase are to be found in the fact that it caused the natural bonds of affection and friendship between man and man to be severed. 'In contrast with the feudal system of the Middle Ages under which everybody had a fixed place in an ordered and transparent social system, capitalistic economy put the individual entirely on his own feet. What he did, how he did it, whether he succeeded or whether he failed, was entirely his own affair. That this principle furthered the process of individualization is obvious, and is always mentioned as an important item on the credit side of modern culture. But in furthering "freedom from", this principle helped to sever all ties between one individual and the other and thereby isolated and separated the individual from his fellow-men.' (Erich Fromm, *The Fear of Freedom*.)* It is in this isolation of modern man that we must seek for many of the answers to the problems of industrial unrest, increasing neurosis and crime, and the pervading sense of helplessness and lack of meaning in the lives of many people today, and, no doubt, it has a good deal to do with the success of totalitarian political groups which, however spurious their claims, are able to offer emotional security and comradeship.

*'[Under capitalism] there must be no discouraging placards "not for sale" set up in the interests of the non-economic concerns of living – of the concerns of kinship, of neighbourhood, of profession or creed. Everything must be open to freedom of contract. The organic bonds grown by society were to be loosened or snapped and all non-contractual relations discouraged.' Canon V. A. Demant, *Religion and the Decline of Capitalism.*

The paleotechnic period became possible with the introduction of coal as a fuel, the development of the steam engine, and the discovery of new methods of smelting iron. It was based on the factory system, in which one or more men provide capital to construct the factory with its equipment, and employ wage-earners who, unlike those of the previous age, were unlikely ever to become employers themselves. The earliest examples of capitalist enterprise existed before the end of the Middle Ages in the mining industry, and occasionally in other industries – in 1371 a weaving factory at Amiens employed 120 workers, and a printer in Nuremberg about 1450 employed the same number. 'In the early sixteenth century the famous Jack of Newbury built a weaving factory with more than 200 looms, employing about 600 workers. Before 1660 such large-scale enterprise, requiring the accumulation of considerable capital, became more common, especially in England. The capital required for mining rose from £100 or so in early Elizabethan times to several thousands under the Stuarts. Blast-furnaces involving several thousand pounds of capital appeared in the mid seventeenth century. In 1649 two capitalists spent £6,000 on a copper-wire mill at Esher. A London brewery under Charles I had a capital of £10,000. All these, however, are but hints of the great change-over to the factory system that took place in the eighteenth and nineteenth centuries.' (S. Lilley, *Men, Machines, and History*.) The beginning of the paleotechnic age may be dated from about 1750, when the perfecting of the steam-engine made possible really large-scale manufacturing and made necessary even larger supplies of capital and labour. Workers were drawn in from their small village communities to the growing industrial towns where their living conditions were soon reduced to a level which is today barely credible. Women and young children laboured alongside men for long hours and lived amongst surroundings of filth, overcrowding, and disease. They came from a familiar social and family background and were compelled to work with others recruited from all over the country in factories situated, with complete disregard for all human needs, around the areas where coal, iron, and other technological requirements were easily available. Such new industrial areas were often based on a single form of occupation, with the result that any slump in the local industry brought all to the verge of starvation. Housing and sanitation were at an appallingly low level of construction and efficiency, and the amenities of the countryside were carelessly destroyed. Work was torn out of its social context. No longer an integral part of the worker's life, it became meaningless, a hateful activity to be evaded whenever possible. It became the fiction of the time that the employer had not bought the worker, but merely his labour, and hence the worker's health or living conditions were no concern of his. During the early years of the Industrial Revolution, at least, machines were better cared for than the workers, since the latter could easily be replaced when they were worn out, and machines were more difficult to obtain.

From about 1825 onwards, the factory system was in full swing in several European countries, and, as time went on, the industrial units increased in size. This led to further developments within the system. The factory owner could no longer gather enough money to finance his own business, and joint-stock companies and corporations began to arise so that investors were able to pool their resources. The individual owner began to die out in many industries and a class of managers arose to manage companies which they themselves did not own. A second result was that, in view of their intolerable position, the workers began to band themselves together into unions for collective bargaining and in order to put pressure on managements to improve their conditions. We need not here consider the development of trade unionism, which had its counterpart in the Journeymen's gilds of late medieval times, was explicity made illegal by the Combination Act of 1799, and finally made legal once again in 1824 through the influence of Francis Place. The Tolpuddle Martyrs were sentenced to transportation in 1834, not for the act of forming a union, which was, of course, no longer illegal, but on a technical point that they had administered illegal oaths. (An excellent account of the early history of the trade unions will be found in Henry Collins' *Trade Unions Today*, Chapter 1). Nor need we discuss the process of reform and the work of Lord Shaftesbury, who did immense service towards lessening the horrors of child labour and was very largely responsible for the Factory Acts of 1833 and 1842.*

The ideology of the paleotechnic period was derived from many and varied sources, and the work of many great men was utilized to support its rationalizations. When, in 1859, Darwin set forth in his *Origin of Species* a theory of evolution based on the concept of the 'survival of the fittest', his thesis, although criticized by theologians and churchmen as a threat to religious belief, was wholeheartedly accepted by the industrialists. (Or, at any rate, they accepted what they took to be its practical implications.) It was now made to appear positively antisocial to help the weak or the poor. Herbert Spencer, for example, asserted that each individual had the right to attempt to preserve himself, but, since the fittest only survived and the less fit were doomed to perish, men must be free to compete and so prove their fitness for survival. Competition and ceaseless struggle were accepted as the fundamental laws of life. What Darwin's theory was to the biologist, the doctrine of *laissez-faire* was to the economist. According to this doctrine, originated by the Physiocrats and supported by Adam Smith, Ricardo, and others, free competition and a free market were expected to lead to the maximum benefit of mankind; 'man's selfishness', it was said, 'is God's providence'. The philosopher Jeremy Bentham (1748–1832) enshrined this doctrine in ethical and psychological terms which influence our thinking to the present day. Bentham was essentially a humanitarian whose well-known dictum that good is 'the greatest good of the greatest number' failed to take note of the obvious fact that 'goods' differ in quality. All human actions, he asserted, are self-interested and are basically motivated by the desire to obtain pleasure and avoid pain. Such self-interested actions are, in the long run, to the advantage of society. A worker will undergo labour and suffering (the two seemed to be inevitably associated) only if the reward in terms of wages is sufficiently great or the punishment in terms of poverty sufficiently unpleasant. Beyond this point, as we have already seen, he

* For accounts of these see J. L. and Barbara Hammond's *Lord Shaftesbury*, and David Thomson's *England in the Nineteenth Century*, both published in the Pelican Series.

would cease to do any more. This doctrine of psychological hedonism preached the importance of 'enlightened self-interest' as the basis of a moral code, and it is easy to see how well it fitted in with the attitudes of the nineteenth-century industrialist. 'Bentham's theory of motivation and his desire to use this motivation for the general welfare accorded with the humanitarian movement. But, paradoxically, the resulting conception of the "economic man" who is motivated solely through pleasure and pain became the great all-encompassing dogma of the industrialists, who found in it the inescapable law of all social behaviour, and hence the moral justification for every act of self-interest. The slogans of humanitarianism were often used in the rationalization of the hard practicalities of the Industrial Revolution, and even today the assumption of the self-evident and obvious correctness of ethical and of psychological hedonism runs through the thinking of "practical men" in industrial society.' (Dr Gardner Murphy, *A Historical Introduction to Modern Psychology*). Bentham's thesis was, perhaps, put most succinctly by Pope:

> Thus God and Nature formed the general frame,
> And bade self-love and social be the same.

Many of the attitudes typical of the paleotechnic revolution found ethical expression in the Protestant religion. Marxists, indeed, have asserted that Protestantism is basically an ideological justification of capitalism. Whether or not this is so, there can be no doubt that a relationship between the two existed, as Max Weber, in *The Protestant Ethic and the Spirit of Capitalism*, and R. H. Tawney, in *Religion and the Rise of Capitalism*, have from different viewpoints been able to show. It suited the rising commercial class to free themselves from the restrictions imposed by the Catholic Church of medieval times on capitalist enterprise, but the real state of affairs went much deeper than this. It was that the Protestant and the capitalist were both individualists, they both ignored the spirit of community. The Protestant, in effect, stood the soul naked and isolated before its God without the Church or the Communion of Saints to intercede. Religion was regarded as a personal matter between each man and his God. The capitalist merchants and manufacturers wanted to be free from the codes and controls of the gilds and corporations, from the idea of fixed status and manorial institutions. They wanted to substitute for the concept of the 'just price' the idea that the price of a commodity, or the wages of a worker, was what either could obtain in the competitive market. 'The trader became a Protestant, not because he put it to himself that Protestantism squared better than Catholicism with his business interests, but because he was already thinking individualistically in connexion with the everyday problems of life, and a religion which emphasized his individual relation and responsibility to his Maker gave him the kind of spiritual attitude that he wanted. It was not in the least that his religion was insincere; he was but following the example of men in all ages by re-making his religion after the model of his desires and values.' (G. D. H. Cole, *The Meaning of Marxism.*)

What has just been said is not, of course, contradicted by the perfectly true statement that the early Protestant Church was primarily a revolt against a too worldly Catholic Church, and was intended as a return to a more spiritual religion. According to Sombart, Protestantism was, to begin with, 'in every respect a grave danger to the spirit of capitalism'. But, true as this may be, there can be no doubt at all that, as it later developed, the Protestant faith came to be associated with the rising commercial class and was found to be readily adaptable to the new outlook based on the principle that 'God helps those who help themselves'. From this point of view, it soon came to appear that wealth was a sign of Divine approval, poverty a sin. Whereas in the Middle Ages the poor had been thought to 'represent our Lord in a peculiarly intimate way', and it was even necessary for a religious manual to explain that the rich, as such, were not *necessarily* hateful to God (R. H. Tawney), the new industrialist began to look on the poor as having reached that state by reason of laziness, immorality, or lack of thrift. 'Convinced that character is all and circumstances nothing, he sees in the poverty of those who fall by the way, not a misfortune to be pitied and relieved, but a moral failing to be condemned, and in riches, not an object of suspicion – though like other gifts they may be abused – but the blessing which rewards the triumph of energy and will. Tempered by self-examination, self-discipline, self-control, he is the practical ascetic, whose victories are won not in the cloister, but on the battlefield, in the counting-house, and in the market' (Tawney). A strange joyless way of life came into being which made it clear that men are not here on earth to enjoy themselves, but to work and earn their living by 'the sweat of their brow'. Capital which had been the servant of man became his master. Money which had always been thought of as a means to an end, became an end in itself.* The capitalist, amassing huge sums of money, giving his whole life to his work (often enough to produce objects almost completely useless to society), and yet making little use of his wealth for personal ends – unless it was to pay his physician for treating the diseases his own relentless energy had produced – is a very peculiar phenomenon indeed. Yet, whatever his defects, this was the type of man who created modern industry – a colossal achievement which has changed the face of the world more in the past hundred years than in the previous thousand.

So far we have been considering the psychological attitudes of management as they developed in the paleotechnic era. But how did the worker feel about his changed status? His attitude to his employer, Nietzsche tells us in *The Joyful Wisdom*, was one of fear mingled with contempt. 'People want to live and have to sell themselves; but they despise him who exploits their necessity and purchases the workman. It is curious that the subjection to powerful, fear-inspiring, and even dreadful individuals, to tyrants and leaders of armies, is not at all felt so painfully as the subjection to such undistinguished and uninteresting persons as the captains of industry. In the employer the workman usually sees a crafty blood-sucking dog of a man, speculating on every necessity, whose name, form, and character are altogether indifferent to him.' Lewis Way, in a book entitled *Man's Quest for Significance*, describes how the worker whose job had been relieved of all social significance, all meaning, finally began to accept it at the value placed upon it by the factory owner. The

* ' . . . the main problem set by the capitalist phase of history [was] the achievement of great economic advantages at the cost of colossal social dislocation. [Capitalism] in its total aspect means the running of a society as an adjunct of the market relationship.' Canon Demant, *op. cit.*

hours spent at his job were so much time taken from his real life and given to his employer in return for the privilege of being able to live the rest as he chose. Work was, as he had been taught, the antithesis of all pleasure and happiness; it was no longer performed for the greater glory of God, for the master-craftsman in whose house he lived, for the honour of the craft, or even out of purely personal pride, but was merely for the sake of earning money to do other things. Taking this attitude, the worker was irresponsible, indifferent to the quality of the work he did, and unaware of how, if at all, it helped to satisfy social needs. So long as he was paid, he was indifferent to the type of work he was supposed to do. Sometimes, and to an ever-increasing degree, the employer took the same view – so long as his goods were sold their quality or their usefulness were immaterial considerations. But behind this façade of indifference the worker felt himself humiliated and hostile. Given no responsibility, he showed none; treated as an automaton, he behaved as such. He began to make a virtue out of servitude and refused to take any part in social life but a passively hostile one. He worked as slowly as possible without attracting unwelcome attention from his supervisor, he made deliberate mistakes, either by straightforward sabotage or by interpreting orders too literally. This type of behaviour set up a vicious circle as the manager noted his irresponsible behaviour and further reduced the worker's need to use his own initiative. In line with the suggestions of Taylor and others, work was simplified and attempts were made to make it foolproof and proof against sabotage. Finally, we come to the stage in which the worker becomes almost completely passive and the employer is at his wit's end to know what to do. Fearing his workers (although he would not care to admit it), he dare not given them any responsibility. The only way he can think of to stimulate them to work harder is more money and, in recent times, more 'welfare'.

We can now see more clearly the historical origins of our modern problems. The industrialist has taught his employees that work is a painful and unpleasant necessity, and is now distressed that they believe him; he has treated them as machines, and is surprised when they behave as such. He asserted that fear of starvation was the main incentive to work, and now a thought-less government has removed the fear and the incentive by the 'Welfare State'. Vainly the industrialist seeks for other means whereby the workers may be bribed to work – he produces wel-fare schemes, holidays with pay, dances, outings, free medical treatment, and so on – some of which are excellent ideas, others merely an insult to the intelligence. In short, he satisfies all possible physical needs and leaves the psychological ones – responsibility, pride of craft, self-respect, status, and a sense of social usefulness, still unsatisfied.

In recent times industry has changed in many respects from the early days of the Industrial Revolution. There are, however, two major changes which date from about the beginning of the present century (although their origins may be noted at a much earlier period), which we cannot fail to take into account. The first is the development of the mass-production technique, the second the growth of the large industrial enterprise. Mass-pro-duction as we know it today appears to have been used in the United States towards the end of the nineteenth century in the production of railroad freight cars, but its use on a really large scale was, of course, due to Henry Ford when forty years ago he utilized the principle to turn out his 'Model T' cars from a factory in Detroit. Since that time, the mass-production principle has swept throughout the world and has become a basic principle for the organization of all manufacturing activities. Even out-side the factory, the concept of mass-production is utilized (although without the mechanism of the assembly-line, the conveyor belt, and interchangeable parts) in many other spheres: in agriculture (as in the Russian collective farm or the mechanized cotton plantations of the Mississippi Delta), in scientific research (as in the work done during the war on the atom bomb), in film-making (as Dr Powdermaker notes in her book, *The Dream Factory*), and in the clerical work of a large office. In fact, as Peter Drucker points out, mass-production is to be regarded not only as a mechanical but also as a *social* principle, a principle of human organization, according to which human begins are organized for a common task. As employed in the factory, it has two important implications. Firstly, that nobody, generally speaking, in the mass-production organization has a specialized skill – the man who has spent his whole life in a shoe factory may be a perfectly efficient worker in an electrical equipment plant after only a few days' training. The unit of work is not the product, but a single operation or even a single movement. Secondly, that the worker is now completely divorced from the product and the means of production. Without the factory organization, the worker himself can do nothing; it is the organization rather than the individual worker which is productive under the new system. Since organization has become so important, new skills have become necessary. What is now required is not so much manual skill or knowledge of tools or materials, but partly technical and theoretical and partly social skill. The modern manager is primarily concerned, not with machines and materials, but with handling people, and it is a basic principle of modern management, as with the modern worker, that the same man is equally capable of running a shoe factory or a steel mill. This need for social skills is a further reason for the interest shown in problems of motivation and morale at the present day.

The second significant change in modern industry is, as has already been mentioned, the growth of the large enterprise. It is unnecessary to discuss the economic and other reasons for this change, which, whether we approve of it or not, must be accepted as a fundamental fact of modern industrial organization. Whether it takes the form of the privately-owned corporation, the government corporation in a nationalized industry, or the Soviet 'Trust', the large enterprise is very much the same institution. Although both in this country and the United States the majority of workers are employed by relatively small firms, the existence of the large enterprises must be taken into account for at least three reasons. To begin with, they present a problem in human relationships within industry which it is important we should face up to – the problem of how to reconcile effective leadership with the essentially impersonal character of the big concern. Next, it is worth while considering the part they play in the industrial life of the nation: a part out of all proportion to the number of people they employ. We need not discuss the influence of the large enterprise in the economic field, which is considerable, but it is evident that such firms assume technological leadership, do much of the research, develop the new methods, the new products, the new tools. Finally, it is this type of concern which establishes the social pattern of industry for the whole nation; which is, as a recent writer has said, 'the breeding ground of industrial experiment'.

Much has been said against mass-production (which, it is often forgotten, has been instrumental in raising the standard of living of millions of people throughout the world to a level never before known in the history of man), and even more has been said in criticism of 'big business'. But, although we may sympathize with the motives of the critics, it is necessary to realize that any schemes which envisage a straightforward return to simpler conditions are completely unrealistic. We could not, even if we wished, turn the clock back, and there is no responsible person who supposes for a single moment that the psychological problems of mass-production or the large enterprise can be solved in this way. There can be little doubt that the mass-production technique will be increasingly used all over the world and that the large enterprise, nationalized or otherwise, will grow in importance. In the rest of this book, therefore, we shall take these institutions to be an accepted fact of industrial life which can neither be ignored nor wished away. The solution to such problems lies, not in a return to the past, but in the ability to adapt the new technological organization of industry so that it corresponds more closely with human needs.

2

HUMAN NATURE AND SOCIETY

WE have already seen how the changing technological basis of labour gradually brought about what is usually described as the Industrial Revolution. The great shift in population and industry that took place in the eighteenth century was due to the introduction of coal as a source of mechanical power, to the use of the steam engine, and to new methods of smelting and working iron. Out of this coal and iron complex, a new civilization developed. This paleotechnic or industrial civilization created new concepts of the nature of man and society, which, although their development was gradual, ultimately led to an ideology totally different from that which had prevailed during the eotechnic or medieval period. Whereas eotechnic society had been a society of small towns and villages predominantly agricultural, its industry based on the work of small craftsmen, merchants, and peasants, its religion all-pervading, and its members' status largely determined by birth, paleotechnic society was in all these respects something quite new in human history. Large cities replaced small villages or towns; the unskilled and uprooted labourer the skilled craftsman; the large factory the small home industry; unrestricted competition replaced co-operation, and an individual's position in society became dependent upon his own unaided efforts in the struggle for status.

Naturally enough, the new outlook had a considerable influence upon thought in the social sciences which were beginning to develop from the middle of the eighteenth century onwards. Prior to that time, what we now know as sociology, psychology, and anthropology had made little use of scientific method, and were, in fact, merely branches of theology or philosophy based on arm-chair speculation or travellers' tales. During the last quarter of the eighteenth and the first quarter of the nineteenth centuries, such writers as the German Herbart and the Scotsmen Thomas Brown and James Mill (father of the better-known J. S. Mill) had attempted to found a scientific psychology based upon the concept of the association of ideas, but, as we have already noted, the serious application of experimental method in the field of psychology did not begin until Wilhelm Wundt in 1879 opened his research laboratory at the University of Leipzig. It is true that, to the layman, the results of this early experimental work were likely to appear somewhat dull and uninspiring – as William James unkindly said, German experimental psychology could only have arisen amongst a people who were incapable of being bored. But it is necessary to realize that those aspects of human behaviour which lend themselves most readily to experiment are precisely those which tell us least about human personality as a whole; one may readily carry out laboratory experiments on memory, attention, vision, hearing, and sensation, thereby gaining much useful information – but the same cannot be said of those aspects of the mind which most nearly concern us – for example fear, hate, love, or guilt. This obvious limitation of early experimental psychology was perhaps most apparent to physicians and others who found themselves confronted by the problems of psychiatry, which, following the humanitarian revolution initiated by Pinel about 1792, was slowly becoming a more or less respectable branch of medical science. The psychiatrist, unlike the academic psychologist, was impatient. He could not always wait until science had validated his methods, because, like the revolutionary, he wished not only to understand but to change the world, or at any rate that part of it which confronted him in his clinic or consulting-room. In short, the bias of the psychiatrist, as of any other physician, was basically empirical, and this bias is significant because it led to the development of theories of personality such as those of Janet and Freud and all their many offshoots which, whether or not they are true, undoubtedly go far beyond what is positively known. It is important that the reader should note this basic dichotomy in the field of psychology, and should realize that psychology, psychiatry, and psycho-analysis are not synonymous terms, as is so often supposed, nor do they have the same attitude concerning scientific method. Psychology, it is true, is the study of human behaviour, but the psychologist ordinarily takes the view that his science can only be built up by the gradual accumulation of knowledge in many separate fields of human action, and, as we have already seen, the fields most readily open to such research are likely to pertain to such matters as perception, learning, memory, intelligence, and so on – to the simpler aspects of behaviour. 'The psychologist', writes Dr Zangwill in his *Introduction to Modern Psychology*, 'may be said to nibble at personality; he does not venture to swallow it as an indigestible whole', and Professor Notcutt in *The Psychology of Personality* goes so far as to say: 'Even now, the study of personality belongs to the adventurous and not wholly respectable frontier regions of psychology, which it is not altogether wise to explore without a safe academic reputation in some entirely reputable field, like colour vision, or the ability of rats to learn their way through a maze.'

Psychology, then, is the study of human behaviour; it is based wholly upon scientific method, and although most psychologists are quite prepared to take one or another of the many theories of human personality as a working hypothesis, very few would be prepared to suggest that it is anything more than a useful frame of reference. Psychiatry is a branch of medicine which deals with the treatment of mental disorders, and even if there is a good deal of agreement amongst psychiatrists about certain fundamentals, its approach is fundamentally empirical. Psychoanalysis, on the other hand, is a word which refers exclusively to the theories and methods of psycho-therapy discovered by Sigmund Freud, and a person who accepts and practises these methods in their entirety (having received an appropriate training) is a psycho-analyst. Whilst most psycho-analysts are also psychiatrists, by no means all psychiatrists are psycho-analysts. This does not mean that psychologists or psychiatrists in general reject Freudian theory – on the contrary, nearly all modern psychiatry is largely based upon Freudian concepts. But psychiatrists certainly do not accept the theory in all its details, rather they pick and choose what they find useful; without the concepts of infantile sexuality, of a personality which develops during the first five years of life within the complex relationships of the family circle, of mental conflict as the root of neurosis, of the unconscious, of mental mechanisms in explaining behaviour, of the importance of sex and aggression – all of which were originally formulated by Freud – modern psychiatry could hardly exist. In psychology, too, most psychologists (unlike Dr H. J. Eysenck, whose criticisms of psycho-analysis the reader will find in *Uses and Abuses of Psychology* published in this series) take the view that Freud's work was of fundamental importance and believe that it has revolutionized the whole field of the science. Typical of the general view is that of Dr Zangwill who writes in the book from which we have already quoted: 'The academic psychologist, in virtue of his scientific training, is necessarily something of a sceptic. He has been taught to react with healthy suspicion to broad generalizations founded on imperfect evidence. He argues that the theories of Freud cannot be tested by any of the methods which science has slowly and laboriously evolved to disentangle truth from opinion. The standards of evidence upon which the principal theories of psycho-analysis are based cannot, by any stretch of imagination, be held to fulfil the requirements of scientific precision. But this does not mean that Freud's theories are necessarily wrong. Indeed, in so far as the outcome of clinical observation furnishes valid evidence, his views have turned out to be more often right than wrong . . . As a result of Freud's researches, psychology today differs from psychology of fifty years ago in a manner so fundamental as to justify the comparison with biology before and after Darwin.'

Freud, however, in spite of his great contribution to psychology, shared with other social scientists of his time the outlook of the paleotechnic period, and in what follows, an attempt will be made to trace the manner in which our concepts of human nature and society have changed during the past few decades. Facts, of course, are always facts, although we may agree that how they are regarded, and even whether or not they are perceived, is likely to be strongly influenced by the prejudices of the times. But it is the assumptions lying behind the facts and the frame of reference into which they are fitted that most clearly

44

show the prevailing ideology. During the Middle Ages, although the prevailing philosophy of mind had been one of dualism – that is to say, one which affirmed the independent existence of both body and soul – it would appear that body and soul were nevertheless thought of as being intimately related during life. Thomas Aquinas, for example, appears to have thought of man as a 'besouled' organism, rather than merely a body *plus* a soul. The soul of course, was believed to survive bodily death, but was nevertheless thought to be linked to the body in a peculiarly intimate way during life. During the seventeenth century, however, Descartes, presumably hoping to bring human biology within the sphere of the natural sciences, suggested that spirit and matter, body and mind, were totally different entities, interacting in some way which was never clearly explained, and thus Cartesian theory opened the way to the view that the body was basically a machine, whilst the mind or soul moved ever farther away from human ken. Once mind and matter had been separated from each other it was but a short step from Descartes, the devout (but doubting) Catholic, to the thorough-going mechanistic materialism of the eighteenth and nineteenth centuries. The typical philosophical theory of mind during the paleotechnic period, then, was that which Professor Ryle has described as the theory of 'the ghost within the machine', but, so far as the scientist was concerned, the 'ghost' was merely a polite concession to conventional morality; in fact, man *was* a machine. In the field of medicine, the influence of Descartes came to be felt in the views of the seventeenth- and eighteenth-century schools of iatromathematics, iatrochemistry, and iatrophysics, all of which interpreted illness as a failure in function of part of the machine, and merely differed as to whether the defect could best be explained in terms of mathematics, chemistry, or physics. Another medical school known as Vitalism, although claiming to be violently opposed to those we have already mentioned in that it accepted the existence of the soul, was in practice no different from its opponents – the body remained a passive machine guided, in this case, by an immortal spirit, which, since it was clearly out of therapeutic range, really played little part for all practical purposes when it came to dealing with the sick patient. Nineteenth-century medicine, under the influence of Virchow and others, was totally mechanistic.

Freud, as is well known, was a materialist, who believed that in the course of time all mental activity would be explained in terms of physics and chemistry. He described his theories as a 'mythology', and clearly supposed that they would ultimately be replaced, not by other psychological theories, but by the advancement of knowledge in neurology and physiology. Psycho-analysis is fundamentally a *biological* theory of personality. That is to say, it is founded upon certain preconceptions concerning man's biological nature and in particular upon the theory of instincts. 'In Freudian theory,' says Erich Fromm, 'those passions and anxieties that are characteristic for man in modern society were looked upon as eternal forces rooted in the biological constitution of man.' In this respect, of course, Freudian theory was in no way different from many other contemporary psychological theories; McDougall, for example, gave a list of no less than seventeen 'propensities' or instincts which were alleged to form the innate basis of human behaviour. In fact, Freudian theory, which postulated only two instincts, sex and aggression, had at least the advantage of simplicity. Now this emphasis upon the instinctual basis of human nature led to the belief that certain traits common to individuals in the industrial civilizations of Western Europe and Northern America were innate in human nature. The waging of wars, competition and the striving to dominate, the patriarchal family, Christian attitudes to sex, the activity of men and the passivity of women, the Oedipus complex, the Puritan conscience, and so on, all came to be regarded as rooted in biological traits and therefore universal and inevitable. Animals, as is well known, demonstrate clearly-marked instinctual reactions; man, as Darwin had shown, was an animal amongst other animals; so why should not men have instincts too?

It is now realized that much of this discussion of instincts is based upon verbal confusion; for the word 'instinct' may be used in at least two widely differing ways: (1) it may be used to refer to a *specific and fixed reaction pattern* which is determined by the structure of the central nervous system (much of the complex behaviour shown by such creatures as ants, bees, and wasps, fish and birds, comes into this category), or (2) it may be used to refer to what are now more generally known as 'biological needs' or 'drives'. When, for example, we say that the nest-building habits of birds, the migrating cycle of the salmon, or the social behaviour of ants is 'instinctive', we are using the word in the first sense to imply that the behaviour in question is largely inherited, more or less automatic, and has little or nothing to do with intelligence – in fact, it is typical of 'instincts' in this sense of the word that they are not modifiable, or only very slightly modifiable, by experience. Modern biologists and psychologists are agreed that such behaviour is a disappearing category in man and the higher animals, since intelligent and flexible learned behaviour is, in the course of evolution, replacing inborn, inflexible, and unlearned behaviour. Virtually, *men have no instincts* in this, the original, sense of the word. In the second usage of the word, we are discussing *needs* such as sex, hunger, sleep, thirst, and so on; but, although the existence of such needs or drives does explain why men *initiate* certain actions (e.g. why they want to eat, drink, or obtain sexual satisfaction), it does not in any way explain *how* they do these things, why they sometimes do them when they do not wish to, or do not do them when they do wish to. That man possesses certain needs is a biological fact; how he satisfies them is a social or cultural fact. The modern view is that human behaviour cannot be understood purely in terms of the satisfaction or frustration of biological drives, because social life generates new needs which may be as powerful, or even more powerful than, the original biological ones. That men give away their last crust of bread, permit themselves to be destroyed rather than give up their convictions, are patriotic, religious, and so on – these forms of behaviour cannot be wholly explained biologically, but only in terms of society and culture.* There are, it need hardly be said, certain constants relating both

* 'In Middletown during the depression years of 1929 and 1935 purchases of food declined markedly while gasoline sales remained at a near-normal level. In this case secondary motives are displacing the primary ones . . . the so-called secondary motives are seen to be stronger than the primary roots out of which they developed; the person-as-a-whole – as formed by the culture – has become the regulator of the parts.' L. E. Cole, *Human Behaviour*.

to man's biological needs and the situation of the human being *vis-à-vis* his environment which inevitably limit his way of life and which no social group could afford to ignore. Thus women, not men, give birth to children; all children are born helpless and must therefore be supported by the family (or a family substitute) for some years; in most climates clothes are necessary, and at all times human beings need food, water, shelter, and a minimum of warmth. Even apart from these biological constants, there exist others which are the universal result of social interaction. If a society is to exist as a society, there must be rules regulating behaviour which reflect a spirit of give and take. Whatever the appearances, all societies must be based upon co-operation – indeed, the failure to realize this obvious fact was one of the more obvious fallacies of paleotechnic civilization, which did not understand that no society can exist on a basis of all-out competition. Competition presupposes a pre-existing state of co-operation; for, as Stuart Chase has pointed out, if more than 5 or 10 per cent of the members of a group did not for the most part do what was expected of them, the group would simply cease to exist. In order to co-operate, individuals must know where they stand and what is their duty in relation to the society as a whole (i.e., they must have a clearly-defined status and function), and they must be able to communicate with each other (i.e., they must have language). As they are related not only to each other but also to their natural environment, to the universe, this relationship also must be defined (i.e. a body of religious belief or some similar ideology, whether mythology, philosophy, or scientific knowledge, tends to arise). As a result of all these constant factors in the social, biological, and material environment we find that all known societies possess the following institutions:

(1) Language.
(2) Materials, shelter, food, clothing, and the knowledge of how to deal with them.
(3) The status of the individual within the group is defined so that he knows his duties, his functions, and his expectations.

(4) Art forms, tales, poems, sculpture, architecture, etc.
(5) Mythology and scientific knowledge.
(6) Religious belief and practices.
(7) The family and social organization (although, of course, the family takes many different forms in different societies).
(8) Rules regulating property, trade, barter, and money.
(9) Government.
(10) War, although a very ancient and widespread element, is *not* found amongst all societies.

In company with most other psychologists of his time, Freud seems to have supposed that there was a universal 'human nature' capable of explaining all human behaviour, and that this nature was basically biological. As we have seen, there are indeed certain more or less fixed constants which must apply to any human society, but there can now be no doubt that the concept of a more or less fixed 'human nature' is a figment of the imagination. This assumption began to fare badly in the 1930s when the American anthropologists Margaret Mead and Ruth Benedict produced a series of studies which effectively demonstrated how very flexible 'human nature' is when observed against differing cultural backgrounds. Margaret Mead found, for example, that the storm and stress which is taken for granted as typical of adolescence in Western civilization does not occur amongst girls in Samoa where custom permits early sexual experience. Similarly, sexual differences between men and women cannot be said to be wholly due to innate biological factors, as Freud supposed, if, as Mead found in New Guinea, neighbouring tribes with differing cultures show variations in masculine and feminine traits which, in some cases, amount almost to a reversal of the rôles as we know them. 'The Arapesh ideal is the mild, responsive man married to the mild responsive woman; the Mundugumor ideal is the violent aggressive man married to the violent aggressive woman. In the third tribe, the Tchambuli, we found a genuine reversal of the sex-attitudes of our own culture, with the woman the dominant, impersonal, managing partner, the man the less responsible and the emotionally dependent partner.' These cultural differences extend into all fields of personality: the Arapesh are co-operative, unaggressive, and gentle towards their children, the Mundugumor un-co-operative, aggressive, and harsh. Aggression is so distasteful to the Arapesh that it almost seems to take the place filled by sex in Victorian society – anger, boastfulness, and even any sign of mild competitiveness or self-assertion, are strongly disapproved of, and the sight of anyone in a rage shocks them as profoundly as if in England someone were to tell a smutty story at the vicar's tea-party. Arapesh children are never punished, and during their early life it is incessantly suggested to the children that everything is 'good' – good sago, good house, good uncle, and so on. Amongst the Mundugumor, on the other hand, 'social organization is based on the theory of a natural hostility that exists between all members of the same sex, and the assumption that the only possible ties between members of the same sex are through members of the opposite sex.' Ruth Benedict found that the Zuñi Indians of New Mexico resemble the Arapesh of New Guinea in their lack of assertiveness and competitive spirit – the Zuñi try to lose a race, and insist upon not occupying positions of dominance. Whereas the unfortunate capitalists of Europe and America compulsively collect wealth on the assumption that it is perfectly natural to do so (doubtless as a result of McDougall's acquisitive propensity), to the Kwakiutl Indians of Puget Sound the main problem is how to get rid of it; prestige is obtained in this tribe by burning money or tearing it in pieces at the so-called 'potlatch' ceremonies. The Dobu of New Guinea live in such a state of persecutory suspicion, as would seem to justify in Europe or America the diagnosis of paranoia, and in Bali, says Roheim, we find 'the unthinkable – a schizophrenic culture'. Most of us are aware, or would be had our school-books not been so carefully expurgated, that the ancient Greeks regarded homosexuality favourably, and even psychiatrists with little knowledge of the social sciences cannot fail to note how, in Britain, social change has brought about changing fashions in mental disorder – for example, hysteria, once the prevalent neurosis of Victorian times, is now almost unknown in its pure form, whereas anxiety neurosis is rapidly increasing. At a later stage in this book we shall have to discuss the important problem of the selection of leaders in industry, but at this point it is difficult to deny oneself the luxury of suggesting that one method we have not as yet tried which might prove extremely effective, at any rate in eradicating a certain type of industrial 'leader', is that employed by the Zuñi. In this happy tribe, we are told, ' . . . when leaders are required, groups of men are locked up and virtually imprisoned until someone's excuses against being put in authority have been battered down. Once chosen, the leaders are regarded with little respect, have little power, and at any sign of authoritarian behaviour, they are hung up by their thumbs until they confess to their crime.' However, we must reluctantly drag ourselves back to reality from these pleasing sadistic fantasies to note that the important point about such anthropological observations is the extreme variability of 'human nature' which they demonstrate, a variability which biological theories of personality fail to explain. In the words of Ruth Benedict, we have come to realize that 'most of these organizations of personality that seem to us most incontrovertibly abnormal have been used by different civilizations in the very foundations of their institutional life. Conversely, the most valued traits of our normal individuals have been looked upon in differently organized cultures as aberrant (abnormal). Normality, in short, within a very wide range, is culturally defined.'

We must now examine a second assumption which Freud shared with other psychologists of his time, the origins of which have already been traced in Chapter 1. This is the belief that there exists a basic dichotomy between man and society. Human nature, it is supposed, is, at the roots, evil – man is 'naturally' antisocial, and it is the function of society to domesticate him. In Freudian theory, society is pictured as a conglomeration of human atoms, each at war with the other, each separated irrevocably from his fellow-men by the limiting membrane of his own skin. In order to keep this rabble quiet, some expression of the crude instincts may be permitted, but ordinarily these must be checked and refined, and through the thwarting of the sex-impulse and its deflexion to symbolic ends there arises, by the process described by Freud as 'sublimation', what we know as 'civilization'. If we grant this assumption, it follows that there must exist an inverse relationship in any society between the satisfaction of man's instincts and the level of cultural attainment, so that the more suppression the more elaborate the culture (and the greater the incidence of neurosis) and the less suppression the less neurosis (but also the less civilization). Neurotics are those who have fallen by the wayside in the drive towards a civilized society; for whereas criminals rebel openly against their society neurotics do so in secret. All behaviour is basically self-interested, since love is merely sublimated sex and kindliness a reaction-formation against one's latent sadism. But although the more positive emotions of love, friendliness, and generosity are in some sense 'secondary' and derived, the negative ones of greed, cruelty, and aggressiveness are allegedly innate and primary. This suggestion is so preposterous that Karen Horney, one of the American group of neo-Freudians, felt bound to comment: 'That over-kindliness may be a reaction-formation against sadistic trends does not preclude the possibility of a genuine kindliness which arises out of basically good relations with others. That generosity may be a reaction-formation against greediness does not disprove the existence of genuine generosity.' Erich Fromm specifically derives the social aspects of Freudian theory from the ideology of the Industrial Revolution. He writes: 'Human relations as Freud sees them are similar to the economic relations to others which are characteristic of the individual in capitalist society. Each person works for himself, individualistically at his own risk, and not primarily in co-operation with others. But he is not a Robinson Crusoe; he needs others as customers, as employees, or as employers. He must buy and sell, give and take. The market, whether it is the commodity or the labour market, regulates these relations. Thus the individual, primarily alone and self-sufficient, enters into economic relations with others as means to one end: to sell and to buy. Freud's concept of human relations is essentially the same: the individual appears fully equipped with biologically given drives, which need to be satisfied. In order to satisfy them the individual enters into relations with other "objects". Other individuals thus are always a means to one's end, the satisfaction of strivings which in themselves originate in the individual before he enters into contact with others. The field of human relations in Freud's sense is similar to the market – it is an exchange of satisfaction of biologically given needs, in which the relationship to the other individual is always a means to an end, but never an end in itself.' (*The Fear of Freedom.*)

Much of this gloomy picture is beyond the reach of scientific discussion for the simple reason that it is based upon mere value-judgements which could not conceivably be settled by any factual observations. We cannot usefull/ discuss, for example, whether man is basically antisocial or society basically repressive, because these are pseudo-problems with no discoverable meaning. Man, it is true, is born without morals, since morals arise only in social interaction, and society certainly encourages some of his traits and discourages others, but without society he would not only not be human in any meaningful sense of the word, he could not even survive. As Professor Sprott tells us in his *Social Psychology*: 'It is a mistake to think of the "person" as a pre-fabricated structure waiting at birth to be erected, well or ill, by the adults in charge of it. *Prior to an infant's earliest contacts with other human beings it simply does not exist as a "person" at all.*' No modern sociologist or social psychologist would accept the atomistic view of society which Freud seems to have accepted as natural, because it is not nowadays believed that human beings exist in a random state, bumping against each other like marbles in a boy's pocket. They are invariably organized in one form or another, and the individual is always related to the larger national or tribal society through the mediation of smaller and more intimate social groupings. The most fundamental of these is the primary or face-to-face group, about which we shall have a great deal to say in subsequent chapters. In an important sense it is true to say that it is not the individual but the primary group which is the basic unit of society. At this stage, we shall merely mention the existence of primary groups, emphasize their significance in the life of man, and contrast them with the more formal and deliberately organized secondary groupings which play much less part in the actual development of character. The most familiar primary groupings are the family, the play-group, the neighbourhood group, the work group, and the group of elders in the village. 'These groups', writes Professor Kimball Young, 'are primary in several senses. They are the first groups in which the individual builds up his habits and attitudes. They are fundamental to the development of the social self and the moral sense, and give one the basic training in social solidarity and co-operation.' (*Personality and Problems of Adjustment*.) Any national or tribal society, therefore, is built up from a network of primary groups, and it follows that the theory, prevalent during the eighteenth and nineteenth centuries, that society consists of a horde of basically selfish and unorganized individuals – the so-called 'rabble hypothesis' – is totally untrue.

One aspect of social organization which not only demonstrates the falsity of the 'rabble hypothesis' but requires to be emphasized for the purposes of our argument is the fact that the culture or way of life of any society is a patterned whole which can never be regarded as a patchwork quilt of unrelated elements. 'The different parts of a culture are all related to one another and do not function separately; the culture of any one area or people is thus like a machine or an organism with all its parts interlinked.' (Ogburn and Nimkoff: *A Handbook of Sociology*.) That this is so is demonstrated by the way societies respond when an attempt is made to introduce a new trait into their culture, whether the trait is a new belief, a new tool or invention, or a new custom. When this happens one or other of the following reactions is likely to follow:

(1) It may fit into the pattern and be accepted.
(2) It may clash with the existing pattern and be rejected.
(3) It may be found unsuitable in its original form, but capable of modification or substitution so as to make it acceptable.
(4) If a trait which conflicts with deep-seated elements in the cultural pattern is forced upon it, whether by conquest or extreme environmental pressure, the society may disintegrate, or it may, after a period of disintegration, manage to restructuralize itself around the new trait. Disintegration may also result from the suppression of a cultural trait which has played an

important part in a particular society (e.g., the banning of head-hunting by the British authorities in New Guinea led to the beginnings of disintegration in the tribal society which had been based on this custom, but the situation returned to normal when the spearing of a wild boar was substituted for the original practice).

There are many examples of this selectivity of cultures to new traits – a selectivity which could certainly not exist were the 'rabble hypothesis' true. The Plains Indians, who valued dreams and delirium, readily accepted alcohol from the white man; the Hopi, who valued regularity and order, did not. Hunting societies accept firearms, fishing societies do not. Tribes which value uniqueness in objects reject mass-produced goods. 'The acceptance of any new culture element entails certain changes in the total structure configuration. Although the full extent of these can never be forecast, certain of them are usually obvious. If the new trait is of such a sort that its acceptance will conflict directly with important traits already in the culture, it is almost certain to be rejected.' (Ralph Linton: *The Study of Man*.) Malinowski, Radcliffe-Brown, and other anthropologists of the Functionalist school, have suggested that each custom, belief, or trait in a society serves some function within the culture as a whole. Thus, although a culture element may have no objective use, it may nevertheless serve a subjective function. For example, the performance of magic rituals during work does not add to the success of the work in any objective manner, but it does contribute to the assurance and peace of mind of the worker, to what is generally described as his morale, and, as we shall see later, the distinctive dress, 'mythology', or beliefs of a working group in modern industry help to increase its social solidarity, and thereby its effectiveness.

It is apparent, of course, that whereas the Zuñi, the Mundugumor, or the Arapesh tribal societies have shown little change over many centuries, there are other societies, of which our own is one, which have radically altered even in the past fifty years. There are two reasons why this is so, as Professor W. F. Ogburn of Chicago tells us in his book *Social Change*:

'Primarily,' he says, 'the cause of social change is the making of inventions, mechanical or otherwise, and secondarily, the diffusion of inventions already made.' Each new invention (as contrasted with new discoveries), is for the most part a combination of old elements – that is to say, it is dependent upon principles already known. It therefore follows that the more of such elements there are in a particular culture the greater will be the number of possible new inventions. Technical progress moves at an ever-increasing rate for just this reason. Roughly speaking, as Ogburn shows, material culture grows according to the exponential principle (i.e., it grows like compound interest).

But, as we have already noted, each technical invention has an effect on those who use it, or, to say the same thing in another way, each invention becomes an aspect of the material environment to which the society must adjust itself.* This process of adjustment happens in three stages: (1) the invention or technique is created and accepted into the society, (2) individuals react towards it, and, finally (3) cultural institutions and beliefs are altered to allow for it. For example, the invention of the steam engine replaced manual work and water power in workshops (stage 1); it made the workers adjust to a new situation in which the machine and not the man set the pace (stage 2); there were more accidents, and ultimately workmen's compensation laws came into force (stage 3). In the sphere of belief, the idea that the worker had to take care of himself wholly upon his own responsibility had to go. (This was, of course, only one effect of the introduction of the steam engine, and a large part of Chapter 1 was taken up with describing the other results – the development of paleotechnic society). Another aspect, and a very significant one, of the impact of modern industrial technology upon society, has been the break-up of the family as a social unit. In pastoral or agricultural communities, the family is not only a biological unit – it is also a unit of production, and children, being junior members of the productive unit, sharing in the work of the family, are social assets to their parents. This association of biological and psychological with socially productive unit disappears under

---

* Cp. Hegel's statement: 'Man, in so far as he acts on nature to change it, changes his own nature.'

industrialism. Children are no longer an economic asset, but an economic liability, and an increase in industrialization runs parallel with a decline in the birth rate. The home and the family are no longer the focal point of modern society. Peter Drucker, in his book *The New Society*, describes graphically the impact of the new mass-production techniques on ancient and long-established societies: 'The sweep of mass-production technology is undermining and exploding societies and civilizations which have no resistance to the new forces, no background or habit-pattern of industrial life to cushion the shock. In China the mass-production principle, swept into the hinterland from the coastal cities by the forced migration of industries during the Japanese invasion, is destroying the world's oldest and hitherto its stablest institution: the Chinese family. In India industrialization has begun to corrode the Hindu caste system: ritual restrictions on proximity and intercourse between castes simply cannot be maintained under factory conditions ... In America the Old South, hitherto least touched by industry and still living in the ruins of its ante-bellum rural order, is speedily being "tractored off". Indeed, conversion of the Southern farm into a rural assembly line seems on the verge of "solving" the Southern race problem in a manner never dreamed of by either Southern Liberal or Southern Reactionary: by pushing the Negro off the land into the industrial cities.'

This rather long digression into the nature of society has been made for three reasons. Firstly, in order to make it quite clear to the reader that any society, whether at the national, tribal community, or even at the single factory level, is of the nature of an organism. One cannot do just anything by way of changing it; for it can only be changed in terms of its existing organization and structure, and in terms of its needs. Secondly, it is necessary to create a healthy scepticism in respect of what one can, and cannot, do in the way of social change. Many years ago, Herbert Spencer, in his book *The Study of Sociology*, described the process of attempting to change a society and likened it to the novice's attempt to beat out a dent in an iron plate. The novice hammers at the offending dent and soon succeeds in making it quite flat, only to find that another dent has appeared near the opposite edge of the plate. 'Where it was flat before it is now curved. A pretty bungle we have made of it. Instead of curing the original defect, we have produced a second.' 'Even a sheet of metal', continues Spencer, 'is not to be successfully dealt with after those common-sense methods in which you have so much confidence. What, then, shall we say about a society? "Do you think that I am easier to be played on than a pipe?" asks Hamlet. Is humanity more readily straightened than an iron plate?' A whole series of social experiments, from the Prohibition Laws in the United States to the attempt to foist a democratic constitution upon a basically undemocratic Germany at the time of the Weimar republic, demonstrate that, however good our intentions, good intentions are not enough without knowledge. Thirdly, it is important to realize that all we have said here of national or tribal societies relates with equal force to the factory society. To send supervisors on a course to learn a more democratic approach, when they have to return to an autocratic factory, is in no wise different from the similar attempt to 'democratize' German policemen and return them to a society which is autocratic from the family upwards – both experiments will fail. To introduce new types of machinery which demand a totally different method of social organization in order to work them – to do this without adequate preparation – is, as we may see today in the British coal-mines, to court disaster. To ignore the little peculiarities of industrial groups – their 'rituals', customs, their concepts of what is, or is not, done, may lead to much the same effect as the banning of head-hunting amongst the New Guinea tribesmen, namely, the partial or complete disintegration of the group.

The nineteenth-century Rationalist approach assumed that individuals or societies could be changed by argument, by reason. It was assumed that when one had a good idea all that was necessary was to convert enough people and the idea would become reality. Alternatively, if one were in a position of power, the idea might be made reality simply by passing a law. This position is no longer tenable, because it is becoming increasingly apparent that many problems, both in industry and elsewhere, are such that they can only be radically solved at the national, the

European (or American), or even the global level. Well-meaning moralists who talk as if all that were necessary to make people 'good' or 'industrious' is to tell them not to be 'wicked' or 'lazy' are scientifically illiterate Canutes ordering the ocean to retire. Increasing cruelty to children, crime, and divorce rates, whilst filling the Sunday newspapers, are not signs of merely individual wickedness (or, at any rate, it is not profitable to think of them as such). They are symptoms of a diseased society. Take, for example, the problem of gambling, superstition, and belief in luck which is nowadays so prevalent. Gilbert Murray has pointed out that 'the best seed-ground for superstition is a society in which the fortunes of men seem to bear practically no relation to their merits and efforts. A stable and well-governed society does tend, speaking roughly, to ensure that the Virtuous and Industrious Apprentice shall succeed in life while the Wicked and Idle Apprentice fails. And in such a society people tend to lay stress on the reasonable or visible chains of causation.' But in a society in which promotion does not seem to bear much relationship to ability or performance, and, even more so, when there is mass unemployment with skilled and experienced men out of a job, people begin to feel that their fate is out of their control and come to depend on 'luck'. The moralists who so bitterly complain of certain forms of behaviour are, in fact, not infrequently those who have played a large part in bringing about the social circumstances which lead to the acts of which they complain. People, to be sure, are no worse than they ever have been, but it takes a moral giant to go against the tide of circumstance – and few of us are moral giants.

A final point of distinction between the picture of man prevalent during the eighteenth and nineteenth centuries and that of today is that we no longer think of man as a machine either with, or without, a 'ghost'. Modern science is neither mechanistic nor vitalistic, since it regards body and mind as inseparable.* 'Mind' is not thought of as a separate entity, but simply as an abstract noun which is used to refer to certain processes going

* In point of fact, the mechanistic hypothesis is by no means so opposed to vitalism as most people assume. If we begin by postulating that the human individual is a machine, then we have to introduce the concept of 'mind' in order to explain why he does not in all respects behave as such.

on in living matter at a certain level of development. 'Mind' exists in the same sense that 'digestion' exists, not as a 'thing' but a process, and, as we shall see later, it is now an accepted fact in modern medicine that prolonged emotional stress may eventually lead to organic disease with structural changes which may ultimately prove fatal, in fact, to what is known as psychosomatic disease. This does not occur as the result of what used to be described as 'mind over matter' – except in a very metaphorical sense – it occurs because what we subjectively experience as an emotion is a physico-chemical state of the body. Thus resentment repressed over a long period of time may lead to the disease of hypertension or high blood-pressure (the blood-pressure is normally raised during anger), or chronic anxiety may lead to gastric ulcer (the muscles of the stomach contract during anxiety). These psychosomatic or 'stress' diseases, which include not only certain cases of high blood-pressure and gastric ulcer, but also colitis, many skin diseases, some serious heart diseases, exophthalmic goitre, some forms of rheumatism, and so on, are, as we shall see later, on the increase in all highly-industrialized countries. Other disorders, which are at least partly emotional in origin, are rheumatoid arthritis, diabetes, the predisposition to tuberculosis, and numerous gynaecological conditions. Industrial accidents are often psychologically motivated, and the so-called 'industrial dermatitis', apart from that due to recognized skin irritants such as strong alkalis and acids or other caustic substances, is almost entirely a psychological problem. It is the modern view that the neuroses, whether psychosomatic or mainly psychological in their manifestations, are social diseases. This being the case, the psychological conditions of work in the factory become even more important. When it is realized that the emotions aroused in industry: resentment, anxiety, fear, and hatred, not only make people unhappy and 'nervous', but may, and frequently do, shorten their lives, the problems of human relations in the factory become even more important. The well-known quotation from John Donne to the effect that 'no man is an island' must be accepted, not as a theological or ethical platitude, but as a realistic statement of scientific fact.

Thus far, we have been mainly concerned with the changing

concepts of the nature of human beings and their societies, and to conclude this chapter we must discuss briefly the modern views relating to the development of the individual personality. Although there is still some room for discussion as to the exact details of what is inherited in man, there is good reason to suppose that the psychological qualities inherited by the individual are relatively simple in nature and only become elaborated when they come into contact with the culture or way of life of the society in which he is going to live. The human personality is primarily the result of an interaction between the hereditary traits on the one hand and culture as presented through the medium of the family on the other. Or, to use a common analogy, heredity supplies the raw material, culture the design, and the family is the craftman whose function it is to model the given material into a more or less close approximation to the design with which society has supplied him. But, unlike the materials with which the ordinary craftsman has to work, the human child is not passive under the moulding process, and the finished result may not be exactly what the parents intended: the basic character traits, as they later reveal themselves, will depend in part upon whether the child conformed willingly, more or less willingly, or rebelled in relation to the first social demands made upon him. In turn, this is related to hereditary qualities of temperament and to the skill and understanding with which the parents carry out their task. 'Systems of child training', writes E. H. Erikson, 'represent unconscious attempts at creating out of human raw material that configuration of attitudes which is (or once was) the optimum under the tribe's particular natural conditions and economic-historic necessities.' The type of character aimed at by any given society is known as the *basic character structure* of that culture, and we have seen that this differs widely from one society to another.

The biological drives of hunger, thirst, and the rest are primary needs which, owing to the utter helplessness of the infant, cannot be satisfied unaided. Since this is so, there arises very early in life the most fundamental of psychological needs – the need to be loved, protected, and cared for. This need, says Professor Kimball Young, is 'the underpinning on which all the later motives and the cultural imperatives are constructed.' In later life, the individual's continued awareness that he cannot satisfy his needs unaided, that his is dependent upon others makes him fight for social status; his status is the sign that he belongs within his social group, his badge of emotional security. Here we have the answer to the problem of the wide variety of traits which have, at one time or another, been supposed to form original human nature: the fact is that each culture, depending upon its total situation, has set a premium on specific forms of activity which are then untilized by the individual in order to obtain the approval and regard of his fellows. Ruth Benedict has expressed this relationship in the following way: 'Man is a highly gregarious animal and he always wants the approval of his fellows. First, of course, he had to get the means of keeping alive, but after that he will try to get approval in forms which his society recognizes. His society may recognize conquest, and he will engage in conquest; it may recognize wealth, and he will measure success by dollars and cents; it may recognize caste, and he will behave in all things according to the position in which he was born.'

The general design of personality, then, comes from the individual's culture – 'personality is the subjective aspect of culture'. But as we have seen, culture, in the early years of life (which are the formative years), does not reach the child directly but only through the mediation of the family. Differences between individuals, therefore, when they are brought up within the same culture or sub-culture, depend partly upon inherited differences of temperament and intelligence and partly upon differences in upbringing and in the family constellation. During the first five years of life, the child begins to learn, not only by what the Behaviourists describe as 'conditioning', but also by a process of trial and error and by acquiring the habits taught by its parents. These habits are established by differential reward and punishment, indulgence and deprivation, or the implied threat of deprivation of affection on the part of the parents who utilize the infant's needs to avoid harm and obtain satisfaction of its organic drives to this end. The habits acquired at this stage relate to sleeping and feeding, bowel and bladder control, and the child's early loves and hates (Oedipus complex) within the family circle. Throughout this period it develops attitudes towards its father and mother, brothers and sisters, which become the proto-type of its attitudes towards all the people it meets subsequently. During the first five years of life, whilst the basic character is being laid down, the child is learning not only control of its excretory and feeding functions but also how to deal with people; if it is not given affection freely, consistently, and unconditionally, it will soon learn more complex and abnormal methods of gaining attention. If being sick produces the required results (i.e., love, or at any rate attention), the child will develop into the sort of person who seeks refuge in real or imagined illness when trouble threatens; if being aggressive or demanding works ('all right, if you don't love me I shall at least see to it that you have to pay *some* sort of attention to me'), the child will utilize these techniques of the delinquent throughout life; if keeping to one-self works ('if I leave people alone, they won't harm me'), this attitude, too, becomes structured into the basic personality. In the words of Dr Camilla Anderson: 'We become acceptable or non-acceptable, helpless or capable, important or insignificant, passive or agressive, busy or lazy, resourceful, or cautious, or sweet, or clever, or polite, or thoughtful, or obedient, or demand-ing, or a thousand and one other characteristics. These are the traits which are produced by the child and structuralized into his very self because of their *functional* value to him in the earliest years of life. Each one was the trait that worked best and got the best results in the particular setting in which he was placed.'

Since the individual's personality is an integrated set of respon-ses to life as he has experienced it – is in short a form of adapta-tion, however, inadequate – he feels a need to maintain it, and therefore the more deep-rooted aspects of behaviour are not easily changed. Even when he is placed in a more favourable environment, each individual tends to interpret his experiences in the ways learned during his early years. It is therefore true to say that the core of the personality is set in infancy and early childhood. The attitudes which arise in the first five years persist throughout life, often modified by later experiences but never entirely obliterated. This core personality is rigid in structure and strongly resists change. On the other hand, the more superficial aspects of personality with which we are mainly concerned in this book change very readily; these aspects which are described as relating to the 'peripheral', 'public', or 'social' personality, will be dealt with shortly. What does not change is the groundwork of the personality: 'Whether a person will become timid or outgoing, cautious or enterprising, self-confident and optimistic or self-critical and pessimistic, aggressive or submissive, dependent or independent, generous or withholding, orderly or careless – all these personality features which make a person a well-defined individual, different from others – depends on the influence of the intimate personal environment (i.e. the early parent-child relationship) on a hereditary substratum.' (Dr Franz Alexander, *Educative Influence of Personality Factors in the Environment*: an essay in Kluckhohn and Murray's *Personality in Nature, Society, and Culture*.) The basic personality is the result of cultural influences as handed on through the medium of the family, of what Dr Halmos describes as *mediated* social-cultural influence, whereas the peripheral personality results from the direct relationship between the individual and his society after the formative years are over. The peripheral personality is based on *direct* social-cultural influence.

Freud believed that the moral compulsions felt by the individual in relation to his society came to him through the medium of his superego, a sort of 'psychic gyroscope', to use the description of Dr Gardner Murphy, which keeps the individual on a straight course. The Freudian account of the origins of the superego is complicated and we need not concern ourselves with the details here. Suffice it to say that, although the child has been learning throughout its early years which actions are rewarded and which are not, in the fourth or fifth year of life (following on the experiences of the Oedipus complex) it starts to learn in a new way. It *identifies* itself with its parents. This term implies a great deal more than mere imitation. The child takes the parents' moral code within its own mind – or, more accurately, certain aspects of their moral code – and makes them a part of itself. Whereas, formerly, the parent stood outside and said 'Thou shalt' or 'Thou shalt not', from this time onwards it is as if an internalized parent within the mind gave the commands. A part of the mind is differentiated from the rest which becomes the representative of society and prevents the individual from doing certain forbidden acts or makes him feel guilty when he has done them. It is the 'still small voice' generally known as conscience. The concepts of conscience and superego do not completely coincide, however, since, firstly, the superego does not cover the whole field of morals but only a few fundamental regulations, and, secondly, there is no implication, as there is in the term 'conscience', that there is some supernatural sanction for the superego's dictates – it is simply the internalized voice of society, handed on by the parents to their children. This process of handing on is an unconscious one and the superego is, for the most part, unconscious; it may often be noticed, for example, that an individual will suffer severe pangs of conscience after he has done some act which intellectually he believes to be quite harmless – he is more, as well as less, moral than he knows.

What has been earlier described as the 'peripheral personality' arises in the social interactions of the individual within his primary, and, to a lesser extent, within his secondary groups. In Chapter 6 we shall discuss the problem of how attitudes change as members move from one group to another, the distinction between membership groups and reference groups, and so on. All that need be said here is that a great deal of behaviour which has been supposed to come from within the individual, to be based on his fixed character traits, is, in fact, a function of the individual within the group. Thus, as was noted in the previous chapter, the worker in a suspicious group behaves differently from the same worker in a happy group or from the way he behaves at home; the agitator who has always been teased and looked on with amused contempt in a happy setting becomes a leader when there is a strike, and, although all doctors, clergymen, and miners are unique individuals, each profession or trade produces certain uniformities of behaviour within its members. All physicians and clergymen, for example, behave in certain respect according to their social rôle – the concept society has given them of how men in their position ought to behave.

There is no law which says that clergymen may not play the saxophone, or that doctors may not go to work in an open-necked shirt without a tie, but such behaviour would clash with what is considered fitting in the rôles they are playing. The wide range of behaviour which may be noted within the same individual is a part of his peripheral personality and is related to his group memberships, his status, and his social rôle. Since this is so, Karl Mannheim can say quite correctly: 'We are altogether too prone to think of ourselves and our fellow-men in fixed terms; a coward is always afraid, a shy girl is always retiring, a bad worker is always lazy and slow. But the coward may be very active within a rioting group and the valiant soldier may be easily cowed by his boss. The shy and blushing girl may be saucy enough to her mother and sisters in the familiar surroundings of her home; and the slack worker may prove to be a very efficient member of a team. Thus the elasticity of human nature seems to be much greater in various group settings. We form such rigid pictures of people only because we are accustomed to see them in so very few established situations.' But this statement of Mannheim's should not be thought to conflict with that of Franz Alexander quoted earlier in this chapter or with what we have said about the fixity of the basic personality. Clearly, people may do very different actions from the same deep-seated motives. We do not suppose that the supervisor who is submissive to those in authority and bullying towards his subordinates has, on each occasion, changed his basic personality. On the contrary, he is acting very much in character in both situations. The manager who is hated by his employees may be civil and even benevolent outside the factory – yet both forms of behaviour may be based on a compulsive desire for power over others. Within his factory, when he has 'got people where he wants them' he may show a naked lust for power, but this technique would not work elsewhere, for he would simply be ignored. He has to buy power outside the factory with gifts, flattery, and in a more indirect manner. The 'lazy' worker may be a highly intelligent man who resents being treated as an irresponsible cog in a wheel, and, when he is not so treated, he may be as hard-working as anyone. The 'bravest' man may be 'cowardly' if he is compelled to fight for a cause he does not consider to be worth fighting for, and the 'coward' may be 'brave' precisely because he is so afraid of appearing foolish in front of others whose opinions he values. It follows, then, that the relatively fixed and rigid basic personality may manifest itself in a wide variety of different ways in different settings. The human personality is both rigid and malleable – rigid in its depths and malleable on the surface. Finally, we may note the strange – and hopeful – fact that it is easier to change the behaviour of groups of people than to change them as individuals. This, of course, has to do with the nature of social controls on behaviour, a point which will be discussed more fully later. At this point, all that need be said is that the moral control exercised by the superego is not only limited in scope (in the sense that it is concerned with only a limited number of moral problems), but there can be little doubt that in many individuals superego control is very weak. The major controlling force in society is not the superego of the individual but the social controls of the groups to which he belongs.

To summarize: the old paleotechnic view in science held that the human body resembled a machine, that every disease was therefore due to a breakdown in one or other of the parts, and that it was the physician's duty to discover the fault and repair it; it held that human nature was explicable solely in terms of biological instincts and was the same the whole world over. Society was regarded as a mass of unorganized individuals in incessant competition with each other, so that the individual and society were inevitably at war; negative emotions were assumed to be primary, positive ones merely derived from the necessity to repress and sublimate the others. Psychology was defined as the study of the individual mind, and the superego was assumed to be the sole source of moral controls (other than the compulsive force of law). The new view holds that the human body is an organism which cannot be defined in terms of non-living categories, it does not think in terms of 'mind' but of mental processes, and regards all disease as a total response to environmental threat, whether from germs, poisons, physical agents, or emotions induced by social interaction. It does not accept instinct as an adequate explanation of human behaviour, and is more interested in how the biological drives are socially modified than in their mere existence; i.e., its explanations are in social rather than biological terms. Society is also regarded as an organism – as a body of *organized* individuals – and man as basically a social animal. All psychology is social psychology, and, without denying the existence of the superego, it is believed that the major instrument of social control is the primary group.

3

THE WORK OF ELTON MAYO

THE inadequacy of the assumptions on which most of the early work in industrial psychology had been based was first shown by the failure of certain experiments carried out at the Hawthorne Works of the Western Electric Company in Chicago between 1924 and 1927. This company manufactures equipment for the Bell Telephone system, and, at the time of the experiments, there had been a good deal of grumbling and dissatisfaction amongst the 30,000 employees of the firm. (It should be noted that, in all material conditions, this was a most progressive company with pension schemes, sickness benefit schemes, and numerous recreational and other facilities.) Efficiency experts who were called in to deal with the trouble attempted by the usual methods – altering working hours, changing the length and spacing of rest-periods, changing the intensity of lighting and other environmental conditions – to find some means of reducing the existing tension and raising production. But these investigations proved to be inconclusive, and, in 1924, the company asked for the co-operation of the National Academy of Sciences which began its researches with an attempt to study the relationship between the efficiency of the worker and illumination in the workshop.

The assumptions which lay behind all these experiments were those of the industrial psychology founded by Taylor, Frank Gilbreth, and their numerous successors. That is to say, it was supposed that the worker must be studied as an isolated unit; that in certain important respects he resembled a machine whose efficiency could be scientifically estimated; and that the main factors influencing his efficiency were (a) wasteful or ineffectual movements in doing his job, (b) fatigue, which was believed to be a physico-chemical state of the body due to the accumulation of waste products, and (c) defects in the physical environment, such as poor lighting, inadequate heating, excessive humidity, and so on. These beliefs, as we saw in Chapter 1, were based partly on the atomistic view of society which arose during the early paleotechnic phase of industry and partly on the mechanistic approach of eighteenth- and nineteenth-century medicine. But, as the Hawthorne research proceeded, they were to receive a severe blow from which they have never since recovered. It is not that the assumptions are to be regarded as entirely untrue – there are circumstances in which the individual may profitably be studied in isolation, and there can be no doubt that bad environmental conditions adversely affect efficiency, or that Time and Motion studies in reducing ineffectual movements may be of material aid. But they are not the whole truth, or even the most important part of the truth. What the Hawthorne researches were to demonstrate was that there is 'something far more important than hours, wages, or physical conditions of work – *something which increased output no matter what was done about physical conditions*'. (D. C. Miller and W. H. Form, *Industrial Sociology*.)

In order, then, to study the effects of altered illumination on work (on the assumption that the better the light, the better the work), two groups of employees were selected. In one, the control group, the illumination remained unchanged throughout the experiment, while in the other the illumination was increased in intensity. As had been expected, the output in the latter group showed an improvement, but what was quite unforeseen was that the output of the control group went up also. As the lighting in this case had not been altered, the result was naturally puzzling to the investigators, who then proceeded to reduce the illumination for the test group. When this had been done, output went up once more. Obviously some factor was at work which increased output regardless of either greater or less intensity of light in the workshop, and further experiments became necessary in order to discover the nature of this unknown factor.

The investigators selected two girls for their second series of experiments, and asked them to choose another four girls, thus making a small group of six. The group was employed in assembling telephone relays – a relay being a small but intricate mechanism composed of about forty separate parts which had to be assembled by the girls seated at a long bench, and dropped into a chute when completed. The relays were mechanically counted as they slipped down the chute. It was intended that the basic rate of production should be noted at the start and that subsequently changes would be introduced the effectiveness of which would be measured by increased or decreased production of the relays. Throughout the series of experiments, which lasted over a period of five years, an observer sat with the girls in the workshop noting all that went on, keeping the girls informed about the experiment, asking for advice or information, and listening to their complaints.

The experiment began by introducing various changes, each of which was continued for a test period of four to twelve weeks. The results of these changes are summarized below:

(1) Under normal conditions with a forty-eight-hour week, including Saturdays, and no rest-pauses, the girls produced 2,400 relays a week each.

(2) They were then put on piece-work for eight weeks, and output went up.

(3) Two five-minute rest-pauses, morning and afternoon, were introduced for a period of five weeks, and output went up once more.

(4) The rest-pauses were lengthened to ten minutes each. Output went up sharply.

(5) Six five-minutes pauses were introduced, and output fell slightly as the girls complained that their work-rhythm was broken by the frequent pauses.

(6) Return to the two rest-pauses, the first with a hot meal supplied by the company free of charge. Output went up.

(7) The girls were dismissed at 4.30 p.m. instead of 5 p.m. Output went up.

(8) They were dismissed at 4 p.m., and output remained the same.

(9) Finally, all the improvements were taken away, and the girls went back to the physical conditions of the beginning of the experiment: work on Saturday, forty-eight-hour week, no rest pauses, no piece-work, and no free

meal. This state of affairs lasted for a period of twelve weeks, and output was the highest ever recorded, averaging 3,000 relays a week.

Stuart Chase, in his books *The Proper Study of Mankind* and *Men at Work*, gives an interesting account of the implications of this piece of research. Briefly they were that production was raised primarily because of a change in the girls' attitudes towards their work and their work-team. 'By asking their help and co-operation, the investigators had made the girls feel important. Their whole attitude had changed from that of separate cogs in a machine to that of a congenial group trying to help the company solve a problem. They had found stability, a place where they belonged, and work whose purpose they could clearly see. And so they worked faster and better than they ever had in their lives.' It has been demonstrated that industry, apart from the production of goods, has also a social function to perform; that the primary group rather than the isolated individual should be the basic unit of observation in all industrial research; and that adequate motivation is more important than the conditions of the physical environment. Chase continues: 'A factory performs two major functions: the economic one of producing goods and the social one of creating and distributing human satisfactions among the people under its roof. A great deal of study by efficiency experts had been devoted to the production function, but very little to the social function until the Hawthorne experiment came along and discovered that the two were inseparable. If a factory's human organization is out of balance all the efficiency systems in the world will not improve the output.'

Further significant results of the investigation were that medical examinations carried out regularly showed no signs of cumulative fatigue, and absence from work declined by 80 per cent. It was noted, too, that each girl had her own technique of putting the component parts of the relays together – sometimes she varied this technique in order to avoid monotony, and it was found that the more intelligent the girl the greater was the number of variations. This, says Chase, should be a warning to Time and Motion engineers who attempt to standardize movements to the exclusion of such small personal touches. The experimental group was given considerable freedom of movement. They came and went as they pleased, and were not 'pushed around' by anyone. Under these conditions, the group developed an increased sense of responsibility, and instead of discipline from higher authority being required, it came from within the group itself. Finally, it was observed that feelings not only counted more than hours of labour – they also counted more than wages. Workers, it became evident, were more concerned about the relationship between their pay and that of their fellow-workers than they were about the exact amount of money they were given. High wages were little ground for satisfaction if somebody in a job which was considered to have lower status than their own was given more. 'Some day,' writes Chase, 'factory managers are going to realize that workers are *not* governed primarily by economic motives ... Underneath the stop-watches and bonus plans of the efficiency experts, the worker is driven by a desperate inner urge to find an environment where he can take root, where he belongs and has a function; where he sees the purpose of his work and feels important in achieving it. Failing this, he will accumulate frustrations and obsessions. "Fatigue" and "monotony" are effects of frustration rather than the causes of it. For their neglect of the human function of production, managers have paid a high price in strikes, restricted output, and a vast sea of human waste.'

The man who was responsible for the Hawthorne experiments was George Elton Mayo, professor of Industrial Research at the Harvard Graduate School of Business. Mayo, an Australian from Adelaide, was born in 1880 and trained in psychology at the University of Adelaide. He first came to the United States on a grant from the Rockefeller Foundation, and was appointed head of the Department of Industrial Research at Harvard in 1926, remaining in this position until his retirement in 1947. It is interesting to follow the development of Mayo's thought from his first researches in 1923 (when he carried out an investigation into the causes of high labour turnover among mule spinners in a textile mill near Philadelphia) to the change of orientation following the Hawthorne researches which influenced all his later work. It is unnecessary to describe the 1923 researches in detail, but a brief account will demonstrate how, although the same factors were at work as in the later experiments, they were missed owing to Mayo's preoccupation with a mechanistic individual psychology and the material conditions of the job. Briefly, then, the circumstances were that, while labour turnover in most departments of this textile mill was 5 to 6 per cent per annum, the turnover in the spinning department was somewhere in the region of 250 per cent. The work in this department consisted in the 'piecer' – the man who attended the machine – walking up and down a distance of thirty yards or more and tying the threads on the spinning frames. In theory, the worker received a bonus each month when production exceeded 75 per cent of a carefully calculated quota (e.g., if it reached 80 per cent, every worker in the department received a 5 per cent bonus on his monthly wage). The bonus, however, remained in the field of theory, since the mule-spinning department had never exceeded 70 per cent of the quota. Special conditions of the job which had a bearing on the attitudes of the workers were, (1) that the workers had a low estimate of the status of their job: 'It doesn't take any brains to be a piecer,' they would say, 'just strong legs'. (2) The job was monotonous. (3) The work was essentially solitary, since the terrific noise of the machines and the distance between the workers made any sort of communication almost impossible.

Mayo began this early piece of research with the introduction of rest-periods which amounted to two ten-minute breaks in the morning and two in the afternoon. The workers were encouraged to sleep for these periods, which initially were made available to only one third of the men in the department. The results were impressive, since labour turnover decreased and output went up. If was further noted that morale had improved and the men were more friendly in their attitude. But what was at that time quite inexplicable to Mayo, was that there was an almost equivalent rise in production and decrease in labour turnover among the two-thirds of the men who had been excluded from the experiment although they worked in the same department. By the end of the first month, production efficiency had reached nearly

80 per cent and the workers received their first bonus. Within four months the level of production was 82 per cent.

At this point, certain difficulties began to arise. The supervisors of the department had never liked the new system, and, it seems probable, shared with many other supervisors a dislike of what they considered to be pampering the workers in the name of science. They believed that the rest-pauses should be earned (that is to say that the men should be expected to complete certain jobs before being authorized to rest), and, when a special rush order was received, they abandoned the rest-pauses completely. (The assumption that, the longer the hours of work, the more goods should be produced, dies hard.) Within five days, conditions were back to what they had been when the experiment started, production was the lowest for months, absenteeism went up, and morale went down. The supervisors were, not unnaturally, upset, and brought back the rest-periods once more, but, this time, strictly on an earned basis. Again the workers failed to respond, and production was back at 70 per cent. The position was a desperate one for the firm, since it looked as if the rush order would never be completed. But, at this moment, the President of the company, in consultation with Mayo, took charge. He ordered that during the rest pauses the machines should be shut down so that everyone in the department would be compelled to rest whether he was worker or supervisor. The supervisors were still more alarmed, for it seemed impossible that the time lost on the job could ever be recovered. But once more absenteeism diminished, morale went up, and production increased to 77½ per cent. Subsequent changes permitted the men to select their own rest-pauses which alternated with each other, so that the machines could be kept running continuously. This was the final phase of the experiment. Production reached 86½ per cent, and several years later the President of the company was able to report that labour turnover had never since exceeded 5 to 6 per cent – that is, it was the same in the spinning department as in the rest of the factory. The problem had been solved.

Mayo's explanation of the results, in view of his later work, was a peculiar one. He believed that the monotony of the job led to 'pessimistic reveries': 'Everyone, worker or executive, probably

75

carries with him a private grief or discontent. Whenever the conditions of work are unsuitable, physically or mentally, the immediate effect seems to be an increase of pessimistic or bitter reflexion.' Furthermore, he supposed that, when carrying out the same movements over a long period of time, postural fatigue and impaired circulation arise which adversely influence efficiency. Both these conditions, it seemed, were such as could be interrupted by the rest-pauses. (We may note here the attitude of early industrial consultants that the solutions to their problems lay within the minds and bodies of individual workers – boredom leads to depressing thoughts coming to the surface, and monotony of movement leads to impaired circulation and fatigue.) We need not necessarily cast doubt on the validity of these assumptions, although it is surely an exaggeration to suppose that the thoughts of the average man are so depressing that he must at all costs perform non-monotonous work in order to keep them out of consciousness. What, one wonders, does he do at home or during a rest-pause when he does not even have monotonous work to keep his mind occupied? In point of fact, there is every reason to suppose that such depressing reveries as exist are, for the most part, due to the poor morale and unsatisfactory psychological conditions in the workshop. One the other hand, the theory of postural fatigue is a fairly reasonable one which would be accepted by most physiologists – all of us, for example, tend to interrupt prolonged sitting or standing in the same position by getting up and moving about. In this way, stagnation of the blood in the dependent parts of the body is prevented and the circulation once more stimulated into greater activity. Such stagnation may be an important factor in the production of certain types of fatigue, but is in no way capable of explaining the results of the experiment. If the results had been due to the factors originally suggested as causal by Mayo, we should still have to explain (a) why the earned rest-pauses failed to raise production, since their purely physical effect could be no different from that of an unearned pause, and (b) why the two-thirds of the workers to whom, in the first instance, the rest-pauses were not applied, showed an almost equal rise in productive capacity and decrease in absenteeism.

In his later book, *The Social Problems of an Industrial Civilization*, Mayo took an entirely different view of his results in this piece of research. He pointed out that, firstly, the mere fact of the research being carried out demonstrated to the workers that their problems were not being ignored. That, secondly, the President of the company had always been popular with his employees, and was never more so than when he took the side of the workers against the supervisors who had put a stop to the rest-pauses. But, finally, and most important of all, a crowd of solitary workers had been transformed into a group with a sense of social responsibility when they had themselves been given control over their rest-periods. 'This led to consultation throughout the group–and to a feeling of responsibility directly to the President. And the general social changes effected were astonishing – even in relationships outside the factory.' What this and many later experiments were to show was the complete inadequacy of the paleotechnic assumptions concerning human nature already discussed in Chapter 1, and attributed, rather unfairly, by Mayo to the economist Ricardo. Mayo described this as the 'rabble hypothesis' of society, and describes what he considers to be its main postulates as follows:

'(1) Natural society consists of a horde of unorganized individuals.
(2) Every individual acts in a manner calculated to secure his self-preservation or self-interest.
(3) Every individual thinks logically, to the best of his ability, in the service of this aim.'

As we have seen, this hypothesis cannot be attributed to any one individual but was part of the ideology of industrialists at a particular stage of industrial development. Its appearance in the spheres of economics, biology, and philosophy, followed rather than preceded its appearance in industry. Mayo's demonstration of the falsity of the 'rabble hypothesis' of society was, however, a major achievement with important implications for industry of which he has written in the book already quoted: 'The ordinary conception of management–worker relations, as existing between company officials, on the one hand, and an unspecified number of individuals, on the other, is utterly mistaken. Management, in any continuously successful plant, is not related to single workers but always to working groups. In every department that continues to operate, the workers have – whether aware of it or not – formed themselves into a group with appropriate customs, duties, routines, even rituals; and management succeeds (or fails) in proportion as it is accepted without reservation by the group as author and leader.'

The initial part of the Hawthorne research in which Mayo had been brought in to deal with the problem following the puzzling results of the early experiments on illumination has already been considered. The brief account given here can do little justice to the elaborate nature of the investigations during which all physical conditions both in the workshops and in the workers themselves had to be kept rigidly under control. The temperature and humidity of the room were taken hourly, while wind, sunshine, and all those other environmental conditions so dear to the heart of the industrial psychologist were also carefully measured. Each worker was medically examined every five or six weeks. When, however, it became evident that what really mattered was the changed attitudes of the employees to their work, an interviewing programme was started with the intention of discovering the nature of these attitudes. Initially, these interviews were carried out by means of direct questioning, each employee being given to understand that he could speak his mind freely. He was then asked point-blank such questions as: 'Do you like your supervisor?' 'Is he in your opinion fair, or does he have favourites?' and so on. But this method was found to have many disadvantages – it tended to arouse antagonism or stereotyped responses, it was likely to produce over-simplified yes-or-no answers, and, while dealing with problems which appeared important to the interviewer, it tended to pass over problems which were important to the worker but unknown to the interviewer. The method was therefore changed to what is known as 'non-directive' interviewing in which the interviewer listens rather than talks, is taught never to argue or give advice, to remain morally quite neutral, and to treat as completely confidential everything that he hears.

As a result of this interviewing programme, various observations were made. It was found, for example, that merely giving a person an opportunity to talk and air his grievances has a beneficial effect on his morale. Thus, a woman who had complained at great length about the poor quality of food in the canteen came along a few days later and thanked an interviewer profusely for taking her complaint to the management and securing such a vast improvement in the canteen meals. In fact, the interviewer had done nothing whatever in this respect. Secondly, it was observed that complaints are not necessarily objective statements of fact (Freud, of course, had discovered this long ago). They are often symptoms of more deep-seated disturbances. Thirdly, that workers are influenced in their demands by experiences both inside and outside the factory. Fourthly, that the worker is satisfied or dissatisfied not in terms of any objective frame of reference but rather in terms of how he regards his social status in the firm and what he feels he is entitled to in the way of rewards. These points will be dealt with more fully at a later stage, but it may be helpful at this stage to give an example illustrating the second point (that complaints are not necessarily objective statements of fact, but may conceal more deep-seated disturbances), which is perhaps the least readily understood of the four. The example is taken from a paper read by Dr D. S. F. Robertson of Unilever Ltd at a meeting of the Association of Industrial Medical Officers: 'Not long ago it was decided in one of our offices to replace the older tungsten type of lighting with fluorescent units. The office contained some twenty men whose work consisted of fine drawing and highly-skilled artistic work.

'Within a short time of the change-over many of the men had visited the medical department complaining of an assortment of symptoms attributed in every case to eyestrain – conjunctivitis, sore eyes, headaches, and even double vision were complained of. Each case was treated on its merits without any attempt being made to investigate further. Within a week a "round-robin" was presented to management from the group concerned to the effect that the undersigned could not continue their work because of eyestrain due to fluorescent lighting.

'Now the lighting was a considerable improvement on the old, and there could be no doubt whatever that the complaint had no basis in fact. Expert opinion was unanimous on this and yet the complaints went on.

'Finally, the troubles were resolved by consultation with all the members of the group participating, and, of course, the fluorescent lighting was only being made the scapegoat for other difficulties mainly due to faulty leadership of the group, but also, it must be said, due to the elementary fact that the group was never consulted on the change before it first took place.

'Since then there have been, I would add, no further complaints of eyestrain.' (*Some Human Relation Problems in Industry*, October, 1950).

To return to the Hawthorne experiment. It had been discovered by this time that social groups formed in a factory workshop were capable of exercising considerable influence over the behaviour of their individual members, and, in particular, over the amount of work they would do. Observers had noted that, in certain departments, output had been restricted by the workers in complete disregard of all financial incentives which the management were offering, and it seemed likely that this phenomenon was due to group pressure on the individual worker. Dr Mayo decided to investigate one of these departments, which was known as the 'bank-wiring' room, in order to discover as much as possible about the restriction of output by those employed in it. There were fourteen men employed on 'bank-wiring', which involves attaching wires to switches for certain parts of telephone equipment, and, of these, nine men attached the wires, three soldered them, and the remaining two were inspectors. Now, the problem in this piece of research was not, as in the previous ones, to alter behaviour or increase productive efficiency, but rather to observe exactly what went on. In other words, it was important precisely that the workers should *not* be changed by the conditions of the research. With this in mind, the investigation was carried out by two men, an observer and an interviewer. The observer was actually in the wiring-room, with instructions to be friendly to everybody, but to give no orders, to avoid giving the impression of being too interested, and to be as non-committal as possible. The interviewer, on the other hand, was never to enter the wiring-room, but to discover as much as possible by interview about the individual workers, their thoughts and feelings, their values, and their family and personal history. His work was to be carried out under strictly confidential conditions, privately, and in another part of the factory. He was, however, to keep in daily touch with the observer.

The results of this investigation showed that this little group of men had developed spontaneously into a team with natural leaders who had risen to the top with the active consent of the group. (These natural leaders, as has been found in numerous similar investigations, do not necessarily or even usually coincide with those put in authority by management, but within the group they have far greater power than the official authorities.) Towards the financial incentives of the company the attitude of the group was one of complete indifference, and, although the incentive plan provided that the more work an employee did, the more money he received, neither more nor less than 6,000 units were produced each day. Yet the group could without the least difficulty have produced 7,000 units daily. Any worker, however, who attempted more than this group-determined quota was soon put in his place. Obviously the values and customs of the group were more important to the individuals composing it than any cash benefits. An informal organization existed which had its own social norms, some expressed verbally, others implicit in actions – for example, the daily output represented a standard never clearly expressed of what the group considered to be a fair day's work. There was an unofficial code of behaviour which exerted a powerful influence over group members and impressed on them the following rules:

(1) You should not turn out too much work. If you do you are a 'rate-buster'.
(2) You should not turn out too little work. If you do you are a 'chiseller'.
(3) You should not tell a supervisor anything that will react to the detriment of an associate. If you do, you are a 'squealer'.
(4) You should not attempt to maintain social distance or

'act officious'. If you are an inspector, for example, you should not behave like one.

Professor P. Sargant Florence comments on this unofficial code that, 'to those who have been "through the mill" of an English public school this social situation will not appear improbable or unfamiliar. All these rules are there observed; though the names given to their violators may be different. Rate-busters have been called swots, chisellers, slackers, squealers, sneaks. Americans apparently had no name for (4) but familiar English slang is swank. This code in the American factory and English public schools was as inviolate as primitive rituals; to break it was taboo – simply not done, or if done the violation would lead to social ostracism. British inquiries into the social relationships within the factory have not been so thorough but also supply an inkling of the importance of the unofficial group "codes" running counter to efficiency. Workers are related to their work less than is supposed by the cash-nexus – or by interest in the work itself (the hobby-nexus) – more by a gang-nexus or status-nexus. His group with its code of conduct, and his standing in the factory hierarchy is equally important to the worker as his wage or his work.' (*Labour*.) It became clear that, in the 'bank-wiring' room, there existed a highly integrated group with its own social structure and code of behaviour – a code which conflicted not only with the intentions of management but also with the express purpose and social function of industry, which is to produce more goods. There are two lessons to be learned from this part of the Hawthorne research. Firstly that no collection of people can be in contact for any length of time without such informal groupings arising and natural leaders being pushed to the top. Secondly, that it is not only foolish but futile to try to break up these groups; a wise policy would see to it that the interests of management and workers coincided to such an extent that the collection of informal groups which makes up a factory would be working towards the same goals instead of frustrating each other's efforts.

The above example shows how an informal group in a workshop had the effect of lowering output from the factory. A final piece of investigation by Mayo carried out at a much later date demonstrates how such groups may co-operate with management in the raising of production. This research was begun in 1943, when Mayo and his associates were asked to investigate the problem of high labour turnover in certain aircraft factories in Southern California. An important part of the social background of this research was that the times were unsettled: many men were being taken from industry into the army, and many tens of thousands of workers from elsewhere in the country were moving into this area in search of work. This, however, was not thought to be in itself a sufficient explanation for a labour turnover of 70 to 80 per cent. It is unnecessary to go into the details of this investigation which, as in the previous case, showed the importance of the informal group or work-team. Briefly, it was found that absenteeism and high labour turnover occurred predominantly amongst those workers who did not make a team, who had not managed to fit into any group (either because of personal peculiarities or, more usually, because they had not been given the opportunity to do so). Having no social background, they had no feelings of loyalty and took little interest in what went on around them in the factory. On the other hand, investigation of a work team which had a production record 25 per cent above the average for the firm, showed up some of the factors which lead to good morale in the workshop. This group of men was recognized by the other workers as being somewhat clannish in that its members felt themselves to be superior to other groups – that is to say, they showed loyalty and pride of membership. The foreman of the department where the group was employed was a busy man and rarely visited it, while his senior assistant visited it only once a day. All the work was in charge of a man who had no official standing whatever, but was the natural leader of the team. This man had both the time (in that he was not distracted by the necessity of dealing with technical problems) and the ability to concentrate on group solidarity. He handled this problem in the following manner: all new employees were introduced to the other members of the team and placed with those who seemed likely to make congenial associates; later, they were taken to the end of the assembly line to see where the part being made in the department fitted into the finished article.

All complaints were dealt with at once by the leader, but if they were beyond his powers to handle he referred them to higher authority. The individual workers were in these ways given significance (they saw how their job fitted into the whole), comradeship (in being members of a team), and an awareness of being fairly treated.

In support of this attitude towards leadership is an interesting report from the Survey Research Centre of the University of Michigan (*Productivity, Supervision, and Employee Morale*) which presents selected findings from a study conducted at the Prudential Insurance Company. The investigators selected those supervisors who were in charge of groups whose production was above average and compared their methods with those of supervisors in charge of groups whose productive capacity was poor. It was found that the supervisors of high production groups were those who:

(1) Were under less supervision from their own supervisors.

(2) Placed less direct emphasis upon production as the goal.

(3) Encouraged employee participation in the making of decisions.

(4) Were more employee-centred.

(5) Spent more of their time in supervision and less in straight production work.

(6) Had a greater feeling of confidence in their supervisory roles.

(7) Felt that they knew where they stood in relation to the company.

Professors Miller and Form in their *Industrial Sociology*, one of the most recent and exhaustive works on the subject, consider the main implication of Mayo's work to be that 'the problem of absenteeism, turnover, low morale, and poor efficiency reduces to the problem of how groups may be solidified and collaboration increased in the large as well as the small work plant. The problem, as the famed sociologist, Charles H. Cooley, would say, is how to build primary group life.'

These two writers go on to summarize in more detail certain other conclusions to be drawn from Mayo's researches:

(1) Work is a group activity.

(2) The social world of the adult is primarily patterned about work activity.

(3) The need for recognition, security, and sense of belonging is more important in determining workers' morale and productivity than the physical conditions under which he works.

(4) A complaint is not necessarily an objective recital of facts; it is commonly a *symptom* manifesting disturbance of an individual's status position.

(5) The worker is a person whose attitudes and effectiveness are conditioned by social demands from both inside and outside the work plant.

(6) Informal groups within the work plant exercise strong social controls over the work habits and attitudes of the individual worker.

(7) The change from an established to an adaptive society (i.e., from the older type of community life to the atomistic society of isolated individuals, from eotechnic to paleotechnic society) tends continually to disrupt the social organization of a work plant and industry generally.

(8) Group collaboration does not occur by accident; it must be planned for and developed. If group collaboration is achieved, the work relations within a work plant may reach a cohesion which resists the disrupting effects of adaptive society.

Although it is undoubtedly true to say that the work of Mayo and his associates Roethlisberger and Dickson forms a foundation on which all further researches must be based, certain aspects of it have been subjected to criticism. Since much of what follows depends on the validity of Mayo's views, it is important that such criticisms as have been made should be dealt with at this point before we go any further. On the other hand, it may be said with a good deal of assurance that such disagreements as exist do not, in general, take the form of contradicting the actual results as summarized above. Rather they tend to take one of three attitudes which we may classify as that of the Industrialist, that of the Social Psychologist, and that of the Sociologist. The Industrialist is likely to believe that Mayo's conclusions are true but irrelevant; the Social Psychologist that they are true but obvious; the Sociologist that they are true but that they do not go far enough. We must now consider these various attitudes in greater detail.

The attitude of the Industrialist, or of many executives, towards the work we have just been describing might be expressed in the words: 'This is all very interesting, but what you psychologists and theoretical people seem to forget is that I have to make a profit and produce the goods. Welfare is quite all right in its place, but it is, after all, a side-issue in industry, not its main function.' This appears to be the view, although expressed in a more moderate form, of Professor Sargant Florence in the excellent little book *Labour* from which we have already quoted. Professor Sargant Florence writes: 'There has been a tendency in American psychology, sociology, and schools of social work to concentrate on the mental attitude both of the employed and the unemployed worker quite apart from the consumer's need or demand for his work. This is economic abstraction in reverse. A manual on labour must not forget what labour is ultimately *for*, and in this book the consumer's demands and needs which an economic system tries to satisfy will be kept in view, as well as the satisfaction of the producer's "human nature".' Although Professor Florence has devoted a full chapter in his book to the work of Mayo which, as the quotation on informal groups and codes shows, he regards as important, he here appears to imply that the producer is being pampered at the expense of the consumer. But, in the first place, this conflict (if one insists on separating consumer and producer as if they were different people), exists in industries which are quite guiltless of any psychological approach and which certainly have never heard of Mayo. For example, when the railwaymen of this country demand higher wages (as they are quite entitled to do) it is the user of the railways, the consumer, who has to pay. In the second place, as we shall see later, there are other critics of Mayo who take quite the opposite view, claiming that he is biased in favour of management and has devised a cunning means of getting workers lulled into a state of satisfaction with their job which causes them to produce more and demand less in the way of financial reward. Obviously, the two criticisms cancel each other out.

But, above all, this sort of criticism completely fails to understand the nature of the investigations by American psychologists and sociologists who 'concentrate on the mental attitude both of the employed and the unemployed worker'. The reason for this concentration on the worker's mental attitude has nothing to do with pampering him or 'forgetting what labour is ultimately for' – it is simply a legitimate piece of research based on the common-sense belief that nobody can stimulate anyone else to work unless he knows how that person is motivated and to what incentives he will respond. The ultimate goal of all such research is the increased satisfaction of both consumer and producer, and so far from it being true that the approach we have been considering leads to greater cost to the consumer, there is every reason to suppose that its application in practice has the contrary effect. Gordon Rattray Taylor has pointed out that in those far-sighted firms which have put the results of these researches into practice 'the results have been astonishing. Not only has friction been reduced, but the technical efficiency of production has been raised, so that output has risen in a double sense. Output per man-hour has risen, and the number of man-hours contributed has risen too.' (*Are Workers Human?*) He goes on to estimate that by the use of such methods Britain could expand her national income by one-half within a period of five years without additional capital investment, and that it would be possible to reduce the price of many manufactured goods by 30 per cent. What reserves of human energy remain untapped in most industrial concerns is shown by certain figures quoted by Dr A. T. M. Wilson in a paper entitled 'Some Aspects of the Rôle of the Doctor and the Research Worker in Industry' which was read at the Ninth Congress of Industrial Medicine in 1949. American shipyards engaged on urgent war-time work found that, under approximately similar conditions with regard to raw materials, methods, and staffing, the time required to produce the same article varied from 60 to over 200 days. In our own country various studies have

shown that comparable organizations of the same size, manufacturing the same article, often show remarkable differences in
output, which, in some instances amounts to 300 per cent for the
same unit of time. The fact is that, in the face of these problems
and the other problems discussed in Chapter 1, most managers
have not the faintest idea what to do other than suggest that 'a
dose of unemployment' would cure our troubles, and, failing
that, the only other solutions lie in higher wages ('money is the
only positive incentive') or 'welfare'. The real pampering of the
workers is carried out, not by those who recommend a new
approach to problems of morale in industry, but by the very
managements who are always ready to spend tens of thousands
of pounds on the sort of embarrassing spoon-fed 'welfare' which
they vaguely suppose to act as an incentive, and, anyhow, salves
their conscience and absolves them from the responsibility of
finding out what is wrong with industry and their own technique
of handling labour problems. Industry has, as we have seen, a
social function to perform quite apart from the production of
goods, but there is not the slightest reason to suppose that one
function need be carried out at the expense of the other – on the
contrary, all evidence supports the view that a satisfactory performance of the social function leads to higher production,
reduced absenteeism, and reduced turnover of labour. That, in
other words, it is the most effective incentive known. There is no
connexion whatever between the sort of spoon-fed welfare we
have referred to and good morale, which is the goal towards
which all these investigations have been directed.

The criticism of the Social Psychologist need not delay us long,
since in accepting the work of Mayo his only criticism is that all
this was known long ago. C. H. Cooley, whose *Human Nature and
the Social Order* was published as long ago as 1902, studied the
organization of primary groups and their relationship to the
individuals composing them. At a time when most psychologists
were taking an exaggeratedly atomistic view of the individual as
an isolated entity, Cooley was going to the other extreme and
expressing a view similar to that of G. H. Mead in more recent
times: 'No hard-and-fast line can be drawn between our own
selves and the selves of others, since our own selves exist only

insofar as the selves of others exist.' (*Mind, Self, and Society*.) Obviously, it is unnecessary to concern ourselves with the question as to who deserves the credit for discovering the importance of groups in social life – as the quotations from Edmund Burke given elsewhere may have indicated, there were people in the eighteenth century who were by no means blind to their significance. That Mayo has been instrumental in rediscovering their importance and applying his knowledge to the problems of industry is the chief consideration.

The most serious objections to Mayo's researches have come from sociologists who, without disagreeing with his conclusions as far as they go, have put forward the following complaints:

(1) That he has investigated the factory to the almost complete exclusion of its social background.
(2) That he shows bias in favour of management.
(3) That, in the field of scientific method, he ignores the importance of theory and adopts an attitude which exalts empiricism, observation, and fact-finding.

In considering the first criticism, it must be remembered that Mayo was not primarily concerning himself with industrial inefficiency as a social problem; he was dealing with the specific problems of a particular factory. He was thus in the position of a general practitioner whose patient has typhoid fever. The doctor is naturally interested to know that typhoid is a disease often spread by infected water, that it may be due in this case to the faulty disposal of refuse by the local authorities, and that the attitude of the local authorities may be a source of danger to others, but, first and foremost, he is concerned to cure his own patient. This may not always be a correct attitude, but it is surely a very natural one. Nor is it strictly true to say that Mayo has completely neglected the larger framework of society. On the contrary, the larger part of his book *The Social Problems of an Industrial Civilization* is devoted to discussing the influence of social change on the structure of industry. Basing his views on those of the French sociologist Durkheim and the investigations of the Chicago school of sociologists, Mayo draws attention to the *anomie* (in Durkheim's terminology), the rootlessness, of modern industrial society which has resulted from the breaking-up of primary group life. He points out that whereas at one time the supervisor in a factory was dealing with workers who belonged to a local community, men whom he knew out of factory hours and who were likely to remain with him for many years or even a lifetime, he now frequently has to deal with vast shifting populations of workers living in lodging-houses and moving from one part of the country to another in search of jobs. Such men have no fixed abode, belong to no community, and have no loyalties. They are the rootless units of a disintegrating society. Although this state of affairs has probably gone much further in the United States than in Britain with its older, more tradition-based and conservative society, it is also quite evident here, and its impact on industrial morale is considerable. The casual observer will easily note how much more difficult it is to maintain good morale in a factory situated in a large industrial area with a shifting population than in a factory situated in a long-established and settled community. In the former type of factory, the manager or supervisor may be in charge of a department through which workers stream in an endless procession, starting work and leaving their job in a few weeks before they have ever been able to settle down. Clearly circumstances such as these make the task of management much harder, since the first requirement for good discipline, high morale, and efficient training in a job is an established factory community.

Nevertheless, it must be admitted that there are strange omissions in Mayo's work and in that of his colleagues Roethlisberger and Dickson. Thus Mary B. Gilson in a review of *Management and the Worker* by Roethlisberger and Dickson contributed to the *American Journal of Sociology* (July 1940) notes that in all this long account of the Hawthorne researches no mention is made of trade unions except a short statement to the effect that they were so seldom mentioned by any of the workers that it was not thought necessary to discuss them. She then points out that between 1933 and 1936 the Western Electric Company paid nearly twenty-six thousand dollars for espionage, and continues: 'We know of no instance where spies have been employed without some fear of unionism on the part of management. We wonder whether the interviewers have the proper technique for revealing the causes of what Mr Mayo terms "futile strife and hatreds". We are also surprised that in twenty thousand interviews the workers are reported to have criticized the company in no instance.' A reply to this review was made in the *Proceedings of the Industrial Relations Research Association* for December 1948 by B. M. Selekman, who wrote that, although these studies were written and published in the 1930s when trade unionism was increasing in American industry, the actual researches were carried out towards the end of the 1920s when there was comparatively little union activity throughout the country. In the Western Electric Company, at this time, there was even less activity than elsewhere. 'Moreover,' he continues, 'whether we like the astounding fact or not – and I must confess that I myself found it hard to swallow for a while – it is the fact that, among twenty thousand non-directive interviews upon which so much of the findings were based, there appeared to be very little articulation on trade union matters among the workers.' In addition to Mayo's failure to discuss the place of trade unions in industry, he has also been criticized for ignoring such other relevant factors as changes in the class and occupational structure of America. For example, in former times there existed a hierarchy of skills in certain industries which led to a social structure in which each worker knew his status. But alterations in technology, in particular mass-production methods, have resulted in a levelling both up and down; for the machine is capable of carrying out processes formerly done by the skilled worker, who is thus downgraded while the unskilled employee is upgraded. An old-established hierarchy has disintegrated with results which have proved disastrous for the skilled craftsman.

It is in some respects unfortunate for us in Britain that so many of the important researches into the social psychology of industry have been carried out in the United States where the situation is in many respects very different from our own. Political and cultural differences between the two countries are obvious, and this makes it even more important that the social setting of such researches should be noted. In Great Britain we could not, even if we wished, ignore trade unions; we cannot ignore the workers' long history of exploitation from the early days of the Industrial Revolution which has led to a tradition of bitter memories difficult to eradicate and therefore still operative; we cannot ignore differences of psychology between the British and American worker (e.g. that the American worker tends to be a 'go-getter' more often than his British counterpart, who, by reason of his traditions, prefers security). Finally, and perhaps most important of all, the worker in America still shares with his management a confidence in the virtues of 'private enterprise' which it would be idle to pretend is shared by the average worker in Britain. Yet, emotional considerations apart, when we discuss the differences of opinion between management and workers, we have to ask ourselves how far the interests of the two coincide in either country. Dr Norman Maier, a leading industrial psychologist in America, appears to have no doubt that the interests of management and workers do not coincide, that there is an inevitable conflict between the two. 'Both management and labour', he writes, 'have certain social responsibilities which they must meet if the system of private enterprise is to operate unhampered by governmental restrictions, or even to survive at all. Since it is more to the interest of the owning classes than to that of the masses of labour to preserve this system, the former, especially, should have an understanding of their responsibilities and take a long-range point of view.' (*Psychology in Industry*.) Obviously Dr Maier is implying (a) that private enterprise is primarily in the interest of the owning classes, and (b) that the owning classes should behave in such a way that the system should survive and be able to operate unhampered by governmental restrictions. (Why, if he believes (a) to be true, he goes on to recommend (b), must remain a mystery.) It seems hardly fair to criticize Mayo for his admittedly inadequate approach to the question of the social framework of industry, since the vast majority of industrial psychologists either never mention it at all, or discuss it only with a view to showing how the *status quo* may be maintained.

We now come to the second criticism – that Mayo has shown a bias in favour of management. The obvious reply to this is that no industrial psychologist has ever shown anything else, and it is therefore hard to understand why Mayo should have been selected for this criticism. Under the circumstances in which all industrial research is carried out, such bias is inevitable. 'It must be remembered that all of the industrial researches which Mayo directed were by permission of and subsequent arrangement with management. It is also a well-known fact that professors as well as researchers in "good" colleges of business administration do not displease the business community. If Mayo, out of a lifetime of service in the interest of industry, should carry either consciously or unconsciously a pro-management bias it should not be considered surprising. These researches were conducted to help *management* solve its problems. Therefore, the *status quo* is accepted.' (Miller and Form, *Industrial Sociology*.) Another critic, Daniel Bell, in an article entitled 'Exploring Factory Life' (*Commentary*, January 1947) writes that Mayo and his associates 'uncritically adopt industry's own conception of workers as *means* to be manipulated or adjusted to impersonal ends. The belief in man as an end in himself has been ground under by the machine, and the social science of the factory researchers is not a science of man, but a cow-sociology.' This important problem will be discussed more fully in the final chapter, but here again, we can only say that industrial psychology has always thought of the worker as 'means to be manipulated or adjusted to impersonal ends', and it is difficult to see why the work of Mayo, which at least equates these ends with the happiness and wellbeing of the worker, should have been selected for special criticism. This critic is, however, right in emphasizing the importance of man as an end in himself and seeing the danger which is inherent in our increasing ability to utilize science as a means of manipulating other human beings to our own ends. It is more than ever important that we should ask ourselves the question: 'Efficiency to what ends and at what price?'

More specifically, Miller and Form point out that, although the *facts* elucidated by the researches are not in doubt, based as they are on scientific method, their *interpretation* may be open to question. Closer investigation, they believe, may reveal a certain pro-management bias. For example, Roethlisberger and

Dickson in the account of the Hawthorne researches already referred to, distinguish between formal and informal organization in the factory; formal organization is that existing on paper (the logical relationships prescribed by the rules and policy of the company), while informal organization is the system of inter-relationships based on likes and dislikes which exists apart from any openly expressed social structure. Although these forms of organization exist for both management and employees, it is apparent that Roethlisberger and Dickson, in discussing the formal organization of management (based on logic), fail to mention their informal organization (which, of course, is based on feeling). They thus give the impression that management is essentially logical. This impression is strengthened by the further observation that, although they discuss the informal and emotional organization of the workers at great length, any formal organization is ignored. It is thus made to appear that, whereas management is rational, the workers are fundamentally emotional and irrational. 'It does not seem to appear to Mayo and his colleagues that the social organization of a factory contains diverse and conflicting *interests* and that real differences in "logic" are held with as cold rationale among workers as among managers.' (Miller and Form, *Industrial Sociology*.)

Further bias seems indicated by Mayo's repeated emphasis on 'social skills' (i.e. practical methods of dealing with the human problems of society), as means of improving production. This essentially managerial point of view is put forward to the exclusion of other ends. Social skills are implicitly regarded as good because they increase production and maintain the *status quo*. 'Again, Mayo's inability to see a conflict of interest in a dynamic society involves him in a limited perspective. The "logics" of his world remain so fixed upon management goals that he is shocked to find the new world is full of "emotional" or "radical" ideas. If Mayo could remove his glasses he might find that these revolutionary currents are not moved in the absence of social skills but with a high degree of coldly calculating social skill' (*ibid.*). Once again, Mayo is being criticized for concentrating on his job, which was to solve the problems of management and which he did in such a way as not, at any rate, to harm the workers but rather to help them in the process. As has already been said, it is a little absurd to ask of an applied scientist who is employed as an industrial psychologist in order to perform a certain task, that he should criticize the whole structure of society in the process. This is not to say that the social background of industry is not important (it is one of the main points of this book that it is of the greatest possible importance), but we are looking in the wrong quarter if we expect it to come from those whose bread and butter depends on their performing a specific task in increasing industrial efficiency.

The third and final criticism, that Mayo's work is too empirical and that he ignores the importance of theory, is a more technical one. In his book *The Social Problems of an Industrial Civilization*, Mayo writes: 'Observation – skill – experiment and logic – these must be regarded as the three stages of advancement.' And elsewhere: 'science did not begin with elaborate and overwhelming systems and thence proceed to study the facts.' He goes on to compare two kinds of knowledge: 'Knowledge-about', based on reflexion and abstract thinking, and 'knowledge-of-acquaintance', based on direct experience. The latter is stated to be the more valuable since it leads to the acquisition of manipulative ability and skill. The superiority of the physical sciences over the social sciences (assumed by Mayo) is due to their emphasis on 'knowledge-of-acquaintance'. In fact, he asserts, none of the social sciences equips students 'with a single social skill that is usable in ordinary human situations'. But, reply Professors Miller and Form, it is useless to collect any number of observations unless they can be related within some frame of reference; mere facts without a theoretical background are valueless.* A review of Mayo's book by the sociologist Wilbert Moore in the *American Sociological Review* makes the same criticism in greater detail: 'Professor Mayo's views as to the proper course of social science inquiry may be most succinctly summarized as radical empiricism. This position rests on two fundamental

---

* Mayo was by no means alone in supposing that science rests on observation unguided by hypothesis. Peters, in his new edition of *Brett's History of Psychology* (Allen & Unwin, 1953), has argued that this error, deriving from Bacon's philosophy of science, has influenced adversely the development of psychology as a science both in its theoretical and applied branches.

misunderstandings: (1) The author is ignorant of the rôle of theory in social research. Rather, he advocates amassing observations, apparently at random. At no place does he indicate how it is that one knows where to begin observing the infinite phenomena of the universe. (2) He is ignorant of the difference between science and technology, and is thus insensitive to problems of ends or values. He pleads for knowledge of the techniques of co-operation, which will settle all issues from those in industry to those in international affairs. Co-operation towards what goals, with what inducements, under whose direction, with what safeguards for participants? The direction and use of research in industry is not so simple as in the case of medicine, to which the author frequently and mistakenly refers as a science rather than as a useful art.' Once again, we must admit the justice of the charge against Mayo, whose books show a quite extraordinary naïveté both as regards the philosophical background of scientific method and the economic and political background of industry. Mayo's work was essentially empirical and practical, but it has nevertheless led to great advances in the field of industrial psychology.

To summarize: Mayo's researches remain revolutionary and are among the most important in the whole field of the social sciences. Since they were first carried out, his findings have been tested many times and in many different countries by different investigators who have confirmed the results. His theses, enumerated on page 85, may be confidently accepted as valid, and their validity is not affected by the criticisms as to method, bias, and the lack of sociological background already considered. At an earlier stage it was noted that the findings of the early industrial psychologists might, generally speaking, be regarded as correct 'other things being equal' in relation to the social structure within the factory. Similarly, in the case of the Hawthorne researches. we may say that they are correct 'other things being equal' in relation to the social structure of the culture within which the factory is functioning.

4

THE FORMAL ORGANIZATION OF INDUSTRY

THE formal and informal organizations within the factory have already been mentioned in the last chapter. The formal organization of a firm is the official hierarchy as it appears on paper, and we must now go on to consider the theory of formal organization, how it works in practice, and what is likely to go wrong when theory is translated into practice. It will, perhaps, be helpful if we take a representative factory, an engineering works employing, say, 1,500 to 2,000 workers, and try to see it as it might appear to someone who knew nothing whatever of industry either from experience or hearsay.

The factory consists of a group of buildings some of which are known as workshops, others as offices, and still others as the canteen, the recreation room, the surgery, and so on. The workshops form by far the larger part of the factory, and, on entering the nearest one, we find that the workers are occupied at noisy machines which mould, hammer, drill, and cut metal into shapes which are obviously intended to form parts of the finished article. This part of the buildings is called the manufacturing department, and it is mostly staffed by men. In other, and less noisy, workshops the pieces from the manufacturing department pass along an assembly line and are fitted together to form the finished article by a staff composed largely of women. These are called the assembly departments. The majority of workers remain most of the day in the same place within very narrow limits, except for the occasions when they have rest-breaks, go to the canteen for meals, or visit the cloakrooms or lavatories. A few individuals, however, will be seen to spend their time walking about and giving orders or inspecting the work done by the employees. These are the foremen or supervisors, of whom there is usually one to each of the sections into which the manufacturing and assembly departments are divided. (Naturally, the lay-out of the factory will vary a great deal according to the type of work done, the way it is divided, and so on. There may also be warehouses, packing departments, or other types of workshop, and the work may be more or less mechanized. In some factories much or most of the work is still done by hand, but in the majority the workers merely tend or feed the machines which do the moulding, filling, drilling, and cutting.)

If the factory is situated in one of the older industrial areas, it is likely that most of the workers and probably the foremen live fairly nearby in typically 'working-class' districts. They may cycle to work or come by bus or tram. At the factory gate they 'clock in' at a machine which registers on their 'clock card' the time of arrival. If they are late, the time lost will be deducted from their pay at the end of the week. In attendance at the gate is the gate-keeper in his lodge, whose job it is to direct traffic, keep out unauthorized visitors, check the lorries and trucks bringing in, or taking out, supplies, and finally to see that the workers as they leave take nothing away from the factory. If there have been many recent cases of pilfering, he may be required to search any suspects before they go out of the gate. After 'clocking in', the workers go to the cloakrooms where they change into special clothing, the nature of which depends, naturally, on the type of work they have to do. Thus in a food factory they will be expected to wear clean white overalls and caps, but in an engineering firm such as this they will put on greasy denims. When ready, they go to their places in the workshop and start work. Their time of arrival may be anything from 6.30 a.m. to 8 a.m., unless the factory is on shift work, when, of course, it will depend on the number of shifts worked and when they begin. In theory, workers are paid by the hour, and may, therefore, be sacked on the spot; their pay is known as 'wages', and is issued at the end of each week, usually on Fridays. If they do more work (overtime) they must be paid accordingly.

An hour or more later, the office or clerical staff arrive. In Great Britain, these are still mainly recruited from the middle and lower middle classes, although many people of working class origin now prefer to train for clerical jobs. The office staff does not 'clock in' – ostensibly because they are not paid by the hour, but it seems likely that at least part of the reason for this is the supposition that, unlike labourers, they do not necessarily dislike work and can be placed on their honour to be punctual. The working classes, as we have seen, are supposed to dislike work and therefore need 'discipline' to keep them in order. Since 'clocking in' has been abolished in many firms, it cannot be accepted as absolutely necessary. The office staff is also treated with greater respect by the gate-keeper and does not have to change for work. They are not paid wages, but a 'salary' which falls due weekly, fortnightly, or monthly (usually depending on status – the more senior staff are paid monthly). Although the receipt of a salary seems to be accepted as a sign of higher social status, the amount received nowadays may be no greater, and is sometimes much less, than that received in wages by the manual worker. Also, the salary is a fixed amount (subject, of course, to periodic increases) which is not related to the amount of time worked. The salaried worker is not ordinarily paid 'overtime', but, on the other hand, he must be given a week's or a month's notice before dismissal. On arrival at work, the office staff go to their desks, which are collected together in various sections or departments as in the case of the machines in the workshops. The supervisors in the clerical departments arc less easily distinguishable, since everybody does what appears to be similar work. In general, the more important an employee the larger his desk, and heads of departments have small offices of their own adjoining the main office. Most of the clerical workers are women, but it is noticeable that few women occupy the positions of higher authority.

Whilst the functions of the workshops are usually fairly clear, those of the offices are less evident, but the inquirer would probably be told that the clerical staff is employed on work such as the ordering of raw materials, planning, record-keeping, selling the finished products, and dealing with pay and statistics.

Also in the main administrative block along with the general office are the rooms belonging to the senior executives. These workers keep 'management hours' – that is to say, they arrive about 9.30 a.m. and officially leave at 5.30 p.m. or 6 p.m. In fact, they may leave very much later, and for most of them work is a full-time business which occupies much of their waking life. The importance of each of these individuals is usually indicated by the size of his desk and the greater or less opulence of his office. Each executive has a private secretary who usually has a room or office furnished according to the status of her chief. Elsewhere in the building, but with positions less clearly marked or stratified in the organization, are the technicians and specialists: the chemist, the doctor, the chief engineer, the sister in charge of the surgery, and so on.

Obviously, then, the factory is arranged in a hierarchy of power; it is a pyramid with the chairman of the board at the apex and the workers at the base. Junior and senior management, clerical staff, and supervisors, occupy intermediate positions. The visitor to the factory would discover in a comparatively short time that all the employees, from the highest to the lowest, show considerable concern about the relative position they occupy in this hierarchy. They respond with great anxiety or resentment to any situation which seems to indicate that their status is in danger. Promotion in the hierarchy is not necessarily desired, but any employee who has become integrated into the structure is sensitive about his position in relation to the other employees. This attitude is seen very clearly in the canteen arrangements, if we note where the workers sit and how they arrange themselves. For example, office and manual workers almost invariably refuse to mix, men and women tend to sit separately, and people from the same department normally keep together, except for the foremen who generally sit at a single table, no matter to which department they are attached. The importance attached to status is seen even more clearly if the firm is one of those in which there are separate dining-rooms for the various levels within the organization: directors, management, clerical staff, and workers, may take their meals separately. Under these circumstances, there may be furious arguments and much resentment over such questions as whether a director's secretary has been unduly favoured in being permitted to dine in the management mess rather than with the other secretaries in the office canteen.

It is the theory of this system that all authority is delegated to successive levels from the one above, being ultimately vested in the Chairman of the Board of Directors. Orders pass down the scale, and information as to what is going on in the various departments passes up, but the traffic in orders and information is a one-way traffic. It is not intended that orders should ever pass upwards or that information about the management should ever pass down. Since all the information from the lower levels deals ostensibly with technical matters relating to production, there tends to be defective communication between workers and management so far as human problems and grievances are concerned. (In reality, of course, a great deal of information concerning personal matters and emotional problems passes both up and down in the form of gossip, but this, being unofficial, cannot, or in theory should not, be acted on.) One of the main functions of Joint Consultation Committees is to deal with such matters as well as with the more technical difficulties which arise from time to time, but unless the atmosphere of the factory is good and a certain degree of mutual respect already exists such Committees are likely to prove dreary sessions during which the workers' representatives rack their minds to produce all sorts of petty complaints but never get down to any of the more serious ones. The Committee will be told that there was no soap in such and such a lavatory last week, that 'Music While You Work' was cut off five minutes too soon the day before yesterday, that Mr So-and-so slipped and nearly fell in a pool of lubricating oil which some engineer had carelessly failed to remove. But, so far as co-operation or frank and mutual exchange of views is concerned, many of these Committees accomplish nothing. We have to recognize the paradoxical situation that the unhappy factory which most needs a competent Joint Consultation Committee is the very factory which can never make adequate use of it, whereas the factory with an atmosphere of friendliness and mutual trust which needs it less can always have adequate Joint Consultation. When a sense of fear and insecurity pervades a firm and workers are scared of being victimized, no complaints other than trivial and formal ones relating to matters of detail will ever reach the management, and the unexpressed resentment will show itself in the more explosive form of periodic strikes (apparently without adequate cause), outbursts of sabotage, high labour turnover, and absenteeism. In one such firm, the management was astonished and disgusted to find that the quite valuable gifts given to the workers at Christmas were thrown into the nearby canal and floated along on the surface of the water, a mute testimonial to what the workers thought of their bosses. Spoon-fed welfare is no substitute for treating people as human beings, and it is often the case that the only way in which workers with grievances can contact management is through their shop stewards and trade union officials.*

The visitor passing through a factory may very easily be led astray by his superficial impressions. Civility, a disciplined appearance, and an attitude of industrious application to the job, of being constantly busy, are not always good signs amongst workers. One of the most eminent of industrial consultants has said that if, on going round a factory with one of the managers, every worker is civil and seems to be busily concentrating on his job, something must be far wrong with the firm. It is quite impossible for every man to be busy all the time, and one of the signs of mutual trust and security in a factory is that, when the boss arrives in the shop, the man who was doing nothing before he arrived is still doing nothing. (Of course, this might also be a sign of a factory in which complete indifference to the opinions of management existed, but other signs would soon make it clear to the visitor which was the real state of affairs.) The workers in an authoritarian type of firm are often cowed into a state of civility and discipline which is superficially most impressive, but, whereas in the good factory the workers are naturally polite and friendly and remain so, the visitor who spends a week or more in an authoritarian firm will often find that the attitude of the employees towards him passes through three stages: (1) the workers, thinking that he may be someone of importance, are unnaturally civil and greet him with obsequious cap-touching and good-mornings; (2) when they find that he is not a *very* important visitor, they will soon become rude and ignore him, or

* 'All men fall into two main divisions: those who value human relationships, and those who value social or financial advancement. The first division are gentlemen: the second division are cads.' If we accept this classification of Norman Douglas, we must reluctantly conclude that many self-styled 'gentlemen' are, in fact, 'cads'.

their greetings will be decidedly less effusive; (3) when, if ever, they discover that he is not a new manager and is quite a pleasant and harmless person, they may finally behave naturally and treat him on his own merits as an individual. The 'atmosphere' of a factory, although intangible, is often immediately apparent whenever one enters the gate, and whereas in one firm the visitor immediately senses an air of freedom, casual friendliness, and co-operation, there are others which, to use the graphic phrase of a well-known industrialist 'stink of fear'.

Promotion within the hierarchy is allegedly based on merit and hard work, but many workers regard this thesis cynically and believe that promotion is based on what is variously described as 'pull', 'influence', or 'crawling to the boss'. Management, of course, deny this and frequently complain bitterly that what they want is more men who are fit for promotion. To the observer it appears that both sides are quite sincere in their beliefs, but since they base their judgements on widely differing sets of values, no agreement is possible. Granted that management and workers are far from sharing common interests, it is natural that management, who possess all the authority, will tend to put into positions of responsibility men who share, or give the impression of sharing, their views. Equally naturally, given the basic conflict of interests, the workers will feel that those who have been selected for promotion are 'bosses' men'. This fundamental difference of outlook is clearly seen in the selection of foremen, who, it is evident, should be chosen largely because of their ability to lead and hold the respect of the men in their department. In reality, they are often chosen for precisely the opposite reason: that they have *not* shared the attitudes of their mates, that they have told tales or 'sneaked' on them, and that they possess many of the unpleasant traits which, it is to be feared, are associated in the authoritarian firm all too frequently with the type of individual who is termed a 'trusted servant'. It is not meant to imply that loyalty is not an excellent, and indeed essential trait, but a man who is not loyal to his own immediate working group is neither likely to be able to control that group nor to be loyal to any other group. The matter is not so simple that we may safely assume that the workers in limiting production, demanding higher wages, and 'acting dumb', are in the wrong and that, therefore, those who do not follow the group in this respect are in the right. As we have already seen, it is impossible to explain such attitudes in terms of neurosis, laziness, waywardness, or original sin. It must be assumed that, in behaving the way they do, the workers are convinced that they are justified in doing so; that it is largely environmental influences which determine their actions; that, in effect, almost anybody in the same position would behave in the same manner. The same is, of course, true of management attitudes, and the dilemma of the foreman in many factories is that he is the man situated at the point where these two conflicting sets of attitudes meet. In the unhappy firm, the foreman who faithfully represents management opinion is *ipso facto* disqualified from being accepted by his men as a leader. If, on the other hand, he is accepted by his men, he will almost certainly come into conflict with management. The job of supervisor is not only one of the most important in industry; it is also the most difficult.

Another problem about promotion is that the structure of industry has changed in such a way that it is no longer entirely justifiable for management to hold out the carrot of limitless advancement and insist that 'there is plenty of room at the top'. If by 'democratic' one means that any worker can by application and energy have a good chance of reaching the highest levels within a firm, then there can be little doubt that industry is now less 'democratic' than it was, say, twenty years ago. Management has become specialized to such a degree that promotion from the shop floor is no longer so likely to happen as it once was. The capable worker may become a charge-hand, a foreman, or he may even attain a higher position in junior management, but in many large firms the members of senior management are recruited from the universities. One reason for this is that specialization is increasingly common and specialists in technical subjects must as a rule take a university degree. Perhaps, indeed, specialization in technical subjects has gone too far, and C. I. Barnard has suggested in his book *The Functions of the Executive* that the duties of management should be concerned essentially with the co-ordination of human, rather than technical, activity.

In any case, it is doubtful whether high qualities of leadership are likely to be found amongst those who have been promoted just because they passed on orders efficiently, did as they were told, and behaved as a good charge-hand or supervisor under existing conditions is all too often supposed to behave. A very similar situation may be seen in the army, where the work done by Officer Selection Boards during and after the last war made it increasingly clear that the fact that a man has been an N.C.O. or Warrant Officer for many years is an indication that he is unsuited to be a Commissioned Officer rather than the reverse, as has often been supposed. This had little to do with differences of education or social class; it is simply that the *kind* of person who makes a good officer is an entirely different *kind* of man from the good N.C.O. or W.O. It became the practice to pick out men who seemed to be suitable candidates for a commission at an early stage in their army career, put them through a Selection Board for further testing as to suitability, and then train the successful candidates immediately as officers. It is possible that a similar technique might be applied, with suitable alterations, to industry; for in a democracy the capable worker ought to have the opportunity of promotion right up to the highest levels, and it seems certain that, under present conditions, a great deal of talent is being wasted. There is good reason to suppose that the really capable men are not always those who are being slowly promoted to supervisor's and charge-hand's jobs, but are often men who are regarded as trouble-makers and agitators who agitate just because they are frustrated in a job beneath their abilities. In an unsatisfactory society, or in a factory with an unhappy atmosphere, the 'good' man is not necessarily the one who accepts the *status quo* – he may be the one who agitates against it.

The formal organization of industry, so far as its theory is concerned, has three clear-cut characteristics:

(1) It is deliberately impersonal.
(2) It is based on ideal relationships.
(3) It is based on the 'rabble hypothesis' of the nature of man (i.e. it is assumed that competition leads to maximum efficiency, that when each man fights for himself

the best interests of the group are served, and that men are isolated units who may be moved about from one job to another depending only on their ability to do the job).

(1) and (2) imply that each member of the organization is supposed to react towards the others, not in personal terms of like or dislike, but in terms of the function they have to play in the whole, the place they occupy in the hierarchy. Thus in dealing with any person within the organization, as in dealing with a king, a judge, or a policeman, such matters as sex, religion, personal appearance, and manner, are supposedly irrelevant; behaviour is determined by relative official status alone. This insistence on formal relationships should, in theory, be an advantage, since its function is to eliminate (or to attempt to eliminate) all individual peculiarities and personal prejudices. It need hardly be said that in this attempt it is never entirely success-ful, and that the network of personal relationships based on individual likes and dislikes which inevitably arises is what has already been described as the 'informal organization' of the factory.

Characteristic (3), based on the 'rabble hypothesis', leads to the claim that formal organization not only avoids human com-plications but has the further advantage of being *flexible*. If we assumed that the worker is an isolated individual in a state of free competition with all other individuals, he will evidently be replaceable. So, for example, if more workers are needed in a particular department, some can be withdrawn from a depart-ment where their work is not at the moment necessary. It is assumed that all concerned will readily see that such a movement is to their benefit, since the theory implicitly equates the good of the organization with the good of the individuals composing it. That any worker should object to being moved from his familiar department and job into a new one or from his own working group into another group of strangers seems utterly illogical and absurd from the standpoint of the theory of formal organization.

The industrial hierarchy, as we have so far described it, con-sists of several layers of authority from the chairman of the board of directors or president to the vice-president, managers, chiefs of divisions, chiefs of departments, foremen, and workers. With the exception of the top and the bottom layers, everyone has a boss and is in turn boss over others; he has a more or less definite job and is responsible to someone who wants it done. This system of authority, known as the 'line organization', represents a basic division in the work structure of the concern. Clearly, the greater the number of levels in the structure, the greater the 'social distance' between people in different parts of the plant. The senior management is likely to know very little of what goes on within the workshops (although many executives delude themselves into believing that they know a great deal). Of course, a manager does not need to know the *technical* details of what goes on in the workshops, since his function is to concern himself with policies and general objectives. These are translated into more and more concrete terms as they pass down the line, until the worker is ordered to cut a specific strip of metal into pieces of specific size. But, although knowledge of technical details is unnecessary, it is coming to be generally agreed that, since management should be primarily concerned with the co-ordination of human activities, some awareness of the emotional attitudes of those under his control is an essential part of the job.

Although the line organization is the most apparent part of the social structure of the factory, it is not the only one. Two other superimposed structures exist which are of importance as potential sources of conflict within the firm. These are the 'functional organization' and the 'staff organization'. Just as the line structure is based on authority, the functional structure is based on the type of work done and the staff structure on specialization. Although the line structure is based to a certain extent on different functions, it is easy to see that many people officially at the same level in terms of power are, in fact, doing different types of work. The way in which the total process of manufacture, assembly, packing, and so on is divided up will depend to some extent on the ideas held by those in authority as to which type of subdivision is most efficient. Thus it may be decided to manufacture each separate component of the complete article in a single department, or departments may be split up according to specialized processes such as packing, drilling, or moulding. This functional organization, then, is based on the subdivision of work within the factory, and its importance lies in the fact that it is naturally more vague in conception than the structure based on pure authority. Because of this, differences of opinion are liable to arise between the various departments as to who should be given priority or whose job is the more important. Workers in the assembly department are liable to look down on those in the manufacturing department and vice versa, although workers in both departments are at the same level in the line hierarchy. For example, in a certain London factory, a strike was threatened because alterations in a cloakroom used by the packing department made it necessary for packing and manufacturing departments to share temporarily the same cloakroom. To the outsider, the amount of resentment shown on this occasion would have seemed quite disproportionate to the cause, but the fact was that the manufacturing department considered itself greatly superior in status to the packing department. Both groups were deeply hurt that it should be suggested that their status was sufficiently similar that they might be expected to use the same cloakroom without loss of dignity on either side. This incident demonstrates once more the importance attached to status in industry by workers, an importance which is tacitly ignored by the theory of formal organization, which can only see status in terms of the line hierarchy. There are, as will be seen, many other potential causes of friction between departments performing different functions in a factory – for example, uneven flow of work between one shop and another ('bottlenecks' is the usual phrase).

A final problem of work structure is what is known as the 'staff organization', the problem of how and where the specialist should be integrated into the whole. Modern industry uses an increasingly large number of specialists, who, in general, come into one or other of two categories:

(1) Specialists associated with the production process whose function is to translate the policy of the executive into concrete terms. These are, in effect, advisers to the executives. For example,

the chief engineer or designer in a motor factory, or the chemist or bacteriologist in a food factory, may be asked whether a suggested policy is within the bounds of possibility, and, if so, how it may be implemented.

(2) Specialists who have no direct concern with production: the physician, the legal and financial experts, those engaged in research, and so on, come into this category.

All specialists and technicians are part of the 'staff organization' and, in theory, since their functions are purely advisory, they have no authority within the line organization. Nevertheless, they must be fitted into the line organization in some way, and W. E. Moore in his book *Industrial Relations and the Social Order* has described the three possible methods:

(1) *In a purely advisory capacity:*
   (a) Either each specialist is placed in a 'horizontal' relationship at whichever level he is thought to be most necessary (i.e. he is situated alongside the line manager who most needs his advice). Or,
   (b) Specialists are brought under the control of one or more high-level executives (e.g. one director may be in charge of personnel matters with the personnel officer, welfare staff, and physician under him; another director may be in charge of finance with its accountants, keepers of records, and so on).

(2) *Integrated directly with the line organization:*
   In this case, all managers would be specialists right down the line, but possessing authority only within their own sphere. (This is the so-called 'functional management' advocated by Frederick Winslow Taylor.) Thus a single worker might be under the control of several managers, each dealing with a particular aspect of his job. In its pure form, direct integration presents difficulties from the point of view of co-ordination, and is rarely used.

(3) *Both methods together:*
   This method is the most commonly used. Some specialists are utilized in a purely advisory capacity in relation to the executive and outside the line organization. Others are

managers within the line organization, where they may supervise a department and at the same time advise elsewhere in their own particular sphere.

There are certain weaknesses in the theory of formal organization, certain points at which, by its very nature, it is liable to break down. Two of these points, neither of them completely separable from the other, may be given the separate headings of problems of co-ordination and human problems ignored by the theory of formal organization. Co-ordination is, of course, always likely to be a source of difficulty in such a complex structure as the modern factory, and the larger the factory or concern, the more this difficulty is likely to present itself. The problem of co-ordination is largely one of communication, for without efficient communication no co-ordinated effort is possible. The word 'communication' may be defined as 'the capacity of an individual (or group) to pass on his feelings and ideas to another individual (or group)', and in recent times social psychologists have been giving an increasing amount of attention to this problem. Elton Mayo, for example, writes: 'I believe that social study should begin with careful observation of what may be described as communication. This problem is, beyond all reasonable doubt, the outstanding defect that civilization is facing today.' (*The Social Problems of an Industrial Civilization*.) While there are many causes of defective communication, we shall be dealing for the moment mainly with those relating to formal organization and the structure of industry as such. These may be classified as defects due to time, to space, and to the natural divisions of the structure. Defective communication due to the time factor occurs for the most part in factories on shift work. Tension frequently arises because the main shift, not unnaturally, considers itself to be the most important; it is the money-maker, while the others merely serve to keep the machines going in order to keep down costs. When the bell or hooter goes at the end of their working day, most workers are in a hurry to get home, and the brief exchange of notes or verbal statements tends to be sketchy in the extreme. Even apart from the matter of prestige, workers in the various shifts have little or no social contact with each other, and are liable to adopt a 'couldn't care less' attitude towards the problems of those they have never met except during the few minutes when shifts overlap. Under these circumstances, a vicious circle of grievances may develop, and there may be deliberate attempts to shelve problems or even to create them for the next shift to solve. The same sort of problem may, of course, arise within the same shift between different sections or work-teams. Since all work is closely tied to a definite time-schedule, a great deal of trouble may arise if one group fails to supply the materials needed by another at the time they are entitled to expect them. When this happens, work-flow is affected, and 'bottlenecks' develop.

Similar results may follow from spatial segregation. The various units of an organization may be widely separated either within the same piece of ground, or, as in the case of a large concern, all over the country. Such segregation, either in space or time, tends to lead to the situation described above in which each department thinks itself the most important and its problems far more pressing and urgent than those experienced by any other. In general, the greater the spatial separation of the units of an organization, the greater the difficulty in co-ordinating work-activity; spatial distance is likely to lead to social distance. Needless to say, the fact that units are in close physical relationship with each other does not, of itself, create good communications and satisfactory relationships, but it at least makes them possible. Physical separation obviously reduces this possibility.

The third type of failure in communication arises when work groups fail to co-ordinate their activities for reasons other than space or time factors. Such breaks are most likely to develop in an organization along what Miller and Form describe as the 'natural' divisions of the structure, that is to say, between functionally separate units such as divisions and departments, line and staff organizations, or various departments and sections at the same 'horizontal' level. Generally speaking, it is easier to co-ordinate units doing similar work than those which are per-forming widely different functions. It is therefore easy to see why conflicts should arise between the various levels of the line organization, since in this case functions differ so widely that it is genuinely difficult for members of one level to appreciate what other levels are trying to do. In this connexion, we have already mentioned the dilemma of the supervisor who is under pressure from above to produce more, and equally under pressure from below to understand the viewpoint of the men he controls and retain their loyalty. Under such circumstances, he is a man with a 'split mind', liable to act in ways which at times appear inconsistent. 'Thus, how a supervisor feels and acts depends upon whether he is looking down or looking up the structure. The different way he acts does not strike him as contradictory or unreasonable. Yet this contradiction makes for segmentation in the structure.' (Miller and Form.) But this is not the only problem; for there are 'horizontal' divergences of interest, whether for the supervisor as head of a section in relation to other supervisors or sections, or for chiefs of divisions or departments in relation to other chiefs of divisions or departments. The basis of this divergence of interests is the further dilemma that each section, department, or division is under pressure, both from higher management and for reasons of personal prestige, to show a good record. Each must try to impress those at the top with its efficiency and high level of production. But these depend on intimate co-operation with other sections, departments, or divisions. How are they to reconcile simultaneous attitudes of competition and co-operation? The head of one department which is not being adequately fed with work by another department will naturally feel resentful that his efficiency may be questioned because of a problem outside his control. Perhaps he may quarrel with the head of the department which he feels to have failed him, and he is likely to shelve the blame on that department not only in the specific situation just described but on other occasions when the fault lies in his own inadequacy. Obviously such a background is hardly conducive to high morale within the factory. But there is another way in which the natural desire to please, raised to an even higher pitch by the atmosphere of competition which pervades industry, may adversely influence effective communication; the desire to make a good impression causes information passed up the line to be distorted. Management is constantly told that all is going according to plan (which it is reasonably assumed is what they want to hear), and, when things go wrong, an attempt is made to 'cover up' in the hope that the trouble will be rectified before it has been discovered. Orders passing down the line may also be distorted, although in a different way – the process of elaboration, of making the general decisions of the executives more specific as they pass down to the workers, may involve errors, delay, or omissions. In such ways, as B. B. Gardner shows in his book *Human Relations in Industry,* each person both up and down the line acts as a sieve or filter, and what arrives at the other end, especially in the case of information passing up the line, may bear very little relationship to the state of affairs as it actually exists.

Problems due to conflict between staff and line organizations, that is to say, between management and the various specialists within the organization, are so common, and the reasons for such conflicts so obvious, that little more need be said. The 'practical' man (and all managers pride themselves as coming into this category) is naturally suspicious of the specialist, who is regarded as being too theoretical, too single-minded in his subject, and lacking in realism. Managers of the old school, brought up to a state of affairs in which specialists were less frequent than they are now, are liable to feel that things went very well in the past without such complications. Perhaps a not entirely irrelevant matter is the feeling of jealousy attaching to those who are able to walk into a position because they have technical qualifications, whilst others, it is supposed, had to 'go through the mill' of practical experience and work hard for their position. The staff organization is, relatively speaking, loosely integrated, since specialists in different fields have no direct connexion with each other, and such a situation added to the other factors we have mentioned creates a sense of insecurity and a tendency to be constantly on the defensive. Specialists are likely to feel that they must justify themselves, prove that their work is essential, and that they must continue to widen its scope. The personnel manager will attempt to show that bad training and selection are the root of all trouble, the doctor that failure to accept medical advice is the cause, the engineering research department that the same trouble is due to out-of-date methods and design in the workshop, and the financial experts that the department concerned could never have been expected to pay in any case. Since all these assertions are, by implication, criticisms of the line organization, further reasons can readily be found for disliking the specialist.

Finally, we may mention the existence of conflicts due to social and cultural differences. Holders of the 'rabble hypothesis' are especially prone to ignore the importance of differing nationalities, religions, and classes among their employees. This, of course, must not be taken to imply that any employee should be victimized on account of his religious, political, or other beliefs, or because of his national or class origins. What is important is that the fact that such a problem exists should be recognized. Many Polish or Italian workers, for example, are being employed in industry, not because the managers are enlightened people who think that a man has a right to work regardless of his nationality, but rather because they are completely indifferent and assume that one pair of hands is as good as another regardless of who owns them. Now, as we have seen, a factory or a society is not ordinarily a mass of isolated individuals (although the development of modern industry has tended to make it so); it is an integrated pattern of primary work-groups. This being the case, it is apparent that the presence of people who speak a different language and have an entirely different outlook will have a very potent influence on the social structure of the factory and will influence the facility of communication within a unit. As a rule, employers refuse to see that any such problem exists, and the foreign workers, instead of being integrated into the structure of the firm, form an indigestible mass which may cause much ill-will and interferes with the co-ordination of work. The unfortunate foreigner, instead of finding himself in a situation which might have assisted his absorption into the community within which he has chosen to live, very soon finds himself developing the attitudes typical of national or religious minorities all over the world. Finding that he is not acceptable to the community, he may become resentful, slip into dubious ways of earning a living, or become a delinquent. It would be absurd to pretend that this problem could be easily solved, but it is in industry more than any other field of the community where the solution might be found, and the foreign worker aided to find his place in a new society. Far from doing this, industry often aggravates the matter, as may be seen in the anti-Irish problems of such cities as Glasgow and Liverpool and the anti-Negro problems of certain states in America, which in large measure have been due to the employment of Irish and Negroes as cheap labour. The failure to understand such problems of religion and nationality may be seen once more in the surprise and impatience shown towards the miners when they are reluctant to accept an influx of Italians to increase the labour force in the coal mines. The miners may well be unenlightened in their attitude, but any sociologist, or, for the matter of that, any thoughtful human being, will see the absurdity of supposing that all that is necessary is to take a number of men from one country, dump them in a totally different one, and simply leave them to solve their own problems. Any group of individuals who are in some respect 'different' from the members of an established community will be liable to cause social disintegration when they are introduced without forethought into that community. There is some evidence that, when foreign workers must be used in a factory, their number should not exceed 10 per cent of the total and that they should be divided up and spread evenly throughout the various groups in the firm. In this way their absorption will be aided and the creation of all-foreign groups which cannot be integrated into the social structure is avoided.*

The problems associated with defective communication are closely linked with the second weakness of formal organization: that by its very nature it tends to ignore certain emotional factors in human behaviour. Designed precisely in order to be rational and logical and to keep the human factor at a minimum, it is liable to come to grief when faced with the irrational and

* We have only to recall the attitude displayed by physicians in Britain and America in relation to their refugee colleagues who wished to make a home here to realize that miners are not alone in objecting to 'foreigners'.

emotional aspects of industrial life. Designed to deal with the predictable, the routine, and the typical, it is at a loss when confronted by the unforeseeable, the unusual, and the illogical. It is unreasonable to suppose that formal organization could be discarded – on the contrary, it is both inevitable and essential. But although no factory can be understood without knowledge of its formal structure, it is quite impossible to understand it on this basis alone. 'The reason this is so is quickly identified. The most important variable in the organization chart has been absent, namely, people. Formal organization looks on the people that inhabit the different offices or positions as constants. It assumes that all of the workers in a plant are unrelated individuals, or that their relations are only those which are specified on the chart.' (Miller and Form.) Since, as we have seen, these assumptions are false, any inferences based on them are also false and unlikely to work out in practice with any degree of success.

Although industry is based on an ideology which exalts the virtues of competition, sooner or later every firm comes to realize that pure competition does not work. Managements try to inculcate ideals of loyalty to their firm; but where loyalty ends and personal advancement begins is never made quite clear. The result is a set of conflicting attitudes which ends by confusing everyone and plays no small part in increasing the incidence of neurosis and personal unhappiness in industrial society. 'Cooperation and competition, group-consciousness and individualism, loyalty and mobility are not necessarily compatible. It is quite possible that such an atmosphere breeds insecurity feelings rather than high teamwork and morale. When a worker feels that at any time one of his subordinates or colleagues may threaten his position, he is filled with distrust and suspicion. Far from developing an atmosphere of uninhibited, spontaneous cooperation, this system breeds a structure of strange contradictions.' (Miller and Form.)

It follows, then, that this sort of atmosphere in a factory has a very definite influence on the attitudes and behaviour of the individual employee. But clearly the degree of competitive feeling in an industry is directly related to the attitude the firms concerned have to adopt in relation to the market. In those industries which are subject to intense competition, in which time and money are of vital importance, there is likely to be an all-pervading sense of insecurity. The problem is not merely lack of money (for it is quite possible, as we have seen, to adopt a humane attitude towards employees without great financial cost), but fundamentally that management in such firms has little time to spare for other than technical matters. What they want, as Constance Reaveley and John Winnington point out in their book *Democracy and Industry*, is a staff of technicians who will attempt as far as possible to eliminate the personal element, the need for skill and thought, on the part of labour; who will, in short, foster automaticity. Employees must be found who do not mind monotonous work, who will be sufficiently intelligent to carry out orders and sufficiently dull not to become bored and troublesome. Insecurity of employment, monotony, lack of interest in the job, and lack of time on the part of management to give any attention to the more social side of factory life, causes the worker in competitive industry to think more in terms of financial rewards than is the case elsewhere. In any case, there are no other incentives available in work of this type, so bonus schemes and other financial rewards are always being devised in order to get him to work harder. The need to increase output results in pressure being applied right down the line, a pressure which is felt most of all by the supervisor who has to pass on the demands of higher management to the workers. Since time-saving is regarded as most important in competitive industry, the supervisor tends to become a strict disciplinarian who relies on authority to see that his orders are obeyed. A good leader requires time to investigate and discuss, but under the circumstances we have just described, the supervisor has to rely largely on snap decisions. The type of foreman who is automatically selected for this task is energetic, ruthless, and driving; he must not be bothered by subtleties and must get things done at any cost. Reaveley and Winnington summarize the situation as follows: 'Competition in industry resolves itself into a struggle to obtain greater output from plant requiring the minimum of skill to operate it. These are the two ends to which the greater part of managerial activity in competitive industry is directed: the provision of plant which can be operated with a minimum of skill, and of a labour force which will operate that plant as nearly as possible to its maximum capacity. It follows that the internal organization of a factory, and through it the lives of the people who work in it, will be governed by the relative urgency of the need to attain these ends.'

In many respects free competition is as intolerable for the factory owner as it is for the employee. There is, therefore, a strong tendency to form combines in order to secure monopoly, to produce a state of what the economist euphemistically describes as 'imperfect competition'. We must now consider what influence this state of affairs has on the conditions of the workers. In the first place, the large concern is no longer compelled to make the most of every penny and every minute, and management are more free to devote themselves to other matters than the sheer struggle to survive. It is, in fact, in such concerns that most of the research into the human and other problems of industry has been carried out; Works Councils and partnership schemes are developed, sickness benefit, pensions, welfare (both in the good and bad sense of the word), and medical attention become possible, and the workers are likely to have continuity of employment. The greater sense of security resulting from these conditions tends to attract a better and more responsible type of employee, and this, in turn, is likely to be reflected in higher standards of management. In many respects, then, the large concern or monopoly has opportunities of solving the human problems of industry (whether or not it makes use of them) which are lacking in small and highly competitive firms. There are, of course, many small firms – usually in industries where competition is slight – which are as well, or better, run than any of the large concerns. Nevertheless it is important for the psychologist to realize that it is possible to over-simplify industrial problems, and that economic pressure is often as important in determining the outlook and conditions within a firm as anything which can readily be changed within the factory itself.

The main disadvantage of the large concern, as is almost too frequently pointed out, is its impersonal nature and the difficulty of communication which is a direct result of its size. The corresponding advantage of the small firm is that problems of communication are less acute and the face-to-face relationship of employees to management should make the resolution of conflicts simpler. But when we hear the large concern of today being unfavourably constrasted with the smaller firm, it is as well to realize that the small firm of today bears only the slightest resemblance to the family concern of fifty or more years ago, which is what the critic frequently has in mind when he makes the comparison. In the small family business, the owner was often director, manager, and supervisor in one. He knew most of his men by their first names and was, in turn, addressed by his; their family affairs were his concern, and he took a personal interest in their lives. These days, however, are almost past, and intense competition and mass-production have radically altered the situation. So much has been said about the problems of communication and the dehumanizing effect of monopolies and large concerns, whether privately or state-controlled, that it is liable to be forgotten that such problems are capable of solution and that much may be said in favour of large concerns. Monopoly-formation or nationalization will, in itself, solve no problems of human relationships, but it seems fair to say that, although in some respects it even creates problems, in others it makes their solution potentially easier. Elton Mayo, in a letter to *The Times* in January 1949, claimed that 'economic nationalization' and 'remote control' within industry and elsewhere is at the roots of much of our present-day troubles. He wrote: 'In the free societies, no less than in the totalitarian groups, there has been for many years a tendency to develop remote control not only of a political order. In 1933, when I was closely studying industrial developments in the United States, I said, with respect to the human problems of industrial civilization, that our political leaders constantly decried the rising tide of "economic nationalization". Interrupted, as it were, in speeches deploring this disharmony, they are forced to act in a manner that accentuates it. Attention is given to tariffs, currencies, price levels, to anything rather than to discovery of means whereby the human capacity to collaborate may be restored. This refers itself once again to the problem of remote control. As controls become remoter, whether in Washington or Whitehall, the effect is to accentuate disharmony at the working level rather than to diminish it. This affects trade unions no less than governments: recently we have seen strikes at Grimethorpe among miners, at the Port of London among dockers, at Euston among porters, and, lastly, among bus-men in London. It is a fact established by the research of many workers that as control becomes remoter, the probability of what is termed disloyalty among the actual workers is greatly increased.' We may grant that 'remote control' is a disease to which the large concern is particularly prone, and that this tends to lead to the symptoms described in this letter is also evident. But there is no reason to suppose that it cannot be avoided. On the contrary, Mayo, in the same letter, gives an example of just how this may be done. He continues: 'I have just received from Yale University the report of an inquiry into the human relations in an industry. In this instance the company had undergone immense expansion but had increased the possibility of direct communication between workers at the bench and the highest business executive: the expansion was successful and was attended by no disturbances. In other words, the continuous inter-communication between highly-placed executives and workers was improved.'

It is often forgotten that what is referred to, in an unflattering sense, as 'bureaucracy' within large privately-owned or nationalized industries is not found there alone. Miller and Form quote an executive as saying: 'We in business have bureaucracy just like the government. Only we call it "system".' However, in the larger concerns a situation tends to arise in which those concerned tend to think in terms of security rather than taking any active steps to deal constructively with problems which confront them. Officials are under pressure to be methodical, prudent, and disciplined, rather than enterprising. If not making a decision is easier than making one and likely to involve less risk of criticism later, no decisions will be made. Emphasis on discipline and reliability may lead, as Robert K. Merton points out in an essay on 'Bureaucratic Structure and Personality' (contained in *Personality in Nature, Society, and Culture*, edited by Kluckhohn and Murray), to a situation in which adherence to the rules, originally conceived as a means, becomes transformed into an end-in-itself; there occurs the familiar process of *displacement of goals* whereby an instrumental value becomes a terminal value. This sterilized, cautious, dreariness of outlook has become all too evident in many of our nationalized industries; for example, in the attempt to have all canal barges painted a uniform colour; in the N.C.B.'s description of the South Wales coalfield as part of the 'South-Western Division'; and in British Railways merging the four main-line railway systems under the same name.

Such an impersonal approach will produce no enthusiasm on the part of the workers, who, as is the way with human beings everywhere, prefer their friends and enemies to be personal. E. G. Chambers points out that 'the ordinary man has a need for a leader whom he can respect and admire and for whom he feels a personal loyalty based on personal relationships.' (We might add that, failing a good leader whom he can admire and respect, it is desirable that he should have a bad leader whom he can loathe and blame for his discontentment.) But, Chambers continues, 'in future many workers will have two sets of impersonal bosses – the State, which really signifies very little to most people, and the T.U.C.' (*Psychology and the Industrial Worker*.) N. M. Davis, in an article on 'Attitudes to Work Among Building Operatives' (*Occupational Psychology*, 22: 1948), found that on sites worked by private contractors, 30 per cent of the workers employed expressed approval of their management; on sites operated by local authorities, approval was expressed by only 10 per cent.

These problems are really of the utmost importance, although there is a tendency for political prejudices to confuse the picture and introduce over-simplifications which imply either that the problems are non-existent or that they can be solved by a return to 'free competition' and 'private enterprise'. As has already been suggested, the large concern, whether privately or state-controlled, will continue to exist and probably to become more common, so the sooner we discover how to run it properly from the point of view of human well-being, the better.

It is a complete fallacy to suppose that rigid bureaucracy is specially typical of very large or state-controlled industries; for there are many privately-owned business of quite moderate size which are just as 'bureaucratic' as any owned by the state. On the other hand, the Tennessee Valley Authority, a state enterprise initiated by the United States Government, proved to be a model of how a democratically-organized enterprise should function – it was decentralized, and the power of decision was vested to a considerable degree in the people on the spot. Numerous large privately-owned combines have, in varying degrees, contrived to avoid the dangers of over-centralization, lack of initiative, and poor communications. Thus Unilever Ltd, which has over 600 factories scattered throughout the world, was sufficiently decentralized to permit the management of one of its plants in Toronto to work out independently a war-time plan with the local branch of the International Chemical Workers' Union, as a result of which working hours were reduced from 48 to 40 hours per week, while labour costs to the company and the workers' pay remained the same. This has been claimed as one of the most impressive examples of union-management co-operation on record by W. F. Whyte of Cornell University, who has described the case in full in an article entitled 'Union-Management Co-operation: a Toronto Case' (*Applied Anthropology*, Summer 1947). The same authority contributes an interesting essay on 'Small Groups and Large Organizations' to *Social Psychology at the Crossroads*, a book edited by John H. Rohrer and Muzafer Sherif, in which he contrasts long, narrow hierarchies, having many levels of authority, with broad or flat hierarchies, having few levels of authority for large numbers of people. The former grows directly out of the inability of manage-ment to induce the co-operation of others and the attempt to solve the problems it has created by introducing another link in the chain of command, another individual to watch and control. One plant, for example, had no less than ten positions between worker and factory manager, and several more to the top of the firm. There were 12,000 workers in this company. Yet Sears, Roebuck and Co., a firm with 110,000 employees, has only four levels between the President and the workers in its retail division. Top-heavy organizations are always relatively inefficient, both economically and in respect of employee morale. Whyte concludes that the issue is one of centralization versus decentralization, and quotes David E. Lilienthal, who was head of the T.V.A., as saying: 'Over-centralized administration is not something simply to be made more palatable, more efficient, and better managed. It is a hazard to freedom. Centralization at the national capital or in a business undertaking always glorifies the importance of pieces of paper. This dims the sense of reality . . . To maintain perspective and human understanding in the atmosphere of centralization is a task that many able and conscientious people have found well-nigh impossible.'

It follows that the overall structure of a firm, its organization, influences the behaviour of the individuals and groups contained in it. Just as the individual's acts can only be understood in relation to the group in which he is functioning, so the behaviour of a group can only be understood in the context of the larger group to which it belongs.

'The social psychologist interested in small groups must be fully aware of the work going on in the larger structures. Otherwise he will attribute to factors within the group influences that really impinge upon the group from outside.' (W. F. Whyte, *Social Psychology at the Crossroads*.)

5

THE INFORMAL ORGANIZATION
OF INDUSTRY

C. I. BARNARD has pointed out that all large organizations may be thought of as having been built up from a number of smaller groups. These small groups vary in size, but average about eight or ten people, the number being determined by the fact that problems of communication become greater as the size of a group increases. Since it is impossible to hold a primary group together in the absence of adequate face-to-face communication, there is a tendency for it to break up or subdivide after it has reached a certain critical size. This process resembles in many respects the cell-division which may be observed under the microscope in the tissues of animals or plants – in this case, too, the cell increases in size until its internal metabolism can no longer be effectively maintained, and, when this stage is reached, it subdivides into two daughter cells. A group of more than ten or twelve people is likely to divide in a similar manner, since, beyond this size, intimate face-to-face contacts between all its members can no longer be maintained. (It is significant, as Gordon Rattray Taylor notes, that throughout history we find that groups of just this size have been formed under circumstances in which high morale was important – the twelve disciples, the cricket eleven, the Communist cell, the army section, and so on.) But the groups which result from this process, assuming that they do not wish to separate altogether, can only be kept in communication by setting up another organization with executive functions. That is to say, the leaders of the unit groups must not only be members of their own working units – they must also join together to form an executive unit which acts as a sort of nervous system in maintaining contact between the individual groups. In biology this phenomenon may also be observed, when, at a certain stage of evolution, single-celled animals or plants no longer subdivide and go their own way but group together in colonies which require a nervous system in order that the collection of cells may function as a single unit creature. 'This simultaneous contribution to two organizations by a single act appears to be the critical fact in all complex organizations; that is, the complex is made an organic whole by it' (C. I. Barnard). When all the unit groups of which a large organization is composed subordinate their purposes to a common goal, we may describe the organization as well-integrated, but if the units are in conflict with each other or try to dominate each other or attain independence of the parent organization, the state of affairs is described as showing a tendency to segmentation. All groups or combinations of groups represent an equilibrium between integration and segmentation, and every large organization has to face the same dilemma: that unit groups must be permitted to preserve their individual identity as much as possible, and that, on the other hand, their individual identity must be reduced to such an extent that all may work together towards a common goal.

The small natural unit groups we have been discussing are what we have already described as 'primary' or 'face-to-face' groups, whilst the larger bodies within which they function (the factory, the combine, etc.) are described as 'secondary' groups. In the former, the individual members are interrelated by a network of personal relationships which may be of any type or degree, but, whether the feeling is liking, disliking, or indifference, each member has a more or less clearly defined attitude towards every other member. The latter are altogether more formal, and the attitude of individual members towards the secondary group is likely to be determined by the degree to which its goals coincide, or conflict with, those of their own primary group. Edmund Burke tells us that 'to love the little platoon we belong to in society, is the first principle of public affections', a statement which carries the implication that all the individual's deepest feelings take place within the bounds of the primary groups of which he is a member; he cannot, as it were, love, hate, or feel any other emotion at first hand towards the state, the army, the Church, or the large industrial concern, which only arouse emotions in so far as their goals are seen to coincide, or clash with, those of his primary groups. It will be seen, then, that if the worker feels that the interests of his firm clash with those of his primary group (in this instance, his working-group), no amount of propaganda or pleading or 'discipline' will cause him to develop feelings of loyalty towards that firm. A situation will arise similar to that in the 'bank-wiring' room of the Hawthorne works in which the working-group went its own way and acted according to its own social norms which did not correspond with the interests of the factory as a whole. *The primary group is the instrument of society through which in large measure the individual acquires his attitudes, opinions, goals, and ideals; it is also one of the fundamental sources of discipline and social controls.* Although some of the individual's attitudes and ideals are acquired actually within the primary group, others come from his culture or subcultures – to a considerable extent, however, it is through the primary group (and especially the family) that these are enforced and handed on. Moral controls are, as we saw in Chapter 2, partially enforced by the superego, but (a) the superego does not cover the whole field of morals but only a few fundamental regulations (e.g., prohibiting incest or murder), and (b) the power of the superego to influence behaviour varies greatly from one person to another. Outside these fundamental regulations, it is the social pressure of the primary group which, in most people, becomes the instrument of discipline and moral control. It is, of course, also the source of certain controls such as those in the 'bank-wiring' room relating to 'rate-busting', 'chiselling', and 'squealing', which, although not moral controls in the ordinary sense of the word, were based on a code of behaviour suited to the circumstances in which the group was placed. The primary group then, is the most potent influence in regulating the individual's behaviour.

What we have just said has two important implications for industry:

(1) In attempting to change human behaviour (within the peripheral regions of the personality, at least), the attack must be made through the medium of the group rather than through the individual. Thus F. M. Thrasher, a sociologist who made a study

of gangs of delinquent boys in Chicago, found that it was impossible to deal with these boys individually, but, when the social norms of the gang were altered, the behaviour of its members also changed. This point, however, will be dealt with more fully at a later stage.

(2) It is most important that the manager should realize that the informal working group is the main source of social control, that he should endeavour to exercise legitimate control through such groups, and that he should avoid breaking them up. The common belief of management that such groups are subversive in their nature and always act according to the psychology of the mob is based on the dangerous misapprehension that any individual or group with opinions different from those of management must necessarily be in the wrong. The average strike, for example, is *not* based on 'mob psychology' or 'bad morale' – on the contrary, it is usually carefully planned and can only be successful if it is based on very good morale. The reason why the manager thinks the strikers' morale is 'bad' is because it does not happen to coincide with *management* interests, but how glad he would be if the same amount of energy and enthusiasm were shown by the workers towards the goals of industry! In short, the actions of the well-integrated primary group are likely to be disciplined, controlled, and, in relation to the situation as seen by the group, fairly logical. The wise manager should hesitate to criticize until he has asked himself whether he has treated his employees fairly, and whether he has taken the trouble to explain the situation fully to them and allowed them to discuss it fully with him.

What is known as a crowd or mob is entirely different from either primary or secondary group-formations, and, in fact, can only exist in their absence. The characteristic feature of the mob is that no personal inter-relationships exist between its members. Everyone remains virtually anonymous and lost in the mass. Indeed, it is this quality of anonymity which is largely responsible for the phenomena of 'mob psychology'. It is precisely because the members of a crowd are unknown to each other with no loyalties or any form of primary group control that these phenomena occur. It is, therefore, in the type of firm where Mayo's 'rabble

127

hypothesis' has almost become a reality, in which labour is casual, disintegrated, and unorganized, that the management nave most reason to be concerned. A crowd, to quote Dr Karl Mannheim in *Man and Society*, 'has as yet no social aim or function, so that the conduct of the individual cannot be determined by his function in it or regulated by the mutual control of its members, for these members have not as yet entered into personal relationships. The effect of the crowd on the individual is purely contagious; it does not subordinate his impulses to functional tasks . . . The reason why we behave as we do in a crowd is that the inhibitions connected with our family, our neighbours, our work, are cast aside; and in the anonymity of the mass, sober citizens throw stones and scared employees fire on the police.' The groups we have been discussing are the opposite of this. They are not temporary associations – they have some degree of permanence. They have particular aims and a definite structure. Their size is limited and their members are known. Within such a group, each member has a specific function and relationships with other members.

Although it is in general the case that primary groups, for the reasons given, are small in size and the larger secondary group is likely to be more formal, purposeful, and rational, Ellsworth Faris has made the observation in his book *The Nature of Human Nature* that there are some large social groups, usually of a political or religious nature, which show many of the characteristics of the primary group. Thus the Society of Friends, although in no sense of the word a face-to-face group, manages to preserve some of the intimacy of personal relationship which is found in the primary group. There is, therefore, no abrupt point of distinction between primary and secondary groups. But the contrast remains a valid one; the secondary group tends to be organized for a formal purpose (in the case of the factory, for the production of goods), its structure is more or less rationally designed towards that end, and its members are not all intimately known to each other. The primary group may have a specific practical goal, and when in pursuit of that goal will organize itself logically to that end, but essentially it is based on social satisfactions and personal choice, and, quite apart from any practical goal, it seeks to maintain itself as a unity. When a secondary group no longer has a practical function, it tends to disintegrate, but for the primary group its own existence is an adequate goal. Charles H. Cooley, who, more than twenty years ago, was the first to study this problem, has given the classical description of the primary group in his book *Social Organization*, which is less well-known than it deserves to be in this country: 'By primary groups I mean those characterized by intimate face-to-face association and co-operation. They are primary in several senses, but chiefly in that they are fundamental in forming the social nature and ideals of the individual. The result of intimate association, psychologically, is a certain fusion of individualities in a common whole, so that one's very self, for many purposes at least, is the common life and purpose of the group. Perhaps the simplest way of describing this wholeness is by saying that it is a "we"; it involves the sort of sympathy and mutual identification for which "we" is the natural expression. One lives in the feeling of the whole and finds the chief aims of his will in that feeling.

'It is not to be supposed that the unity of the primary group is one of mere harmony and love. It is always a differentiated and usually a competitive unity, admitting of self-assertion and various appropriative passions; but these passions are socialized by sympathy, and come, or tend to come, under the discipline of a common spirit. The individual will be ambitious, but the chief object of his ambition will be some desired place in the thought of the others, and he will feel allegiance to common standards of service and fair play. So the boy will dispute with his fellows a place on the team, but above such disputes will place the common glory of his class and school.'

Cooley gave as typical examples of primary groups the family, the play-groups of children, and the neighbourhood group of elders in the village community; to these, as has already been noted, we must add the 'natural' work-group which is the basic unit of informal organization in the factory. The informal organization of industry, however, does not consist solely of the primary working-group, and may be said to exist at five separate levels:

(1) The total informal organization of the factory, viewed as a system of interlocking groups of all types.

(2) Large groups which generally arise over some particular issue of internal politics within the factory (e.g., the question of union or non-union labour, whether or not to employ foreign workers). A diffuse group of this sort may extend throughout all the departments of the factory, and is generally described as a 'crowd' or a 'gang'.

(3) The primary group formed more or less on the basis of a common job in the same part of the factory. Relationships between members are more or less intimate and they are likely to work, dine, and talk together. The group in this case is usually described as a 'clique'.

(4) Groups of two or three particularly intimate friends who may be members of larger cliques.

(5) Isolated individuals who rarely participate in social activities.

As Miller and Form have pointed out, there is a special technique in studying the informal organization of a factory (or, for the matter of that, of a school or orphanage). In the first place, it must be remembered that no amount of study of individual people will be likely to give much information; *the unit of observation is the social relationship rather than the individual.* Roethlisberger and Dickson, who did much of the pioneering work at the Hawthorne plant, started with the false assumption that it was necessary to study each individual in order to get a picture of the group, until they finally came to realize that the group was a unit in its own right and could not be understood as the mere sum of the reactions of its individual members. In other words, the behaviour and opinions of the members as isolated individuals may be different from their behaviour and opinions when they come to be integrated into a group. Examples of this phenomenon will be given later, but for the moment it may be accepted that this is a fundamental axiom of social psychology. (It need hardly be said that no modern social psychologist believes in the old concept of the 'group mind' which was at one time used as an explanation of why group behaviour was more than the mere sum of individual behaviours of group members. The explanation lies, of course, in the changing patterns of interrelationships within the group.) Secondly, it is necessary for the investigator to note which actions are spontaneous and which are determined by formal considerations relating to the performance of the job. If, for example, the investigator interpreted the frequent visits of one worker to another in a distant part of the factory as based on friendship when, in fact, the visit was part of the job, his interpretation of the informal organization of the firm would go far astray. It is useful, therefore, to distinguish between those actions which are fundamentally technical, those which are sociotechnical, and those which are purely social. Thus the actions of a coal miner when drilling a hole in which he places an explosive charge are strictly technical, as are those of an operative at his machine or a chemist at his bench. Whether, under these circumstances, the worker is single or married, black or white, Protestant, Catholic, or Jew, is largely irrelevant. The only social aspect of his job in this sense is the social status or significance that others assign to it since the worker's performance of his job may depend on his reaction to its social status. When, however, technical behaviour involves social interaction, we may speak of sociotechnical behaviour. For example, the operative must 'clock in', go to the cloakrooms to change, report to his supervisor, engage in a certain minimum of conversation with his mates on technical matters, teach a new worker the job, call for his wages at the end of the week, and attend a union meeting periodically. All of these actions, although social in the sense that they involve social interaction, are in effect part of the job. This sociotechnical behaviour shades gradually into the purely social – the social interaction which takes place on a basis of purely personal interest in people as people. Clearly technical and sociotechnical behaviour is an aspect of formal organization, whereas social behaviour belongs to the informal structure of the factory. It is with the latter that we are here concerned. Having distinguished between these different types of behaviour and directed his attention towards social relationships rather than individuals, the social psychologist or sociologist will then

proceed to note how the group members react towards each other –
only secondarily will he concern himself with what they are
producing or servicing. He will listen to what they say, or avoid
saying, what they do, or avoid doing, and observe the extent to
which saying and doing coincide with each other. The ideas,
beliefs, and attitudes on which members agree or disagree will
also be noted. Lastly, he will try to discover how far these observations remain stable or alter with changing situations. While
carrying out his investigations, he must take care to remain, so
far as is possible, outside the group. He must not himself become
a factor in the situation he is observing. If it is impossible not to
become involved, he must attempt to analyse his relationship
towards the group as he would any other person's.

In what we are now about to discuss it should be remembered
that what is being described is the behaviour of informal groups,
not mere mobs of people. The extent to which the behaviour to
which we refer may be observed in a given factory or industry
will depend on the extent to which informal groups have been
allowed to form within it. For although there is no factory which
is completely lacking in any form of social life, there are many
circumstances at the present day which militate against a closely-
integrated society. When labour turnover is high for whatever
reason and casual labour is readily accepted there is little
opportunity for primary groupings to arise except in the small
nucleus of semi-permanent employees which is found in almost
every factory. It seems likely that the tendency to employ part-
time female labour may sometimes have a similar effect; for
women who are primarily housewives working in order to get a
little extra money are unlikely to develop a close interest in
factory affairs. When a worker enters a job with the awareness
that he or she is likely to be permanently employed with the firm,
he will wish to make a success of it and will probably take a real
interest in the social life of the firm. But this rarely applies to
casual or part-time labour, and sometimes (although by no
means always) the same might be said of young women full-
time workers who may regard their job as in the nature of a
stopgap between school and marriage. When people feel strongly
about their firm, even if the feeling is anger or resentment, there

is always the possibility of redirecting their emotions, but when for reasons largely external to the factory they are indifferent, the problem is more difficult to solve. The attitude of shrugging the shoulders and leaving to get another job elsewhere often found amongst this type of worker poses a serious problem for industrial morale. But, as has already been pointed out, this is simply one aspect of a more general state of affairs, which is the 'rootlessness' of modern society, the constant shifting of populations from one place to another. The small town or village community of which the factory is an integral part and within which the whole factory staff have lived most of their lives is becoming less common. As Mayo puts it: 'No longer does the supervisor work with a team of persons he has known for many years or perhaps a lifetime – he is a leader of a group of individuals that forms and disappears almost as he watches it.' Under these circumstances, morale is bound to be low and social life negligible, since nobody stays long enough, or cares sufficiently to attempt to improve working conditions either socially or technically. When a job is regarded as merely a temporary one, why should the worker bother to change its conditions?

It seems likely, then, that well-integrated groups and a genuine social life are most likely to be found under the following circumstances:

(1) In skilled trades (since the skilled worker is less likely to become a casual labourer).

(2) Where the factory is situated in a relatively small and long-established community.

(3) Where casual and part-time labour is not employed, and in firms where a seasonal incidence of work does not necessitate the frequent taking-on and putting-off of large numbers of workers.

Closely-integrated groups are most likely to be found amongst skilled or semi-skilled workers (who take an interest in their job and tend to remain at it), married men (who require stability in their job), and elderly women (to whom the social contacts mean a great deal). It is, of course, possible to create good morale

133

under almost any circumstances, but it is only fair to recognize that even the best management may find some of these problems very difficult to deal with.

The most detailed account of group structures is that based on the work of the American sociologist J. L. Moreno whose book *Who Shall Survive?* initiated a new approach to certain aspects of social psychology. Moreno describes his technique as 'sociometry', and the charts which illustrate the patterns of social interaction within a group as 'sociograms'. Briefly, he classifies the basic attitudes which people may show towards each other as attraction, repulsion, and indifference (compare this with the classification of the psycho-analyst Karen Horney: moving towards people, moving against people, and moving away from people), and the members of the group to be studied are asked to indicate those with whom they would, or would not, like to associate. Their choices are then paired and ranked and the members are regrouped in terms of their preferences. Moreno's early work was carried out at the New York Training School for Girls which he had been asked to investigate because poor morale and lack of discipline had been causing trouble. This school is a closed community with a population of five or six hundred girls living in sixteen cottages each with a 'housemother' in charge. It was arranged that each girl should list the five others with whom, in order of preference, she would like to share the cottage. Although it was impossible to satisfy all demands, it was found that there were many mutual choices, and the final results appear to have been excellent both in terms of improved morale and general satisfaction. Housemothers were also to be chosen, and as new girls came to the institution each housemother who had vacancies in her cottage was asked to interview them separately. The housemother and the girls were both asked to make first and second choices, and the girls were placed accordingly. However, it is unnecessary to discuss the details of this particular case, which, as is the purpose of most of Moreno's work, was primarily psycho-therapeutic in intention. What is important is the information obtained about the basic types of sociological nuclei on which informal organizations are founded. Five principal types of nucleus were noted:

(1) The most elementary and clear-cut nucleus was the mutual first choice of two or more individuals amongst themselves. This might be represented by couples, triangles, squares, circles, or other more complex figures.

(2) Non-mutual choices capable of being represented by chains of any number of individuals (e.g., A chooses B, B chooses C, C chooses D, and so on).

(3) The configuration described by Moreno as a 'star', resulting from the clustering of a large number of choices around a single individual, who might in turn respond by mutual attraction, indifference, or repulsion.

(4) A grouping of great practical importance was that of the powerful as opposed to the popular individual. Thus a popular individual might be the object of a large number of choices both within his own group and from people relatively isolated from the rest of the community, but, in spite of this, he might have very little influence owing to the limited contacts of his admirers. On the other hand, an individual chosen by only a few popular members might have a powerful influence through the extensive connexions of the people to whom he is a centre of attraction.

(5) Lastly, there are the isolated individuals chosen by nobody although they may have chosen a few other persons. Such individuals are frequently maladjusted, and may be the source of maladjustments in their group. In Moreno's terminology, they may form the focal point of cleavages of an inter-personal sort. The reason for this is that such an individual is cut off by his isolation from the currents of feeling by which the behaviour standards of the group are impressed on each member, and, when no such pressures are felt, he is like a ship in the fog without radar to guide it.

These nuclear structures are, of course, interrelated, and they overlap to form an immensely complex system, each member being a part of numerous structures in varying degrees of intensity and completeness. The 'overchosen' members are not merely popular in the superficial sense – they are the protagonists of the needs and desires of large numbers of the population. 'They are the members who are the most wanted participants and who have earned this choice status because they act in behalf of others with a sensitivity of response which does not characterize the average individual in the community (chosen to an average extent). They are found to be the individuals who see beyond the narrow circumference of their own personal needs into the wide range of needs of their fellow-citizens. They are the individuals who go farthest in relating themselves to others and in translating the needs of others into effective outlets.' (Helen Jennings in the article 'Sociometry' contained in the *Encyclopedia of Psychology*, edited by Philip L. Harriman.)

The structure of a group is not static but is rather a dynamic network of forces, which, at varying tempos, is always changing. Members may leave the group and be replaced by others, or events may occur which alter the prestige of particular members. Above all, the structure of the group may change according to the tasks with which it is confronted. For example, a number of people on a camping trip may be organized around a leader who is the best-liked and most popular individual (in the ordinary sense of the word) within the group. But if the party is lost in the mountains, the leader who comes to the fore is the man with knowledge of the countryside and the ability to take the others back to their base. The other members will spontaneously organize themselves around his leadership in accordance with their usefulness in the specific situation. Moreno has pointed out that the choices of the girls at the New York State Training School as to who they would wish as housemates was not always the same as their choice when they were seeking workmates. An individual isolated with respect to the one situation might be found popular in the other. 'The community is found to produce many varieties of leadership – varieties which represent the manifold, diverse needs of its many interacting participants. Similarly many varieties of isolation are revealed.' (Helen Jennings.) It follows that there is no such thing as a 'natural' or 'universal' leader in the popular meaning of the phrase – a good leader is the man or woman who is most fitted to take charge in a given situation. Leadership is not a psychological trait which can be investigated as if it were a property of the individual – it is always a function of the situation and the nature of the group. This point is well illustrated in J. M. Barrie's play *The Admirable Crichton*, which describes how an aristocratic family with a butler named Crichton is marooned on a desert island. Within a short time, the butler has assumed leadership because of his qualities of resourcefulness and his special knowledge, and the other members of the party have willingly restructured themselves around him. Crichton is the man whose potentialities and knowledge fit the new situation. In industry, however, situations do not change quite so dramatically – the possible situations are limited in number. In the formal sense, the leader of a working-group is the supervisor or foreman, who, in ordinary circumstances, is likely to be accepted as leader for the purposes of the job. In so far as he is a good supervisor, he will try to see to it that he is accepted willingly as the appropriate leader in that situation, rather than as one who has forced himself on the group by virtue of his formal authority. But if trouble should arise, the accepted leader may be what is popularly known as an 'agitator' – possibly a group member who is ordinarily ignored or teased as an eccentric or extremist. Other frustrated or resentful men may surround him as the nucleus of the new structure. It is quite possible for a leader who has been voluntarily chosen to be one of the most unpopular men in the group, as happened, for instance, in a certain factory where the supervisors felt their position to be threatened, and their authority undermined, by management. In this case, the man who was regularly elected as chairman of the supervisors' group was a blustering bully who was heartily disliked by most of the others. Yet he was unanimously elected on each occasion since he alone was capable of standing up to the management. Similarly, as we have already noted, a man of the agitator type who is almost insanely suspicious of management intentions *and is recognized to be so* by his fellow-workers may be elevated to a position of leadership when discontent has become general. It often appears that the leader's core personality shows those traits or attitudes which environmental influences have temporarily produced in the peripheral personalities of the led. An excellent example of this observation in the political field was the rise of the Nazi party in Germany. The German people, suspicious and resentful after the Treaty of Versailles, chose as a leader the man Hitler, who was from the psychiatrist's standpoint a paranoiac – a man mentally sick with suspicion and resentment. His henchmen possessed in large measure the same traits – Streicher, Himmler, and Hess were obviously mentally sick paranoid individuals, and around this nucleus of fanatics there came to be attached such opportunists as Goering, Ribbentrop, and the rest.

Under more normal circumstances, the members of a group in industry come together for such obvious reasons as that they are employed on the same job, are of similar nationality or regional origin, or of about the same age, sex, or seniority in the firm. Most of all, they come together because they are placed near each other in the workshop. This is especially the case if mobility is limited by the nature of the job. Since spatial proximity is so important, it follows that to a considerable extent the formal working-group and the informal group coincide. On the other hand, there is a good deal of overlapping. For example, a number of supervisors may create their own informal group, and, although separated during working hours, may meet in the canteen at meal-times or socially after work. Similarly young people or older workers or those who have been many years with the firm may form cliques which do not coincide with the group in which they happen to work. So each worker may be a member of more than one group within the factory and in each his status may be different, the important man in one context being relatively insignificant in another.

An individual's status is based on the degree to which he contributes to the purposes of his group, and since to the members of the primary working-group there are many purposes other than the production of goods, it follows that there are also many sources of status. A man's status may derive from his skill with certain tools, his knowledge of a particular process, his generosity, his ability to make others laugh, or his reputation as a first-aider who knew the correct treatment when an accident occurred. In the informal working group, as in the small village, even the idiot has a certain status and 'belongs'. Within the face-to-face group individual traits are readily observed and become common knowledge, but in the larger secondary group, largely because of defective communication, status cannot so readily be assigned. 'In modern industry the man in one department has little idea of what the man in another does, and how far it contributes to the common purpose. In particular, the manual worker cannot understand what it is that the office staff does, nor the factory hand what the farmer does.' (Gordon Rattray Taylor, *Are Workers Human?*) Under these circumstances, people have to depend on external signs of status which comes to mean status within the formal organization of the firm. A man tends to be assessed by his salary, by his position in the hierarchy, by the size of his desk, by the canteen in which he has his meals, and so on. The amount of significance which is attached to such matters in the average factory is really amazing, and many liberal-minded observers, previously unacquainted with industry, and from brief war-time experience convinced that the army is somewhat undemocratic and authoritarian, are astonished to find on entering certain factories that by comparison the army begins to appear as a tolerant, just, and relatively democratic institution. As Dr Tredgold has noted: 'In the army, for instance, which even nowadays some regard as undemocratic, generals and lieutenants do eat together – and wash their hands together; and though units have sometimes three different messes some firms have six or seven. Badges of rank in industry are not sartorial (or less obviously so) but take the form of the size of the desk (and often the largest desk had the least on it); the size and texture of the carpet; the size (and gilding) of the letters of the name outside the office door; the number (and even the colour) of the telephones; and, of course, the accessibility of the person.' (*Human Relations in Modern Industry*.) Or, to take another example, Gordon Rattray Taylor tells us that in the Civil Service the practice of having external badges of status has become institutionalized, and 'elaborate regulations prescribe at what level in the hierarchy one may have a desk-lamp, a padded armchair, and, finally a strip of carpet in one's office.' In the more authoritarian type of factory, the new recruit to management is likely to have some embarrassing moments when he is attempting to discover where he may wash, dine, or park his car, and black looks will follow him whenever he makes a slip. Management personnel will fight for the right to a telephone, a carpet, a place in the executives' canteen or car-park, not because they want these things in themselves, but because of their social significance. Yet the same people often cannot understand why the worker in the manufacturing department of their firm should object to using the cloakroom belonging to the warehouse whilst building operations are taking place! In every factory there are jobs which appear to the outsider (and often to management) to be 'the same' both in pay and official status, but are regarded by the workers concerned as at quite different levels of social significance. Thus in certain restaurants, those who handle fish are considered to be lower in status than those who handle meat, although both may receive the same wages. Dr Tredgold quotes the case of a lavatory cleaner who threatened to leave because she was asked to clean ovens in a canteen; in this factory the job of lavatory cleaner ranked higher than that of oven cleaner in the informal estimate of the workers. The main reason was that the former, in addition to being a cleaner, had charge of certain materials such as soap and toilet rolls, and had the authority to move out other workers when she considered that they had been talking or smoking too long, in the lavatory. Strangely enough, many of these traditional prestige-ratings are completely unknown to those in authority, who, as a result, may unwittingly make mistakes which seem quite shocking to the workers. The worker may be just as upset when he is moved to another job at the same pay, but with a lower prestige-rating, as is the director who finds the new management trainee in the lavatory reserved for executives. It frequently happens that workers who, for reasons of redundancy, or because of bad health, are moved to another job at the same pay but with lower informal status become deeply resentful. Indeed the status situation is one of the commonest causes of strikes. So, too, individual factories or whole industries vary in the prestige with which they are associated in the minds of workers. A steel-worker or coal-miner expected to work in a canning factory would be just as indignant as a doctor who was asked to work as a male nurse. It should be one of the first principles of good management to ensure that people do not have their self-esteem injured by any action which may lower their status in relation to that of others. Status, it must be remembered, may be lowered not only by demoting a person from one level to another which is held in lower esteem, but also by taking some action which, by raising the relative prestige of one group, indirectly lowers that of another. (See p. 91.) Many industrial disputes have indicated that workers are more concerned with how their wages compare with those of others than with what the amount happens to be in absolute terms. An economist writes: 'Every study of industrial workers has shown that wage rates are not uppermost in their minds. Differences in wage rates between various jobs are very close to the workers' hearts because they establish prestige. But absolute wage rates are only rarely very important. They matter a great deal – they may indeed be the most important thing – in an economy very close to subsistence, that is, in the very early stages of industrialization. They also count in inflation, when incomes never quite catch up with prices. But otherwise wage rates do not rank very high among the workers' concerns.' (Peter Drucker, *The New Society*.)

The concepts of 'status', 'rôle', and 'prestige' are often confused. Generally speaking, status implies a position within a group, rôle the appropriate behaviour which goes with that position, and prestige is something more personal which the individual brings to his status and rôle. A doctor, for example, will always have a certain amount of respect from the mere fact of his official status as a physician, but he may have more or less prestige depending on whether he is a good or bad physician. The distinction is important, since a popular fallacy about promotion is based on this confusion between status and prestige. It is simply not true to say, as is often done, that everybody wants promotion in the sense of higher formal status. What people *do* want is a position in which it is possible to increase in prestige. Thus the average skilled craftsman does not want to become a supervisor or a factory manager – he wants to become a better craftsman *and recognized as such*. That is to say, he wishes to feel that if he

THE SOCIAL PSYCHOLOGY OF INDUSTRY

does his job well the fact will be recognized, not only financially, but also in terms of increased privileges.

Status is sub-divided by anthropologists into the two types of 'intrinsic' (or 'functional') status, and 'derived' (or 'non-functional') status. In the former, the person commands deference on the basis of skill, knowledge, or physical attributes – he is the good craftsman or the knowledgeable first-aider; in the latter, rank and prestige are derived from occupying a certain position or office in the formal hierarchy – the chairman or factory manager or supervisor clearly come into this class. From the present point of view, it is simpler to regard intrinsic status as that belonging to the informal organization of the factory, and derived status as belonging to the formal organization. While the two may often be combined, they are not necessarily related. It has been suggested that modern industry should restore functional prestige to work, and avoid non-functional, derived, or artificially-created prestige – that status, privileges, and pay should correspond to the real contribution made. But this cannot be done until each individual with improved communication is enabled to understand the value of the contribution each other individual makes to the whole. The great advantage of functional or intrinsic status is that it contains room for all: 'respect for father as the bread-winner does not take away from respect for mother, whose claims are based on different grounds. The best dentist in the community is not the less respected because someone else is the best ploughman.' (Gordon Rattray Taylor, *Conditions of Happiness*.) For this reason, functional status leads to less rivalry and more satisfaction than derived status based on power or wealth. Another defect of derived status systems is that, under conditions in modern times, they tend to be what is described as 'mobile'. That is to say, except when derived status is based on birth as in the Middle Ages, it is always possible to move down, as well as up, the hierarchy. Money and power are as easily lost as they are difficult to gain, and their possessor has little security of tenure in his position. With functional status, on the other hand, the individual will always be given credit for what he has achieved in the past, even when he is no longer capable of his former skill. The only way in which functional status may be lost

142

is when the holder behaves in such a way as to forfeit the respect of others. We have noted that in the informal group status is essentially functional. But, for practical purposes, what really matters in industry is not whether status is functional or non-functional; the important point is whether it is accepted by the majority of employees or not. The supervisor who manages to get himself accepted and respected by his working-group has, in effect, transformed his status from non-functional to functional. He is both the formal and the informal leader of the group, and holds his position not only by virtue of authority from above but also by the willing acceptance of those below.

Whilst the working-group rewards its members by giving them status and function, or, what amounts to the same thing, emotional security and self-respect, it also expects the individual member to conform to its customs. These customs may involve the general ideology of the group as a whole, or they may relate to the behaviour expected of an individual occupying a particular status. Conformity may be enforced by ridicule, 'sending to Coventry', or sometimes even by violence; but these sanctions are rarely needed as the group member is usually much too concerned lest he should lose the respect of his comrades. Miller and Form describe the case of a labourer who came to work wearing a light grey felt hat instead of the old cloth cap generally worn at the job. On the first occasion, the rest of the workers teased him, asking him whether he thought he was the boss, but on the second day their reaction was more violent. On the third day, the man came to work in the generally accepted style of head-gear. A similar situation arose when a lorry-driver wore a white shirt and tie to work. In these instances the men concerned were not behaving according to the general concept of what constituted normal behaviour within the group. Great pressure is often brought to bear in order to ensure that those in a particular status-position fulfil their rôle in what is deemed to be a proper manner. It is, for example, not always appreciated when someone in authority tries to behave as an 'ordinary' individual. Gordon Rattray Taylor tells how a popular managing director who came to work in a battered old car was thought to be 'letting the firm down'. People who complain that doctors give themselves airs and consider themselves different from other men and women are often the first to complain that the doctor is being 'unprofessional' when he tries to behave as an 'ordinary' person.

Nearly all informal industrial groups insist on members doing their fair share of the work (i.e., a fair proportion of the work done by the group collectively). This is part of a more general rule that no member shall profit at the expense of any other. Likewise promotion through undue influence is disapproved of, not because it is 'unfair' in the wider meaning of the term, but because it is disloyal to the group. On the other hand, should the group have gained an unfair advantage over other groups (e.g., by violating company regulations), the member who reported this would be strongly censured by his mates. The individual member is protected only where the formal organization is concerned, and when he breaks the rules of the informal organization his action will be generally resented. Some of the common rules of the informal working-group have already been described in the last chapter, but, as Professor Florence has pointed out, it should not be thought that these rules are peculiar to workers or people in industry. Any small and closely-knit group, whether the family, a group of schoolboys in a Public School, or a group of mill-girls, is almost certain to object to the member who tells tales on another member to someone outside the group, to the member who fails to do his fair share of the work, and to the member who does too much and thereby shows the others up. The industrial working-group usually has a fairly clear estimate of what, in the circumstances, is considered to be a 'fair day's work', and it tends to keep production within the range of the average worker. This type of restriction of production is, therefore, based on factors within the group and on the relationship, good or bad, which the group feels to exist between itself and the firm as a whole. When it is felt that the weaker members are unlikely to be penalized and that the firm is fair in its dealings with the workers, restriction of production due to these causes will come to an end. But, of course, many restrictive practices have little to do with conditions within the individual firm, being related to economic and political factors largely outside the control of the management. These will be dealt with elsewhere. In many jobs the exact methods of keeping production within the bounds set by the group have been standardized – for example, informal rules may decide that the worker should lift two pieces of material of a certain size or weight, and only one piece of another size or weight in each lifting operation. Even workers who are unorganized by a trade union are likely to have rules of this sort, and detailed examples of such practices will be found in S. B. Mathewson's *Restriction of Output Among Unorganized Workers* (Viking Press, 1931). Mathewson and his co-workers took jobs as machine-operators, labourers, and in other occupations, living with working people in their home environments, and found that, apart from the restrictive practices which are part of trade-union policy, the most frequent reasons given by the unorganized worker for such practices were rate-cutting, fear of unemployment, excessive speeding-up, and resentment at management.

But it would be a mistake even in the worst factory to regard the informal organization of the working-group solely in the light of the intention of the workers to resist company policy. Miller and Form show that if the 'you're-not-paid-to-think-do-what-you're-damn-well-told' policy of some old-fashioned managers were carried out in detail by the workers, the firm would soon find it impossible to carry on business: 'Without the assistance of informal organization, formal organization would often be in-effective. This is frequently the case when managers try to determine every detail in production. They are too far removed from production to envisage many of the problems that arise. Yet frequently they give orders on the basis of presumed knowledge. If their orders were completely obeyed, confusion would result and production and morale would be lowered. In order to achieve the goals of the organization workers must often violate orders, resort to their own technique of doing things, and disregard lines of authority. Without this kind of systematic sabotage much work could not be done. This unsolicited sabotage in the form of disobedience and subterfuge is especially necessary to enable large bureaucracies to function effectively.' (*Industrial Sociology*.)

The culture of industrial groups derives from many sources: from class origins, occupational and technical sources, the atmosphere of the factory which forms their background, and, finally, from the specific experiences of the small informal group itself. Some of its more important manifestations may be classified as (a) occupational language, (b) ceremonies and rituals, and (c) myths and beliefs.

It is well known that different trades have to make use of a great variety of technical terms in the course of their work. But it is not always recognized how far this process of language-making may become institutionalized. Of the functions of language as the instrument of communication we shall have more to say in the next chapter, but at this point we need only mention the more important sources of occupational language. Such deviations from standard English derive not merely from the use of specialized technical terms peculiar to a given trade, but also from the use of argot (i.e., substitutes for words in daily use), and certain usages based on class differences. Thus many words used by the chemist, by the engineer, or in other specialized trades or occupations are strictly technical in that no everyday word exists to replace them. On the other hand, the words 'bulkhead', 'starboard', and 'port', used by seamen are, properly speaking, argot, since they might be replaced by the everyday words 'wall', 'right-hand', and 'left-hand' sides. Whereas technical words are obviously necessary, the use of argot mainly serves the function of creating group solidarity and as a means of identifying indivi-dual members. In addition, class-differences are evident in the different use made by working-class men of 'blasphemous' or 'obscene' expressions. This is not to say that such expressions are uncommon among the middle-classes, but, by and large, the latter swear and blaspheme under more rigidly defined situations. The factory manager or the average clerical worker will use such expressions at a convivial gathering of men, or under emotional pressure, but ordinarily he will not use them as an everyday jargon. When the factory manager uses an obscene one-syllable word to describe a colleague, it will generally be supposed that his opinion of his colleague is, for the moment at any rate, low. But amongst workers such words have a more everyday use which almost empties them of any derogatory significance and they may often be used as terms of endearment. It has been suggested by some serious-minded psychologist that swearing in the working-classes is a response to conditions of tension and frustration, but it is obviously difficult to test the validity of this hypothesis. The language of the working-group is derived, then, from these three sources, with additions from regional sources in the form of dialect.

All well-integrated groups, whether in the Australian Bush, the South Sea Islands, or a London factory have certain ceremonies and rituals which may be classified as initiation rites, rites of passage, and rites of intensification. Initiation rites for the novice who is joining the working-group may take such forms as teasing or ridiculing him, asking him to do favours or run errands for group members, or sending him for such non-existent tools as a 'left-handed monkey wrench'. The (mainly unconscious) function of such behaviour is to demonstrate to the newcomer his inferiority and ignorance in relation to the superiority of the group members, as a consequence of which the morale of the latter is raised simultaneously with the desire of the former to become fully initiated. The novice's attitude towards the group is tested, and his resourcefulness or lack of it made clear. A recent case in the newspapers described how members of the women's services who became attached to a certain air-force station were 'initiated' by having their blouses pulled up and being stamped on the upper abdomen with the rubber stamp ordinarily used for the station correspondence. (It is not, of course, suggested that this primitive rite is in general use in the Royal Air Force.) Such initiation ceremonies closely resemble those of primitive tribes, although they are obviously less elaborate in content. They carry the implication that, if full membership of the group were too easily attained, it would not be worth having. Rites of passage are the ceremonies carried out when a group member is promoted, demoted, or sacked – when, in other words, he is about to leave the group. 'The function of the ritual may be to manifest group identification and loyalty, to ease the process of separation from the group, to emphasize the finality of the social rupture, or merely to indicate that all past animosities are forgiven and forgotten.' (Miller and Form.) They may take such forms as shaking hands, giving a party, speech-making, joking, giving absurd advice, and so on. Between the rites of arrival and departure there are the rites of intensification – ceremonies which have the purpose of demonstrating the solidarity of the group. The unity of the group may be demonstrated by the way members wear their caps, the way they address each other, the informal meetings to smoke and talk in the cloak-rooms, the private jokes whose significance is lost to outsiders, the dining together at lunch in the canteen, and, on special occasions, the drinking together at factory outings, the parties at Christmas and the New Year, and on other holidays and feast-days. It may be thought that too much is being made of such everyday happenings in the life of any industrial group, and that to compare them with the rites and customs of primitive tribes is absurd. But the important point is that, however attenuated the form these ceremonies may take, no group worthy of the name ever assumes that membership is a mere matter of walking into it. There is no integrated or coherent social group which does not make something of a ceremony of the arrival or departure of members or take part in ceremonies which, in effect, indicate its distinctness from any other group. Nor is there any group worthy of the name which does not regard itself as superior to, or at any rate different from, every other group. There always exists the awareness of what the anthropologist would call the 'in-group' and the 'out-group'. The reasons for this are fairly obvious, since, if an individual's status, prestige, or pride of position come to a considerable extent from the groups of which he is a member – from his family, his working-group, his factory, and, in a lesser degree, from the larger secondary groups of the city, the county, and the nation, then clearly the more important these groups are, the greater is his own personal prestige. His attitude towards his own in-group will be that of the Old Testament writer whose feeling towards his religion or his tribe was expressed in the words: 'I would rather be a door-keeper in the house of my God than a dweller in the tents of wickedness.' This fact has two very important implications for the manager in industry. Firstly, it implies that every man or woman has a great desire to 'belong' within a group and to be able to take a pride in it. This 'belongingness' and pride of membership is one of the social goods which the firm is in a position to supply, and, when the firm is one with a great name in the world or even in the local community, the manager has a great asset on his side. Gordon Rattray Taylor shows very clearly the appallingly ineffectual use to which this asset has been put by some firms. He writes: 'I have only once met an employee of (a certain very famous motor-car factory), but I am perfectly sure that most of the men who work there state the fact with a certain pride. It is therefore almost a miracle of bad management that employers have managed to kill pride in the factory's achievements to the extent that they have.' Large concerns such as Unilever Ltd who hold frequent exhibitions of their products at each of their individual factories have discovered the astonishing enthusiasm and interest shown by the workers when they are 'put in the picture', to use the modern jargon which signifies improved communications. In the Ford factory at Dagenham, the visit of Henry Ford jnr aroused the greatest enthusiasm amongst the workers who crowded round him to shake hands or ask for autographs. Admittedly, this aspect of industrial relations is an aspect which, in itself, will not take us very far, but the failure to recognize its existence does demonstrate how some managements have become so stupefied by their own propaganda, their ideology of the unwilling worker and the carrot and the stick, that they are quite incapable of observing human nature and using their own common sense.

The second implication of this attitude of the worker towards his in-group relates to the problem of filling jobs of low status, of getting people who will do the lowly and dirty work. This, again, is a problem which has, in large measure, been created by management. For, if the manager begins by stating the problem in the form: 'This is a nasty job, a job fit only for a simpleton – how can I find anyone stupid enough to do it?', he is completely forgetting the quite obvious fact that the lowliness or nastiness of a job are subjective estimates, and that what really matters is the prestige of the job, and, even more important, the prestige of the group for which the job is to be done. A doctor or a nurse, for example, or a sanitary inspector, have to do some things which would disgust the most unskilled casual labourer who did not see these actions in their social context. Yet the status and prestige of such people is generally high. But when the supervisor or factory manager puts a man in a 'dirty' job with the, probably unspoken, implication: 'I'm sorry to have to ask you to do this job, but, after all, you are the most unskilled and dullest person I can find, so you must do it,' he is by his attitude lowering the prestige of the job to such a degree that nobody in their senses *would* wish to have anything to do with it. The supervisor or manager of this type would no doubt feel that the job of lavatory cleaner was insignificant and dirty, but the woman who was doing the work, as we saw in the case quoted a few pages back, thought it a very important piece of work and was insulted at the idea that she might be asked to clean ovens in the canteen. The Sanitary Orderly in the army who has to clean out the latrines would hardly feel flattered if it were suggested to him that he was in a position similar to that of the Untouchables in India who do the same task. In point of fact (and this is something else in which industrial management might profitably study army methods), he is given lectures on sanitation and dirt-borne diseases, taught the best methods of doing his job, and therefore considers himself a highly-skilled man doing important work. It is, therefore, foolish on the part of the manager to go round his factory assessing jobs as childish, dirty, or mean on the basis of his own subjective estimates; for, in doing so, he is only further lowering the status of those who do them. At the same time, he should see to it that no job is *unnecessarily* dirty or dangerous, since, although few people object to work which is unavoidably dirty or dangerous, they will certainly not forgive the sort of unpleasantness which indicates neglect of their interests on the part of management.

Above all, it is the prestige of his working-group and his position in it which will influence the worker's attitude to such jobs. If the prestige of his group is high and he is satisfied in his membership of it, the type of work he has to do becomes a minor consideration. The late Professor Mannheim told how a friend of his who dealt with the problem of refugees had great difficulty in finding an occupation for elderly ladies who had seen better days, and resented doing any work which they considered a social come-down. But he managed to form them into co-operative squads to go round cleaning hospitals and schools. As individuals, they would never have dreamed of consenting to do such menial work. But as members of a group they did it enthusiastically. Because each lady was sure of the approval of the members of her group – and would actually have lost this approval by refusing to go along – she could afford to ignore any possible comment by outsiders.

Myths and beliefs are based on the need both to justify the actions of the group and to understand what is going on in the world surrounding it. In part, they are also an attempt to maintain group solidarity by recalling the traditions of the past. The myths may be those of a whole class – management and workers, sociologically speaking, both possess their own mythology – or they may be those of the individual factory or working-group based on its own experiences. Although in many industries the working-group is much less stable than in former times, it is still possible to hear older employees telling of the fabulous strength or skill of a former member of the group, of how, in the 'old days' factory outings were not the petty affairs they have now become when everybody drinks lemonade and behaves as if he were on a Sunday-school outing. In those days group members (long transformed into giants of virtue or depravity) are alleged to have *really* enjoyed themselves and, although they got roaring drunk, were able to be back on the job the next day as if nothing had happened. But nowadays people are soft, they are unable to carry their drink, and, even after such a minor celebration, have to keep running to the Medical Department for aspirins. Or so the mythology goes. Meanwhile, the senior executives recount their own private mythology: 'Ah yes, X was a hard man, but he was just – management stood no nonsense in those days. Why, I remember . . .' – and so on. But there is a more general mythology common to managers as a class which takes the form of such beliefs as that they have reached their position by reason of personal merit alone, that workers are lazy, shiftless, and stupid when they are not cunning, that the 'carrot and the stick' are the only incentives, that 'a little dose of unemployment would cure all our present troubles', and that the natural relationship is that of master and man. Workers, too, have a more general mythology which similarly explains how managers reached their present position (although in a less flattering version), how the workers are always being 'done down', how everything is done for ulterior motives of profit, how management requires little or no skill and could be done equally well, or even better, by any group of workers, and so on. It is not for a moment suggested that all managers or all workers share these ideologies; they simply represent general trends in the thought of their respective classes which may, or may not, be fully accepted by individual members. Nor is it suggested that all of these beliefs on either side are necessarily untrue – but they have not been adopted on rational grounds. They are attitudes which are basically emotional in origin, although they may be based on beliefs which were true enough in a particular situation or at a particular time in history. A dangerous aspect of any such mythology or emotionally-held system of beliefs is that, to the individual who holds it, it is capable of explaining everything. Since all experiences are seen in terms of that frame of reference, it never fails to satisfy. S. I. Hayakawa shows in his *Language in Action* how, for example, the mythology of anti-semitism is capable of convincing the holder of anti-semitic prejudices that he is always correct in his beliefs. He can explain all the actions of Mr Miller, who is a Jew, somewhat as follows: 'If Mr Miller succeeds in business, that "proves" that "Jews" are "smart"; if Mr Johansen succeeds in business it only proves that Mr Johansen is smart. If Mr Miller fails in business, it is alleged that nevertheless he has "money salted away somewhere". If Mr Miller is strange or foreign in his habits, that "proves" that "Jews don't assimilate". If he is thoroughly American – that is, indistinguishable from other natives – he is "trying to pass himself off as one of us". If Mr Miller fails to give to charity, that is because "Jews are tight"; if he gives generously, he is "trying to buy his way into society". If Mr Miller lives in the Jewish section of the town, that is because "Jews are so clannish"; if he moves to a locality where there are no other Jews, that is because "they try to horn in everywhere". In short, Mr Miller is condemned no matter who he is or what he does.' Although this example is taken from outside industry, it is easy to see how it applies to the relationships between workers and management.

If either side of industry relies on a set of fixed ideas, whether they are those of Adam Smith and Ricardo or Karl Marx and Engels, they will never be able to see reality in any other terms and each new experience will merely serve to fix their ideas more firmly. Professor W. J. H. Sprott, although in a different context, has given some useful advice about the place of theories or systems of belief which might well be taken to heart by both sides of industry: 'Theories are not utterances of absolute truth, they are useful devices for understanding. If a theory ceases to be useful, we cast it aside and turn to another; theories are to be *used* rather than believed in.' (*General Psychology*.)

The systems of belief or ideologies we have been discussing show the following characteristics:

(1) They are functionally equivalent to wrong theories (although not necessarily wrong in every detail).

(2) They are not changed by the possession of correct knowledge.

(3) Even extensive first-hand experience is unlikely to change them.

(4) They influence the individual's actions.

(5) They form a more or less coherent whole which cannot be altered item by item.

(6) The sentiments of management towards workers (or vice versa) are determined less by the knowledge of the individual manager or worker than by the sentiments which prevail in the social atmosphere which surrounds him.

The last item in this list of characteristics is, perhaps, worth further elaboration. What it means is that, in general, each member of management within the factory tends to be seen first of all as an official in the service of a set-up which may be regarded as pleasant or hateful by the worker. Only much later, or perhaps never, is he seen as an individual in his own right. For example, the factory physician in a 'problem' factory will find that he is no longer regarded as someone who is out to help others regardless of their official status or whether they are considered as good or bad workers, but rather as a supporter of the hated management.

153

This may be so even when he is himself regarded by management with suspicion as being too progressive or democratic. Thus a doctor who has had the interesting experience of working in more than one firm may find that, although he treats all his patients in all of the factories in the same way, in one firm he is regarded with affection and trust whereas in another he is looked on with suspicion and resentment. In short, the way he is regarded by the employees does not depend solely, as is so often thought, upon his personal qualities as an individual; on the contrary, it tends to be a function of the atmosphere obtaining in the firm. Similarly, the good manager in the bad firm is often regarded with as much suspicion as the bad manager; whatever good he may do is interpreted in terms of the prevailing attitude of suspicion. The atmosphere of the factory is, therefore, immensely important since it determines the way in which any act within its boundaries is interpreted by the employees. Thus, to the worker, almost everything in the factory with a bad atmosphere is regarded as bad or done with ulterior motives. If the sick worker is sent to a convalescent home, it is to 'shut him up' and forestall possible criticism (and, of course, it sometimes is), if the long-service worker is given a presentation, it is because 'so he bloody well should be' after working there; if an employee is stood a drink by one of the managers at some social function, the employee comes to be regarded as a 'ruddy crawler'. Or, to quote an example given in another book by the present writer, the welfare worker in a factory may be surprised to find something like the following situation: 'In two factories there are Welfare departments which may lend a worker money when he is in need of it. In each, the Welfare department is equally well fitted out, in each the Welfare worker is equally pleasant and anxious to help. But the response of the workers who have been given loans is very different in each case. Of course, if you ask them, they will be polite and assume a grateful air, but a little more questioning makes it evident that in one factory the worker is really grateful and happy, in the other he is secretly resentful and angry. Why? The answer lies in the fact that one factory is autocratic, the other democratic in structure. A loan from the autocratic factory arouses resentment, since one dislikes being obliged to someone who is feared and hated. But if one belongs to a democratic group, a "we" group, the loan comes from one's associates and is welcome. All relationships in a resentful factory are tainted with resentment.' (J. A. C. Brown, *Psychology*.) (In point of fact, the above account is probably incorrect in so far as it imply that an autocratic factory *necessarily* leads to the state of affairs described. That an autocratic set-up is likely to lead to such attitudes is certain, but a great deal depends on the social background of the firm and whether or not the autocracy is accepted by the employees. In the democratic state of modern times the worker is less and less likely to accept autocracy within the factory.)

Most of what we have said in this chapter has been concerned with the informal organization of industrial workers, and little or nothing has been said about the informal organization of management. Reasons why little research has been done in this direction have already been given in Chapter 3, but, in point of fact, there is little difference between the informal organizations of the two groups. There are the same cliques which in some cases have a disruptive effect on the total structure and in other cases seem to oil the wheels and make things flow more smoothly. One may see the same fight for status and the same tendency to squeeze out the man whose face does not fit. In some firms the general tone of senior management is friendly (this may be quite genuine or a mask to conceal deep-seated tensions), and one may see the chairman simply by walking into his office. The chairman would be deeply hurt if one did not sit on his desk and smoke and everyone is 'Alf', 'Bob', and 'George'. At its best, to work in a firm like this may be very pleasant. Does one want a seat booked on the train to Birmingham? Old George can 'fix' it through the traffic department. Or some information concerning income-tax forms? Well, Alf can help you there. Even if, in some firms, there is a hint of what Lin Yutang describes as 'old roguery' about these goings-on, the cheerful wink accompanying the deed deprives it of any sense of guilt. Lunch is accompanied by some ragging, some mild obscenity, or even conversation about classical music, politics, and literature. In yet another firm one is all too aware that 'life is real and life is earnest'! A request to see the chairman may result in an interview within two or three weeks (depending, of course, on one's position in the hierarchy), and the chairman expects to be called 'Sir' whilst his visitor gets the impression that he is expected to stand rigidly to attention. Here every manager has two sets of opinions – those he tells to his equals and those he reserves for his superiors (official and non-official opinions). At lunch, one's words, if not one's thoughts, are pure and non-controversial, and although the usual amount of 'fiddling' goes on the guilty ones are fearful and feel guilty indeed. Such attitudes of management in the individual factory are set by those in authority, and their importance lies in the fact that, for better or worse, they ultimately penetrate right down the line: 'Good morale (or bad morale) is not a quality that wells up from below – it is something that trickles down from above.'

6

ATTITUDES AND OPINION SURVEYS

THE very young child, like other animals, apprehends reality directly and it probably appears to him as a 'blooming, buzzing, confusion', to use the expression of William James. Soon, however, the child begins to learn that things have names, that events and objects may be classified, and that by classifying them it is possible to have some measure of control over them. At this stage he will begin to ask his parents countless questions: 'What's this?' 'What's that?' 'What is John doing?' since he realizes, although dimly, that the meaning of a word is determined by the responses people make to it. When a certain form of behaviour is described as 'bad' or 'naughty' what is meant is that when one behaves in this way, one's parents or brothers and sisters will tend to respond in another way which is experienced by the child as being unpleasant. The classification of objects enables one to know what to do about them – for instance, when something is classified under the heading of 'food', we know that it can be eaten. But such classifications are socially defined and may vary from one group to another – for example, locusts do not come under the classification of 'food' in most countries, and therefore to eat them is considered to be disgusting. In other lands, of course, they do come into this category. The result of these processes is that the world is no longer seen as a 'blooming, buzzing, confusion' but as relatively predictable, stable, and orderly. 'Out of the infinite variety of objects and experiences, each one differing from every other one, men can find unity – they can construct categories.' (Lindesmith and Strauss, *Social Psychology*.) The child ceases to think of Fido and Rover as completely separate entities and sees them both as coming into the category 'dog'. Instead of having to wait in order to discover how he should react in each specific case, he is able to make certain generalizations about all dogs as a class. Classification is an aid to action.

The adult human being no longer sees the world with the immediacy of the child, for he has come to live in a symbolic universe which interposes itself in front of reality. Ernst Cassirer has noted that 'instead of dealing with things themselves man is in a sense constantly conversing with himself – he has so enveloped himself in linguistic forms that he cannot see or know anything except by the interposition of this artificial medium.' (*An Essay on Man.*) Wordsworth in his 'Intimations of Immortality from Recollections of Early Childhood' has, it would appear, intuitively traced this progress from the immediacy of vision of the young child, his gradual envelopment in the linguistic forms of his society, to the final stage when he lives in an almost completely symbolic universe:

> Heaven lies about us in our infancy!
> Shades of the prison-house begin to close
> Upon the growing Boy,
> But he beholds the light, and whence it flows,
> He sees it in his joy;
> The Youth, who daily farther from the east
> Must travel, still is Nature's Priest,
> And by the vision splendid
> Is on his way attended;
> At length the Man perceives it die away,
> And fade into the light of common day.

Here three stages of development are traced from the naïve vision of early childhood when 'Heaven lies about us', to the more formal stage when linguistic forms derived from society begin to enclose the boy in a 'prison-house' and determine to an increasing degree that he shall see his environment in the terms approved by his culture. Finally, the vision 'fades into the light of common day' when all reality is seen at second-hand enveloped in a maze of words and categories; it is no longer personal but social. The drug mescaline reduces this dependence on words and categories. See, in this connexion, Aldous Huxley's *The Doors of Perception.*

Whatever its disadvantages, this process is inevitable, since, without socially accepted categories and common agreement as to the meaning of words and concepts, no communication would be possible – we could not even commune with ourselves. All the more complex mental activities depend on the use of internalized language, without which we should be, like animals, tied down to the immediate situation. We could not conceive of the past or the future without the use of thought which is based on language. For example, a chimpanzee is able to solve a problem only so long as all the objects necessary for its solution are within the field of vision. It can join together two sticks to reach a banana outside its cage only so long as the sticks and the fruit are both in sight. The human being, can, as we say, solve the problem 'in his head' by using words as counters to replace objects which are not at the moment within his sensory field; he is like a general who wins a battle by moving coloured pins on a map to represent military formations. That this is so is demonstrated by the work of the neurologist Sir Henry Head on aphasia, a disability in which damage to the brain has caused the loss, in varying degrees, of the faculty of language. One of Head's patients who was quite well able to draw a jug when the object was before him was quite unable to draw it from memory. Goldstein describes another case of aphasia in a man who had been a devoted father and husband, but who, in hospital, showed neither concern nor interest in his absent family. When any attempt was made to discuss them, he merely became confused. Yet when confronted by his wife and children at home, he was as devoted as ever. Without language, out of sight is in a literal sense out of mind, and coherent thought becomes impossible.

The adult symbolic environment is a product of group living, since we accept our concepts and categories from our culture or subculture, and the picture they impose upon reality is not a genuine reproduction of the external world. It is a particular reconstruction based on our own needs and the needs of our groups. M. M. Lewis in his book *Language and Society* notes that the Solomon Islanders have nine distinct words for the coconut, indicating different stages of its growth, but they have no word for coconuts in general. On the other hand, they have only one word for all four meals of the day. He concludes that for these people it is important to distinguish the nine stages of the coconut, but not to distinguish between dinner and tea.

'A concept is a means of preserving distinctions which are of practical importance in the life of the community.' It follows, then, that language structures, whether they refer to real objects or to fictions, (a) form a reconstruction of the world in terms of the needs of an individual or group, and (b) organize the individual's behaviour in relation to the physical environment, to other people, and to himself.

The fact that a particular concept refers to something which has no objective existence does not mean that it can be disregarded. Lindesmith and Strauss observe that when people speak of the German 'race' or the Jewish 'race', they are using terms which refer to nothing real. 'Yet their fictional nature in no way alters the far-reaching social significance of the judgements they make. When there is agreement about things which have no objective existence, these imaginary things, or fictions, assume a quasi-objective character: in the sense that, although the words refer to nothing real, the fictions themselves are real, and thus become the basis for social action.' It is therefore irrelevant to say of the ideologies of workers or management that they are largely myths and have little bearing on the real situation – what matters is whether or not people act on them. 'The true meaning of a term is to be found by observing what a man does with it, not what he says about it.' Professor W. I. Thomas, the dean of American sociologists, has, in this connexion, drawn attention to a sociological principle which managements would do well to take into account in their dealings with their employees. The principle has been described as the 'Self-Fulfilling Prophecy' and, in its simplest form it states that: 'If men define situations as real, they are real in their consequences.' Robert K. Merton, in his *Social Theory and Social Structure*, gives an example of the principle at work: a tough but fairminded unionist in the United States favours a policy of excluding Negroes from his trade union – his views are based, not upon prejudice, but upon the cold hard facts. 'Negroes, lately from the non-industrial South, are undisciplined in traditions of trade unionism and the art of collective bargaining. The Negro is a strike-breaker. The Negro with his low standard of living rushes in to take jobs at less than prevailing wages. The Negro is, in short, a "traitor to the working-class", and should manifestly be excluded from union organizations.' So run the facts, and they are quite true. But, comments Dr Merton, 'Our unionist fails to see, of course, that he and his kind have produced the very "facts" which he observes. For by defining the situation as one in which Negroes are held to be incorrigibly at odds with the principles of unionism and by excluding Negroes from unions, he invited a series of consequences which indeed made it impossible for many Negroes to avoid the rôle of scab. Out of work after World War I, and kept out of unions, thousands of Negroes could not resist strike-bound employers who held a door invitingly open upon a world of jobs from which they were otherwise excluded.' In short, by defining Negroes as scabs and blacklegs, the unionist has made his thesis come true, and, similarly, the manager who defines his workers as 'lazy' or 'irresponsible' people whose only wish is for more money inexorably crushes them into a situation in which his theories soon turn into fact.

The concepts and classifications which are imposed by the individual upon reality come from many different sources: they are formed within the family during early life, under the influence of a religion, a secondary or primary group, or from personal experiences peculiar to the individual. Above all, they come from his culture. Without such frames of reference, the individual would be at a loss to know how to behave. Clearly, life would be impossible if, instead of accepting most of the customs and beliefs of his culture, each man or woman had to decide for him- or herself how to behave at meal-times, in church, when address-ing people, and so on. As we have already seen, each group con-sciously or unconsciously indoctrinates its members in order that they may desire those ends which appear necessary in the situation in which the group is placed. The member is expected to react in a characteristic way in relation to other groups, other people, or particular situations. Such characteristic reactions to situations, people, or groups, are based on attitudes.

The word 'attitude' has been defined by Gordon Allport as 'a mental and neural state of readiness, organized through experi-ence, exerting a directive or dynamic influence upon the indivi-dual's response to all objects and situations with which it related.'

The concept originated in the United States and Allport has described it as 'probably the most distinctive and indispensable concept in contemporary American social psychology.' Thomas and Znaniecki were the first writers to make extensive use of the term, when, in 1918, they published their monumental study of the Polish peasant in America, but the word has been used by later writers in ways which seem to indicate some lack of agreement as to precisely how it should be employed. Bogardus, for example, defines an attitude as 'a tendency to act towards or against some environmental factor which becomes thereby a positive or negative value', while Muzafer Sherif uses the word to refer to 'the main body of what is socialized in man'. In Sherif's definition, attitudes are the main constituents of the ego. Others have seemed to imply that 'attitude' and 'opinion' are practically synonymous terms, but, while opinions often reflect attitudes, it is evident that what a person says does not always correspond with what he does. As Emerson has somewhere remarked, it is sometimes the case that 'what you are sounds so loudly in my ears that I cannot hear what you say.' Here the term attitude will be applied to a concept which is used in order to explain the different ways in which people respond to their environment. Since a given stimulus does not always lead to the same response, it must be assumed that conditions within the organism are important in influencing behaviour. At the simplest level, the stimulus of a pin-prick nearly always leads to the same response of rapid withdrawal, but at a more complex level the sight of food is a stimulus which leads to quite different responses according to whether the individual is hungry or replete. At still more complex levels, behaviour is no longer a simple matter of stimulus and response, but depends largely on how the individual experiences the stimulus. The concept of attitude postulates a hypothetical mental structure in order to explain what goes on between stimulus and response, what causes the stimulus to be experienced in the way that it is. When, for example, the employees in a certain department show resentment because they have seen two supervisors talking together, it is obvious that their response cannot be fully explained in terms of the objective stimulus. It must be assumed that they have an *attitude* of suspicion towards management which makes them feel in such a situation that they are being discussed and adversely criticized. But although the concept of attitude is most likely to be used to explain behaviour which is in some respect out of the ordinary, all complex behaviour is based on the way in which experience has taught the individual to see his environment. Although this is a fairly obvious statement, it is one which is frequently ignored in practice. The factory manager, for instance, is often surprised to find that his factory which seems to him to be a friendly, attractive, and interesting place, is not so regarded by his employees. The answer quite simply is that the employees are not experiencing the same factory – in terms of their needs the factory is an entirely different place from that experienced by the manager. For each separate group within the building the factory is a different place, and even each individual sees it in terms of his own attitudes and mental outlook. This means that it is impossible to understand any act without considering how the situation appears to the individual. When seen within its proper context, all behaviour is capable of being understood, whereas in isolation it can readily be made to appear ridiculous. When the more sensational papers in the daily press publish articles describing the absurd behaviour of industrial workers (we rarely read of the equally absurd behaviour of management) – that they went on strike because one worker refused to shave off his beard, or some such story – it is liable to be forgotten that this is precisely what has been done. It is as if we had looked out of our study window into the park opposite and, observing a man dancing up and down shouting and contorting his body in a peculiar way, had decided that he was obviously mad. But, if we had taken the trouble to go a little nearer and had seen that he was being attacked by a swarm of bees, his actions would have been readily understandable. In the sense that some behaviour is ill-adapted to deal with a given situation, we are entitled to describe some actions as irrational, but no behaviour is irrational in the sense that it is incomprehensible or has no cause. This is a fundamental principle of psychology which has been expressed by Dr Norman Maier in the following words: 'From a psychological point of view, we know that all behaviour is *caused*. Since this is true, we must recognize that, no matter what a man does, he does it for good and sufficient reason. When we change the reason for, or the cause of, his behaviour, then, and only then, will his behaviour change. Instead of seeking causes, however, when things go wrong, we usually blame someone, and thereby, sometimes unconsciously, attempt to protect ourselves from criticism for perhaps having helped to bring about the undesirable results. It is plain that this natural reaction is not the correct or scientific approach to an understanding of human nature. In fact, by blaming, we merely avoid the issue. The solution to the problem of undesirable behaviour is to find the causes of that behaviour and then to remedy the situations which constitute those causes.' (*Psychology in Industry*.)

What is here implied is that *all* behaviour is capable of being understood no matter how simple or how complex it may appear to be. The delusions and hallucinations of the insane, the dreams of normal people, obsessional thoughts or acts, phobias, and the symptoms of neuroses, are all caused and capable of being understood. But, as has already been pointed out, abnormal psychology plays little part in the understanding of industrial behaviour (unless we are attempting to understand the actions of abnormal individuals who are in a position to impose their eccentricities on others). An obvious reason why this is so has already been mentioned elsewhere: it is that since the average industrial group is a cross-section of the working population, each member with his own history and peculiarities which differ from those of others, we cannot explain undesirable group behaviour in terms of individual abnormal psychology. Should this point be regarded as so self-evident as not to need any elaboration, the excuse for mentioning it must be that in some quarters there seems to be a tendency to talk as if nations, classes, or groups of people may be literally insane in the psychiatric sense: that Germans may suffer as a nation from paranoia, and other groups from abnormal laziness or aggressiveness. This is a dangerous attitude of mind, since it readily leads to the assumptions that (a) the group referred to is 'abnormal' whereas we (the observers) are 'normal', (b) that, somehow or other, the behaviour noted is mysterious and sense-less, and (c) that an elaborate 'psycho-analytic' approach is necessary to deal with the situation. Possessing such beliefs, the group which is making the diagnosis is enabled to feel morally superior, to ignore the part its own actions have played in bring-ing about the undesirable result, and to suppose that some elaborate 'treatment' (which does not involve a reorganization of its own beliefs) will be necessary to cure the other group. This sort of attitude can readily be observed amongst manage-ment in industry which often seems to regard the behaviour of workers with the combination of helplessness, slightly amused embarrassment, and moral superiority that might be observed in a man who takes his obviously senile and eccentric uncle to see a psychiatrist. Their attitude seems to say: 'Of course, *I* had nothing to do with this, but I want to do the best by the old boy, so if you will undertake to cure him I shall be only too glad to foot the bill – money is no object in such a deserving case.' But what is forgotten is that the position of management in relation to workers is not that of the man with a senile and mentally unbalanced uncle – it is, rather, that of the parent who takes his problem child to the Child Guidance Clinic, and is distressed to find that the psychologist works on the principle that 'there are no problem children, only problem parents'. Most of the work in modern child guidance is taken up with the treatment of the child's parents who are the cause of its misbehaving, and if the parents refuse to co-operate in admitting where *they* have been mistaken, nothing can be done for the child.

It follows, then, that the social psychologist or sociologist who is called in to deal with the problems of an industrial concern will, in the first place, seek the sources of the trouble in the actual situation and in quite ordinary human terms rather than psychiatric ones, and, in the second place, will deal with the whole social structure but pay special attention to its manage-ment. Unless management are prepared to admit their share of responsibility in bringing about the undesirable results, he can do nothing. The inescapable fact is that it is the job of manage-ment to manage, and, while there are many factors both external and within the factory over which they have little control, this cannot absolve them of their responsibility. It is management which has the power to set the situation and create a good or bad atmosphere, whereas the employees have no such power, or only very limited power, to do so. It is the 'bad officers' and the 'problem parents' who must be dealt with first.

The attitudes of the individual or group determine how a particular situation is assessed. What appears to the supervisor as 'loafing' may appear to the worker as 'resting' – if he is the person concerned. What to the supervisor is 'observing the worker on the job' is to the worker mere 'spying'. Each is viewing the situation from a different frame of reference, and with a different set of attitudes. For industrial purposes, the important questions about attitudes are, firstly, how they may be discovered and measured, secondly, whether they may be changed, and how.

The simplest method of discovering and measuring attitudes is by means of a simple census of opinions. For, although an attitude is not quite the same as an opinion, the opinions of a group or an individual give a fair indication of their attitudes. The Gallup poll is an example of this type of test, the main disadvantage of which is that the results give us no possibility of measuring the degree of feeling in the individual, but only the direction of the attitude and its numerical frequency in the group under consideration. If, for example, a population is asked whether it is opposed to some projected form of legislation, there is no means of telling whether the feelings of those who are opposed are strongly felt or not. Yet the legislation, if passed, might be relatively unaffected by a large number of people who were only mildly against it, and seriously hindered by a much smaller number of people who were strongly against it. A second method, exemplified by Bogardus' Social Distance Scale for measuring racial attitudes, attempts to rectify this defect by constructing a scale ranging between the two extremes of approval or disapproval. But in this method the scoring is arbitrary and depends upon the investigator's judgement of what steps or intervals should be included. The most accurate scale is that devised by Thurstone in which a large number of statements relevant to the subject on which attitudes are to be measured are collected. These are analysed experimentally in order to ensure that no ambiguity is present and that they are diagnostic in representing a position for or against the issue involved. Each statement is assigned a value in the scale between 0 and 12 according to the amount of positive or negative feeling involved and these values are based on objective experimentation. The whole scale may contain forty or fewer statements, and the individuals being tested are asked to put a cross in front of all the statements which express their sentiments. These are later assessed in terms of the values previously assigned to each item, the person's score being the average of the scale value of all items marked by a cross. For the use of industry, the National Foremen's Institute of America has issued a book *How to Make a Morale Survey* by Eugene J. Benge which gives details of the process modified to suit the factory situation and contains sample tests. While this particular book is mainly concerned with the discovery of whether morale is good or bad in the factory, it is also possible to utilize attitude tests in order to discover the views of employees on particular issues such as projected changes within the firm.

As samples of the types of questions asked, the following may be taken as representative of some of the sections in the survey:

1. How do you like your present job?
   - ( ) A. I don't like it.
   - ( ) B. I'd prefer something else.
   - ( ) C. I just accept it - neither liking nor disliking it.
   - ( ) D. All things considered, I like it pretty well.
   - ( ) E. I like it very well.

2. Is the atmosphere of your work-place:
   - ( ) A. Extremely hot, cold, draughty, or dusty.
   - ( ) B. Usually unpleasant.
   - ( ) C. Occasionally unpleasant.
   - ( ) D. Generally satisfactory.
   - ( ) E. Excellent most of the time.

3. For the most part, fellow employees in my department are:
   - ( ) A. Unfriendly.
   - ( ) B. Indifferent to me.
   - ( ) C. All right.
   - ( ) D. Co-operative.
   - ( ) E. Very friendly.

4. In his attitude towards you personally, is your *immediate* supervisor:
   ( ) A. Always unfair.
   ( ) B. Often unfair.
   ( ) C. Sometimes fair, sometimes not.
   ( ) D. Usually fair.
   ( ) E. Fair at all times.
5. In comparison with other employers in your community, how well does the company treat its employees:
   ( ) A. Most other employers are better.
   ( ) B. A few of the other employers are better.
   ( ) C. About as well as the average employer.
   ( ) D. Our company is better than most.
   ( ) E. Our company is decidedly the best of all.
6. When desirable job vacancies arise, how are they usually filled:
   ( ) A. By employing people outside the company.
   ( ) B. By promoting favoured employees who are not specially qualified.
   ( ) C. By giving first chance to an employee of long service.
   ( ) D. By taking the most available qualified person.
   ( ) E. By choosing the most deserving based on both ability and service.

There are three possible objections which may be made concerning the use of such tests in industry. The first is that attempting to find out what employees are thinking is a sign of weakness and something with which the competent employer who has adequate control over his men need not concern himself. The answer to this objection is that control based on fear and authoritarian discipline, for reasons already given, is no longer possible, and that, even if it were possible, it is inefficient and shows lack of respect for the dignity of man. The only other type of control is legitimate authority based on co-operation, and this necessitates knowledge of what others are thinking. It is a complete misunderstanding of attitude tests in the factory to suppose that they are given so that subsequently the workers may be spoonfed and given all they ask for. What they do is to indicate (a) certain abuses or legitimate complaints which are based on objective data and need to be remedied, and (b) certain complaints which are based on mutual misunderstanding which may also be remedied by discussion and explanation. For example, if the majority of workers replied to the questions in group 2 by adversely criticizing the atmosphere in their work-place, the reply might be to call in the engineers and have something done about it. On the other hand, the reply might be: 'We're sorry about the state of affairs, but we applied for a building licence some time ago and haven't yet had permission to go ahead.' In either case, the workers would have been treated like adults and given satisfactory explanations for a legitimate grouse. Yet another possibility might be that careful investigation revealed no objective ground for complaint with the atmosphere in the workshop so far as temperature, dust, and draughts were concerned, but a great deal of ground for complaint about the 'atmosphere' in the more metaphorical sense. The grouse might have been relating to an inefficient supervisor, and the objection to the physical conditions a displacement of affect from the real cause of the trouble. In any case, the survey would have been instrumental in revealing an area of tension in the factory, and tension means inefficiency.

The second objection is that such tests are unnecessary because the management know already what the workers think and feel. This belief is so common (and so rarely justified) that it might well be placed in the category of 'famous last words'. Benge quotes the case of a textile mill in which the managing director assured him that the firm was 'one big happy family', that he knew each employee by his first name, and that he was so close to the picture that he could be in complete command of the situation. Two weeks later, the employees went on strike, badly damaged the machinery, and sabotaged work in progress. The mill closed and never reopened. In another case, also noted by Benge, the president of a successful company began to note signs of growing unrest, but dismissed the matter with the statement: 'If it gets any worse I shall give them all a 10 per cent rise in wages – all they want is money.' Two months later, the employees were being given another 10 per cent rise, and in another month a rise of 5 per cent. Still later, wages went up once more by 10 per cent. After that, the workers went on strike. It would not be worth while quoting such cases were it not that they are so common. The fact is that, no matter how much tact or knowledge of men the factory manager may have, it is most unlikely that he will have any real knowledge of what his employees are thinking. In another 'happy little factory' which employed only about two hundred workers, and was run by a factory manager who prided himself on his knowledge of men and women, a young girl went to the medical department with a rash on her face. The nurse in charge looked at it and made the remark that it 'looked like impetigo'. To her astonishment, the girl ran out of the room back to her workshop and, within ten minutes, the women in the department were proceeding to walk out literally seething with rage. The nurse was, of course, blamed by the management, but the fact of the matter was that the real source of the trouble lay with their own attitude to the workers. The girl had associated the word 'impetigo' with scabies and other 'dirty diseases' which were much publicized in wartime, but the other workers walked out because they had long felt that management regarded them as dirty, common, and inferior. When the girl announced to them what the nurse had said this seemed tantamount to saying: 'You are a member of the sort of group who might be expected to have a dirty disease.' Certainly the nurse had unwittingly lit the fuse, but the explosive charge had been laid by the management over a long period of time.

The third objection to attitude tests is the more scientific one that they are likely to be inaccurate, (a) because the employees may fear to answer the questions honestly, and (b) because opinions may not necessarily be closely correlated with actions. Difficulty (a) is largely dependent on how the test is carried out, but provided that its complete anonymity is made clear no such problem is likely to arise. Difficulty (b) has been thoroughly investigated by many psychologists both in industry and elsewhere who have correlated the results of such tests with the actions of the testees. All investigations have demonstrated that the tests are reasonably accurate.

There are, of course, other means of discovering employee attitudes. Those leaving the firm may be interviewed, suggestion systems may be used, and an effective Works Council should be able to bring to the knowledge of management some, at least, of the views of the employees. Skilled interviewers may, in a 'guided interview', attempt to discover the workers' opinions concerning a number of previously stipulated points, or in an 'unguided interview' allow each worker to talk more or less at random about factory affairs. In America, some concerns have offered prizes for essays on such subjects as, 'What I Would Do to Improve Our Company'. On the whole, however, the attitude test or opinion survey gives more accurate results at the cost of less trouble than any other method. (In including Works Councils under the heading of methods for discovering the attitudes of employees, it is not meant to infer that such councils can be replaced by the use of opinion surveys – or, indeed, that any of the methods mentioned are substitutes for each other.)

There is one final objection to opinion surveys which, although it is irrational and often remains unspoken, represents a rather common attitude of management. This is the fear of their employees which may be expressed in such sayings as, 'Let sleeping dogs lie', or, 'better let well alone'. Many managers seem to picture themselves as seated on top of a smouldering volcano which may at any moment begin to erupt, and instead of solving the problem by attempting to release the tension they proceed to suppress it still further. Perhaps one reason for this attitude, at least on the part of junior management, is the feeling that they are under continual observation from senior management who might interpret even the slightest relaxation of control as a sign of incompetence. Under such circumstances they are sincerely afraid to hear any expression of opinion from their subordinates – they fear the worst, but do not want to hear it in detail. Yet, in a situation in which tension is high the most dangerous thing to do is to allow it to accumulate and the safest action is to allow it to be released. In any case, the process of release is rarely so dramatic as had been expected. Gordon Rattray Taylor tells somewhere of a group of rather truculent workers who, apropos of some dispute over wages, demanded to know what profits the firm had made in the preceding financial year. When, with some trepidation, the managing director had told them, their only response was: 'Oh, is that all', and the subject was closed. In another firm, a whole department was moved almost overnight to another part of the factory. The workers had been told nothing of this impending move (although it had been arranged by the management some time before), and, to make matters worse, the new site was at the top of a building which had no elevator and the workers were mostly elderly men and women who were likely to find the climb difficult. There was, not unnaturally, much resentment about this – many workers reported to the medical officer demanding certificates to say that they were incapable of the climb, and all resented the way in which the move had been carried out. The manager of the department, who was young and inexperienced, was most upset at the turn events had taken and asked what he should do. He was advised to call the workers together and explain (as he should have done before), the reasons for the move, ask the workers for their comments, and endeavour to answer their questions. At this suggestion, he was even more upset. He could not possibly do that, he said, because some of the older and tougher workers were quite capable of calling him a fool. The obvious reply to this was that, either he was a fool (in which case he had no reason to complain), or he was not (in which case he ought to be glad of the opportunity to explain just why this was so). In the end, he took the advice and found that, when he had explained why the move was necessary, the workers were extremely friendly and co-operative. Their sole comment was: 'Why didn't you tell us in the first place – if we'd only known we wouldn't have minded at all.' Morale in this department was subsequently considerably higher than it had been before the incident had happened.

Morale surveys serve at least three useful functions within the industrial concern:

(1) They are a means of uncovering specific sources of irritation among the employees at an early stage. Often these are relating to matters which can be easily rectified when they are known and thus later trouble may be avoided.

(2) The mere fact that opinions and resentments can be expressed in this way acts as a safety valve which, even in a factory with rather poor morale, may drain away much resentment. (It would, of course, be wrong to carry out a survey unless it was intended to do something constructive about any

grievances which were revealed, but it is nevertheless true that the survey *in itself* relieves tension and tends to raise morale.)

(3) The opinions revealed by the survey may be utilized when policies are being formulated, when changes are being made, and in the training of supervisors. Many firms, for example, spend thousands of pounds on 'amenities' which are neither desired nor needed by their employees, yet quite simple matters which would cost little or no money are ignored because they remain unknown. When the workers evince little enthusiasm for new and unwanted amenities, management feel aggrieved and murmur bitterly about the 'ingratitude' of their employees. Yet no manager would be delighted if some autocrat at his local golf club had a huge cocktail bar erected in the clubroom regardless of the fact that most members drank beer and had complained for years that the roof of the verandah where they habitually sat let in the rain.

When we come to consider the important question as to how far it is possible to change an individual's attitudes, it is obviously important that we should decide how deep-seated the attitude with which we are concerned happens to be. What we have described as personality traits belong to the basic or core personality structure, which means that either they are temperamental in origin (i.e. constitutional factors based on physique, brain structure, or glandular pattern), or that they originated in the first five years of life and are therefore deeply embedded in the individual's mental structure. In adult life temperamental traits cannot be changed at all, and the traits originating in early life can only be altered by such special techniques as psychoanalysis. In industry, however, we are dealing primarily with the attitudes of groups which are a part of the peripheral personalities of their members and are social or situational in origin. They arise mainly from the actual situation of the working-group. This is, of course, an over-simplification, since each member of the group is also influenced by his individual experiences, by the fact that he is a Catholic or Protestant, Yorkshireman or Londoner, Socialist or Conservative, British or Italian, and so on. For example, the fact that an individual is aggressive may be due to the fact that he was shouted at by his supervisor five minutes before (situational cause); because he feels that the group of which he is a member is being victimized by the management (situational and social cause); because the sub-culture of which he is a member tends to make him so (he may be a Jew or Negro, or a Catholic in an anti-Catholic area); because his culture makes him so (he might be a Dobuan or a Mundugumor tribesman); because of his peculiar experiences in his family during early life (his father may have been a bully and aggressiveness as a response to this has become structured into his basic personality); because aggressiveness is a temperamental trait (for example, in the epileptic character). Only in the first two instances can we, by simple means, take any action. Corresponding to these levels, H. J. Eysenck has distinguished four degrees of depth in attitude structure. At the lowest level, we have haphazard isolated statements of opinion which may or may not accurately represent a person's views on a given subject. Secondly, we may have the same statement made repeatedly, which would seem to indicate that it is more than a passing fancy and that over a period of months it may remain fairly steady. These two levels are *opinions* rather than genuine attitudes. Thirdly, when it can be shown that a number of separate statements dealing with the same issue tend to correlate highly together (e.g. on Thurstone's scale), we may claim to have isolated an attitude in the strict sense of the word. Finally, attitudes may be intercorrelated to form concepts of a higher order. For example, militarism, nationalism, antisemitism, pro-capitalism, and interest in formal religion tend to intercorrelate to define an attitude which might be called 'conservatism' (the word is not here used in its more limited political sense). This latter would be at the highest level in the hierarchy of attitude structures, and is what is described by Eysenck as a 'primary social attitude'; it is, in effect, what we have described as a personality trait. Professor J. C. Flugel in his *Man, Morals, and Society* and H. J. Eysenck in his *Uses and Abuses of Psychology* give some interesting evidence as to the existence of a 'radical–conservative' factor by virtue of which the individual tends to hold views which accord with a radical or conservative pattern, and which apply to a number of distinct fields which at first sight might appear to be logically independent. It seems likely that W. S. Gilbert was not far wrong when he wrote that every boy and every girl is 'either a little Liberal or else a little Conservative.' For example, there seems to be a close correlation between such attitudes as loyalty to a leader, a desire to uphold the family, stress on authoritarian discipline, antifeminism, patriotism, belief in private property, support of traditional religion, and belief in the importance of class-distinctions. These are what might be described as 'right-wing' attitudes. On the other hand, there is also close correlation between the opposing attitudes of loyalty to the group, suspicion of the traditional family, disapproval of authoritarian discipline, feminism, a cosmopolitan attitude, dislike of class-distinctions, anti-religious views, and socialism. These observations, however, are based on experimental work which clearly requires further confirmation. If it is true that what we have described as 'right-wing' attitudes are deep-seated, that belief in authoritarian leadership, class-distinctions, and 'firm discipline' are intercorrelated factors in a basic character-trait, then obviously a man holding these attitudes is unlikely to be a successful exponent of 'democracy in industry'.

It has been noted already that all social groups develop some form of organization which defines the status and function of each member, prescribes attitudes towards those in the in-group and those in the out-group, and requires some degree of conformity both in behaviour and aspirations from its members. These standards set the tempo and determine the characteristics of the group in action. The relationship of the individual to his group varies: he may be a fully conforming member, or he may be unabsorbed, being physically *in* the group but not *of* it, an isolated unit who always has great difficulty in 'belonging' within any group. Others, while accepted as members, may direct their energies towards changing the group in some respect. Finally, some may be members of a particular group but accept their standards from some other group. The group from which an individual takes his standards is known as his reference group, whilst that of which he is a member is known as his membership group. Ordinarily, the group to which the individual relates himself is his own membership group, but this is by no means always the case. In relation to social class, for example, it is possible for an individual to be in the economic sense a member of the working class and yet to take the middle class as his reference group. This is particularly likely to happen in competitive societies in which movement both up and down the social scale is possible and people may be, from time to time, in various marginal positions.

Muzafer Sherif has studied the effect of the group in establishing social norms at the simple level of perception by means of what is known as the 'autokinetic effect'. In this experiment, use is made of the fact that in a dark room in which no physical points of reference are visible, a point of light which is, in fact, quite stationary, appears to the observer to move. The apparent movement of the light is very responsive to suggestion both from the person conducting the experiment and from the individual himself. In other words, the fact that external structure is lacking in the situation allows maximum play for internal or social factors to take effect on the individual's judgement. From this simple arrangement it is possible to discover some of the laws of social interaction at an elementary level. When first placed in this situation, the individual sooner or later comes to establish a range and norm of movement (or apparent movement) which is peculiar to himself, and varies from the range and norm of apparent movement of other individuals in a fairly permanent and stable manner. When, after this norm has been established, he is then placed in the room with other individuals (who also have each their own norms), it is found that the norms and ranges tend to converge. But the convergence is not so close as when the group has first been put in the room together before any individual norms have been established. In this second case, the group collectively establishes a range and norm specific to itself. If, as may happen, there is a rise or fall in the norms established in successive sessions, it is always a group effect, and the norms of the individual members rise or fall towards the common norm in each session. This effect, as Sherif points out, is not due to the group following the norm of an influential person or leader: 'Even if the group norm gravitates towards a dominating person, the leader represents a polarization in the situation, having a definite relationship towards others which he cannot change at will. If the leader changes his norm after the group norm is *settled* he may *thereupon cease to be followed* as occurred several times in our experiments.' (*An Outline of Social Psychology*.) Finally, when a group member faces the situation alone, after the range and norm of his group have been established, he perceives the situation in terms of the range and norms that he brings from his group. It is of interest to note that a majority of subjects always insisted that their judgements were made without the influence of the other members of the group. Sherif's conclusions are that (a) in the course of interaction relative rôles emerge for group members, (b) that attitudes peculiar to the group arise, (c) that these group norms or attitudes shape the reactions of the individual member even when he is no longer actually within the group, and (d) that group standards rise or fall as a function of group interaction and not individually.

One of the most detailed studies of attitude change was made by T. M. Newcomb and is described in his book *Personality and Social Change*. The study was carried out in an American student community known as Bennington College in which the prevailing tone in economic and political matters was strongly liberal. Most of the students at Bennington came from conservative families, and the purpose of the investigation was to observe the shift in attitude from conservatism towards liberalism as they became members of the community, and to note whether any specific personal factors interfered with or facilitated this change. The vast majority of the students did alter their political outlook, and within a comparatively short time had become liberals in accordance with the norms of the group. But amongst those who did so change there were two separate categories; the first, which was in the majority, consisted of those students who tended to conform with the others and who in another community would also have accepted the group norms even if they had been other than liberal. The second category consisted of those who were self-dependent, above average intelligence, and had based their liberal attitude on an intellectual foundation. Some of the latter were psychologically stable, others less so. Both of these two categories, however, had this in common: that they had achieved independence of their families. The first had then become dependent on its own age-group, whereas the second, as we have seen, was self-dependent. Those students who did not change their attitudes and remained conservative were found to be extremely dependent on family ties. They again could be subdivided into two categories. The first category consisted of those who were definitely unstable, insecure, and frustrated, the second consisted of students who were reasonably well-adjusted but uninterested in social life or prestige within the group. Taking all the students together, it was found that 65 per cent of those who changed attitudes were definitely stable and only 15 per cent showed signs of instability. Of those who did not change, 32 per cent were quite stable and 37 per cent had been markedly unstable at the time of entering the college.

The relevance for industry of what we have been discussing may be summarized as follows:

(1) Attitudes originating in the basic personality structure (personality traits or traits of temperament) cannot be changed by any ordinary means. Group attitudes (i.e. those in the peripheral personality) may, however, be changed under certain circumstances.

(2) It is in general useless to try to change the attitudes of group members individually. The group must be dealt with as a whole. The obvious reason for this is that, since the attitudes are a function of the group and its situation, it is useless to attack them in the individual member.

(3) It is also largely useless to attempt to change attitudes by lecturing or logical arguments. 'Attempts at changing attitudes or social prejudices experimentally by the dissemination of information or factual argument have been notably unrewarding. Some investigators have been unable to obtain any change. Others have obtained various degrees of shift in the desired direction, although there were almost always some cases showing negative

or no change . . . these changes are apt to be discrete and rather ephemeral.' (Sherif, *An Outline of Social Psychology*.)

(4) It is not possible to change any attitude into *any* other attitude: 'What we can do is to change attitudes which are remote from reality into attitudes more closely based on reality.' (Gordon Rattray Taylor.)

(5) The more unstructured a situation is (i.e. the less factual information that is available about it), the greater the likelihood that attitudes will become based on emotion and consequently remote from reality.

(6) When individual members do not accept the attitudes of their group, this may be (a) because they are above average intelligence and have factual information which conflicts with the group attitudes, (b) because they are neurotic and therefore unable to relate themselves satisfactorily to others, (c) because their reference group is other than their membership group.

Combining (2) and (3) it will be noted that lecturing *at* people or dealing with them individually is not likely to lead to success in changing their attitudes. From (4) it may be concluded that attitudes cannot be changed if they are closely based on reality. (If, for example, an attitude of resentment is produced by an environment which almost anyone in the same culture or sub-culture would experience as frustrating it can only be altered by removing the frustrating factors in the environment.) Point (5) shows that although factual information cannot change an attitude once it has been formed, the more clearly structured an environment is the less likely is it that unrealistic attitudes will be developed. From this it follows that, as Elton Mayo has said, the more intelligent a company's policy, the greater is the necessity that the policy should be freely communicated all down the line. A company with an intelligent policy has everything to gain and nothing to lose by ensuring that the total picture is clearly structured in the minds of its employees. Vagueness and lack of factual information lead to rumour and gossip, as war experiences have clearly shown.

In order to avoid misunderstanding perhaps a little more should be said concerning the relationship between an individual's beliefs and those of his primary groups. It is not intended to imply (a) that those who disagree with the views of their group are always neurotic, nor that (b) the individual is never convinced by logical arguments. Of course, *single individuals* are quite often convinced by a reasoned statement into changing their views, but here we are concerned with the problem of altering the opinions of large numbers of people, and whether we like the fact or not, it has been frequently demonstrated that a *majority* of people in a group will not change their views on rational grounds alone. There are several reasons why this is so, but to mention only four, we may note (1) that attempting to change a person's views into views which conflict strongly with those of his group is, in effect, asking him to set himself against the group, and, since to most people the respect of their group is more important than the holding of an opinion, we are not likely to be successful in most cases; (2) the views may be a function of the situation confronting the group (i.e. they are objectively valid); (3) lecturing *at* people is, in a sense, a form of verbal attack which many people inwardly resent, and, in trying to change a man's views, we are attacking something which is a part of himself, we are asserting that he is wrong and we are right; (4) reason, however important a part it may play in society, does not play a major part in most people's lives. Concerning the relationship between neurosis and unorthodox views, it is probably true to say that, whereas unorthodox people are by no means always neurotic, neurotic people are usually unorthodox. Neurosis is a form of rebellion against society, and, as Freud long ago pointed out, the neurotic is a criminal turned upside down; the criminal rebels consciously the neurotic unconsciously. It seems to follow that, in an established society as opposed to a society which is in a state of disintegration, many of those who hold unorthodox views are neurotic. In a disintegrating society, of course, there are a great many conflicting views which are simply due to the prevalent state of mental confusion. The number of cases of neurosis in such a society, as we shall see later, is also high.

Lecturing, logical argument, and the individual approach are, therefore, unlikely to lead to success in changing group attitudes, and the most successful method of doing this has been shown to be the use of *group discussion*. That this is so has been so frequently demonstrated that we need only quote two examples from the many which will be found in most textbooks of industrial psychology. The first is taken from an article by French and Coch in the journal *Human Relations* (1: 512–22; 1948), the second is from a report by Alex Bavelas quoted in Maier's *Psychology in Industry*.

The Harwood Manufacturing Company in Marion, Virginia, manufactures pyjamas. It employs about 600 workers, mostly women of average age twenty-three, who are paid on an individual piece-rate basis. Output is measured on the 'standard minutes' system which means that every operation scores a certain number of units, which, with a competent operator, may add up to about sixty units per hour. The company had been having trouble with the morale of its employees, and this manifested itself in the form of poor output, high labour turnover, and aggressive attitudes towards management, supervisors, and time-and-motion study experts. Because of these difficulties, management decided to try a new approach. They selected four groups of workers, all roughly equal in skill and averaging sixty units per hour. The time-and-motion experts were asked to inform the workers concerning changes which were to be made in the job and the new rates which had been proposed in order to increase efficiency. Group number one was treated in the ordinary way, being simply told their scores as assessed by time-and-motion study and left to carry on with their work. Groups two and three were called to a group meeting and it was explained to them that it was necessary to reduce costs. Their advice was asked as to how the process might be simplified and they were told that the operators would be trained in the new method *before* establishing a rate for the job. In the mutual discussion with management these groups produced a great many helpful suggestions and decided on a final plan which was mutually approved. They also helped in designing the changes and setting the new rate. Group four attended this discussion, but was treated slightly differently in that it was arranged that a few members were to be selected for training, the rate was to be established on the basis of their performance, and they were then to train the rest of the group. When results were assessed, it was found that group one never produced more than an average of fifty units and 17 per cent had left their job within the next forty days. Groups two and three achieved a rate of seventy-four units and none of the members of these two groups left their jobs. The compromise group achieved a rate of sixty-nine units. As a control experiment in order to confirm these results, management brought together the first group (which in the meantime had filed a protest with their union that the new rate was unfair), and treated them as they had done originally in the case of groups two and three. Within a week the rate for this group was seventy-three units, and no complaints or resignations had been received.

In the second experiment, conducted by Alex Bavelas under the direction of the late Professor Kurt Lewin of the University of Iowa, the circumstances of the factory were somewhat similar to the foregoing. The average rate of production had been sixty units per hour, and the workers were asked to discuss the problem of production amongst themselves and decide on a future target. The target suggested by the workers as a result of these meetings was eighty-four units per hour to be attained within five days. Although the previous ceiling had never been higher than seventy-five units, the proposed goal was achieved and was finally stabilized at eighty-seven units per hour. In control experiments, it was found that asking, telling, ordering, or lecturing groups of workers in order to get them to produce more had no results – it was only when a group decision had been arrived at that an increase in production occurred.

The reasons why this is so are quite simple. People do not like to be ordered about like automatons; they like to participate in a common task. They like to work for 'us' rather than 'them'. Above all, goals set by someone else have little emotional appeal for the group, but, when the goal has been set by the group itself, it becomes a point of honour to see that it is fulfilled.* Mutual discussion and common agreement lead to the group identifying

* In Sherif's terminology the goals become 'ego-involved'.

182

the goals decided on with its own, and its total energies are canalized into achieving that end.

Many experiences outside the field of industry have demonstrated that lecturing or telling people to do things has singularly little effect in comparison with the method of group-discussion. This principle has been used in the army, in schools, in the treatment of neuroses, and in many other situations. During the war, experiments carried out on such matters as getting housewives to use the cheaper sorts of meat (offal), or getting mothers to give their infants orange juice regularly, showed vastly different results according to the methods of propaganda used. When given a lecture on the subject, it was found that a certain number of women took the advice offered and subsequently served the foods suggested in their own homes. But when they were asked to discuss the matter among themselves with the expert merely supplying information when it was asked for, it was found that *ten times* as many women carried out the suggestions which had been arrived at by mutual discussion and decision. The same method was also used in the army in campaigns against venereal disease, and the statutory lecture on this subject by the unit medical officer was found to be greatly inferior in its effects (as measured by the later incidence of V.D.) to the effects following group discussion with the medical officer standing by as the expert whose opinion might be asked for when required.

The late Professor Kurt Lewin in a collection of essays entitled *Resolving Social Conflicts* has enunciated certain fundamental principles of re-education. Firstly, he points out that (as has been noted already) extensive first-hand experience or correct knowledge are not, in themselves, likely to have much effect in changing wrong beliefs. So, for instance, the man who hated Jews could always justify his beliefs no matter what situations he experienced; the manager who believes that all workers are lazy can always find reasons why a specific worker is not. Secondly, regarding the futility of trying to alter beliefs by lecturing at people, Lewin quotes Gordon Allport as saying: 'It is an axiom that people cannot be taught who feel that they are at the same time being attacked.' An individual who is being re-educated against his will inevitably reacts with hostility, and this state of mind is quite incompatible with receptivity. Even if he does accept the truth of what he has been told, the information reaches only the level of the official system of values (the way I ought to feel), and fails altogether to reach the level of emotional acceptance (the way I really feel). This discrepancy gives rise to guilt feelings and tension and arouses hostility once more; there is nothing more irritating than to feel that we have been proved wrong over some deeply-felt issue. Thirdly, systems of belief cannot be changed one item at a time. 'Arguments proceeding logically from one point to another may drive the individual into a corner. But as a rule he will find some way – if necessary a very illogical way – to retain his beliefs. No change of conviction on any specific point can be established in more than an ephemeral way so long as the individual has not given up his hostility to the new set of values as a whole, to the extent of having changed from hostility at least to open-mindedness.'

The fact is, Lewin says, that 'the re-educative process has to fulfil a task which is essentially equivalent to a change in culture. The group must be changed as a group and the individual member accepts the new system of beliefs by accepting belongingness to his group. It is not true to assume, as the reader may have done, that the examples of change in attitudes already described are due to the cunning of the re-educator who is clever enough to deceive the group into supposing that the change in attitude is due to their own efforts when, in reality, he has manipulated them according to his own wishes. On the contrary, these attitudes were reached because (a) the group was not under threat and (b) the attitudes were *in fact* closer to reality. The whole implication of people (management and workers) getting together to discuss a problem by this method must be: 'Look here, we're all probably wrong in some respects – let's get together and try to find out the real state of affairs.' In short, it is assumed that when people feel free from threat and free to discuss matters openly, they are likely to discover the real facts for themselves. When they have done so, the facts, as Lewin points out, become *their* facts (as opposed to other people's facts), and they are likely to act on them. It is also not asserted that the group is in some mysterious way omniscient or never mistaken. But if the truth cannot be found and accepted in this way, it will certainly not be accepted in any other.

In conclusion, it must be repeated that no amount of saying the right things to people will make up for doing the wrong ones. Management are not judged by what they say, but by what they do. Thus it is a waste of time to assert on all possible public occasions that 'our employees are wonderful', when the factory environment is saying much more clearly quite the opposite. When employees are treated in an off-hand or contemptuous manner, when lavatories are dirty or accommodation inadequate (without good reason), when workers are looked on as irresponsible children, no amount of 'welfare' can cancel out the negative attitudes thus created. Group attitudes cannot be made more favourable against the overwhelming pressure of reality.

7

WORK, ITS NATURE, CONDITIONS, AND MOTIVATION

THE orthodox view of work which has been accepted by most managers and industrial psychologists is a simple one, and fifty years of industrial psychology and more than a century of managerial practice have been founded upon it. Regarding the *nature* of work, the orthodox view accepts the Old Testament belief that physical labour is a curse imposed on man as a punishment for his sins and that the sensible man labours solely in order to keep himself and his family alive, or, if he is fortunate, in order to make a sufficient surplus to enable him to do the things he really likes.* Regarding the *conditions* of work, it is assumed that improving the conditions of the job will cause the worker's natural dislike of it to be somewhat mitigated, and, in addition, will keep him physically healthy and therefore more efficient in the mechanistic sense. Finally, regarding the *motivation* of work, the carrot and stick hypothesis asserts that the main positive incentive is money, the main negative one fear of unemployment. Of recent years, these views have been modified in many ways. It is conceded that some people – for example, managers, professional men, and craftsmen – may like to work, that improving the working environment may have a wider connotation than was formerly thought, and that incentives may also include 'welfare' and social activities. Full employment has forcibly caused those who run industry to reconsider the carrot and stick theory. But, nevertheless, the basic postulates survive almost unchanged. It is still supposed that most people do not

---

* 'No society can long continue in health by merely paying for work which it cannot make satisfying. Because the Victorians regarded work in industry as necessarily hard and disagreeable, they made little effort to introduce tolerable conditions into mines, and mills, and foundries, and were content to think of industry itself as an economic necessity instead of as an element in society.' Christopher Salmon, in a B.B.C. lecture.

186

work willingly, that money is the most powerful incentive, and that the job of the industrial psychologist is to determine the influence on the worker of such environmental factors as temperature, noise, humidity, good or bad illumination, and so on. Time and motion study, by eliminating inefficient movements, will make the worker a more effective machine. In point of fact, much of what goes by the name of industrial *psychology* would be more appropriately called industrial *physiology*.

Now modern research has shown that these views are incorrect, and it is most important that they should be recognized to be so. As has already been pointed out, they are entirely incorrect when we observe the nature of work against a historical and cultural background and they were never more than partly true even at the height of the paleotechnic stage. In this chapter we shall give reasons for supposing that the following statements are nearer the truth, and should, therefore, form the basis of any new approach to industrial problems:

(1) Work is an essential part of a man's life since it is that aspect of his life which gives him status and binds him to society. Ordinarily men and women like their work, and at most periods of history always have done so. When they do not like it, the fault lies in the psychological and social conditions of the job rather than in the worker. Furthermore, work is a *social* activity.

(2) The morale of the worker (i.e. whether or not he works willingly) has no *direct* relationship whatsoever to the material conditions of the job. Investigations into temperature, lighting, time and motion study, noise, and humidity have not the slightest bearing on morale, although they may have a bearing on physical health and comfort.

(3) There are many incentives, of which, under normal conditions, money is one of the least important. Unemployment is a powerful negative incentive, precisely because (1) is true. That is to say, unemployment is feared because it cuts man off from his society.

It is a futile task to attempt to define exactly what we mean by the term 'work'. If the definition is in terms of pay, the hard-working housewife is excluded; if it is in terms of pleasure or choice, it can easily be shown that for some people work and play are virtually the same thing. Dr May Smith (*Introduction to Industrial Psychology*) believes that the final end of work is to live, and that therefore those who exchange their activities of body or mind for the means to live are working. She then goes on to ask: 'Can one imagine a person with a fortune continuing in routine repetitive work, or in the majority of industrial processes?' The answer to this question, which is clearly intended to be a rhetorical one, is that one can. In a group of London factories known to the writer three men have at different times won large sums of money from football pools and, after a short period of leisure, have returned to their ordinary work – two on 'routine repetitive work' and one as a fitter. Yet the money they had received was quite sufficient, if suitably invested, to enable them to live comfortably for the rest of their lives. In another firm which retires its women workers at the age of fifty-five on a quite generous pension, many of these women may be seen standing by the factory gates each evening waiting for their friends to come out. They continue to attend any social events run by the firm, and when part-time work is available during the busy season, are always ready and willing to apply. The most cynical individual who interviewed these women could not get the impression that they are primarily concerned about money (in fact, in addition to their pension, nearly all of them are doing other part-time jobs and have quite enough money). It is clear that, so far as they are concerned, the factory is a social centre. (For confirmation of this view, see F. Zweig: *Women's Life and Labour*.) If one begins with the assumption that the sole incentive to work is money or fear, then such behaviour is incomprehensible. The belief that money is the sole, or even the most important of several, motives for work, is so foolish that anyone who seriously holds this opinion is thereby rendered incapable of understanding either industry or the industrial worker. Fundamentally, work is a social activity with the two main functions of producing the goods required by society and binding the individual into the pattern of interrelationships from which society is built up. We have seen that status and function are of crucial importance to the psychological well-being of the individual, and it is for the most part in the working environment that status and function are assigned to him. (Professor John G. McKenzie, in his book *Nervous Disorders and Religion*, has said that his own experience of neurotic troubles has led him to believe that there are more morbid complexes and character-structures connected with the need for social status than any other of our needs, and Kingsley Davis, in an investigation of seventy cases of neurosis in hospital, found that all but four showed clear evidence of status involvements. (Kingsley Davis, article on 'Mental Hygiene' in *A Study of Interpersonal Relations*, edited by Patrick Mullahy.) Any definition of work which leaves out the fact that it is a social activity is no definition at all. Recognizing this, Professors Miller and Form note that 'the motives for working cannot be assigned only to economic needs, for men may continue to work even though they have no need for material goods. Even when their security and that of their children is assured, they continue to labour. Obviously this is so because the rewards they get from work are social, such as respect and admiration from their fellow-men. For some, work becomes an avenue for securing ego satisfactions by gaining power and exerting it over others. For all, work activity provides fellowship and social life.' Industry is the main source of status, both in the formal and the informal sense (derived and intrinsic) in Western cultures, and, when we are trying to 'place' a stranger, our first question is 'What does he *do*?' This being the case, it will be seen that industry has a second task which is just as important as maintaining efficiency and raising output; it has to administer the institution which determines the social status of most men and women in modern cultures. The non-material social rewards which industry has it in its power to grant are so valuable that we are brought back to the fundamental problem for the industrial psychologist, which is not, as has been supposed, the discovery of methods whereby indifferent people may be pushed by bribes, threats, or gifts into doing a dreary job a little less carelessly or even a little enthusiastically. It is to find the answer to the question: 'What has happened to change an important, necessary, and potentially pleasurable social activity which is capable of satisfying both material and psychological human needs into a source of strife, resentment, and boredom?' That this question appears to be utopian and eccentric to many people only demonstrates how far industry has been deceived by its own propaganda, or perhaps it would be fairer to say, by that of its Puritan ancestry. For the idea of disliking work has never occurred, as the most superficial study of history or anthropology would make clear, to the vast majority of human beings who have ever lived. That there are often many aspects of work which men do not like, is self-evident, but there are few people who are not more unhappy without work than with it even when we exclude the financial reward altogether.

Since the validity of this thesis is likely to be doubted by a large number of those engaged in industry, it may simplify matters if some of the reasons for accepting it are classified under separate headings:

(a) As we have noted already, many men and women work when it is no longer financially necessary. The men who returned to work after winning large sums of money from football pools are not exceptional cases. One of the commonest, and saddest, calamities in industry is the case of the man who works hard all his life and dies one or two years after retiring from sheer misery and lack of things to occupy his mind. Even in the factory which is not a very happy one, the manager has only to look around him with an open mind to see that many, if not most, people do not like to be retired and tend afterwards to maintain contact with the firm on a social basis like the elderly women already described.

(b) Another common factory event which makes nonsense of the idea that money is all-important, is the frequency with which workers who have been given a new job with higher pay ask to be returned to their old job with its lower wages. If dislike of work and love of money is universal, this sort of behaviour fails to make sense.

(c) Even under the existing conditions, which are far from satisfactory, most workers like their jobs. Every survey of workers' attitudes which has been carried out, no matter in what industry, indicates that this is so. Thus a report on Neurosis in Industry brought out by the Medical Research Council discovered that of 3,000 workers (a random sample from about 30,000 workers in the light and medium engineering industries), 58 per cent reported that they liked their job, and only 13 to 14 per cent that they disliked or were bored by it. Where care had been taken in placing workers by means of adequate vocational guidance, it was found in another industry that 83 per cent were contented while only 2 per cent found the work unsatisfactory. Of 1,200 single women who were employed, K. B. Davis found that, in relation to their work, 78.3 per cent stated that their life was 'happy', 63.7 per cent that it was 'satisfactory', and 65.1 per cent that it was 'successful'. (K. B. Davis, *Factors in the Sex Life of Twenty-two Hundred Women*, 1929.)

(d) The pride and interest shown in the affairs of certain concerns (e.g. the Ford Company, Unilever Limited) by those employed in them when an adequate information service has publicized the company's achievements, is quite genuine and unaffected. If workers are treated as human beings, they will behave as such; if they are treated as automatons or unwilling slaves, that is how they will act.

(c) The most compelling evidence as to what work means to the worker comes from a study of unemployment. If it is true that people only work for money then, provided that they are given an adequate 'dole', it would not matter what they were asked to do. But one has only to recall the outcry which arose on all hands when it was suggested that unemployed men should do something for their dole such as digging holes and filling them in again to realize that the normal individual does not need to be told that doing futile tasks is no 'work' at all but is felt as a personal insult. If the worker has to feel that what he is doing has some sort of significance, that his job is a link between himself and his society, then the theory we have been criticizing is obviously absurd. What the job means to the worker is well expressed in the words of an unemployed father and husband to a social worker (P. V. Young, in *Interviewing and Social Work*, 1935): 'What do you think all these things do to me? They certainly don't add to my esteem or happiness. At times I

191

boil inside, but mostly I just feel licked. I never imagined that the peace of my home and the control over my children depended on my job. Why, the job just rules your life. Oh, we are still a family, but the ties are greatly weakened.' Lord Beveridge has said that the greatest evil of unemployment is that it makes men 'seem useless, not wanted, without a country', and K. G. Collier notes that many middle-aged unemployed men accustomed to a regular occupation have preferred to take any sort of job – even at a wage less than the dole – for the sake of getting back a recognized status. That many jobs are not very interesting or socially satisfying may be granted, but few workers are so frustrated that they regard their job as completely futile. How to add to the significance of the job will be discussed later, but it must be recognized that men work both in order to live and in order to feel useful, wanted, and to attain a social status. There are tens of thousands of men and women who like their jobs, whether, as in the case of true craftsman, from an intrinsic love of that particular job, or, as in a far larger number of cases, from motives directly associated with its successful execution. Work may be liked because it gives the worker comradeship, promotion, or social standing, all of which are in a real sense part of the job. There are, of course, others whose attitude to work is based on genuinely extrinsic interests, who, for example, are simply trying to get as much money as possible in order to carry on some absorbing hobby at home or elsewhere. These are the socially unattached people who are self-sufficient, but they form a very small proportion of the total working population. Still others are unattached and miserable, the group of neurotic men or women who want to 'belong' but, for various reasons, fail to do so. That the number of workers in this group is increasing is one of the serious problems of modern industry.

The second aspect of work we have to discuss is the working environment, the material and psychological conditions under which it is carried out, and here again the observer has only to look around him to see that, however desirable good working conditions in the material sense may be, they have little or no direct relationship to good morale. It ought to be abundantly clear that bad conditions of work *in themselves* have practically no bearing at all on the morale of the workers or their attitude to the job. For example, the troops in Burma or the Western Desert during the war worked under the most appalling conditions, yet their morale was very high. It is no adequate criticism of this statement to say that this was in the army and during wartime, since what is clearly demonstrated is that high morale and good environment are not directly related. In any case, there is hardly any factory which does not within its own walls demonstrate the same fact; for there must be many firms in which the most superficial observer may note that it is often the men or women doing the dirtiest jobs who are the most contented and show the highest morale. Thus in a London slaughter-house where pigs are killed, there was a small room in which the internal organs were sorted and washed prior to utilizing them for other purposes – intestines for sausage skins, glands for chemical extraction, and so on. The room was below ground level, dimly lit by artificial light, cold and damp – a perfect epitome of how a workroom ought not to be. Its floors were covered with blood, water, and the contents of the animals' intestines which smelt collectively extremely unpleasant to the casual visitor. Yet in these far from ideal surroundings six girls worked cheerfully laughing and singing throughout the day. A medical officer, new to the factory, and somewhat shocked by what he saw, recommended that the girls be replaced by men and transferred to other departments since building restrictions did not permit any immediate improvement of conditions. But this well-meant recommendation aroused such a storm of protest that it had to be withdrawn almost immediately. What, the girls wanted to know, was wrong with their job? Why should they be picked on? Weren't they doing their job well enough? If the management were dissatisfied with their work, why could they not say so right away and give them a chance to do something about it? These girls formed a happy working-group and were all on friendly terms with each other, they believed that they were doing a skilled job, and they were under the control of a good supervisor who let them take their own time over the work and praised them judiciously. Yet in other departments in the same factory, well-lit, well-heated, and under the best conditions in the material sense, hundreds of other girls worked and grumbled over their jobs. There was nothing special about the six girls in the small room – twenty years earlier there had been another six, and individuals had come and gone, but morale had never been other than good.

It need hardly be said that this is not a plea for bad working conditions, or an attempt to deny that the physical environment is of the utmost importance and that bad conditions adversely influence health and happiness. But there can be no doubt that good physical conditions may coexist with bad morale, and bad conditions with good morale. Good physical conditions of work may make good morale better but they will not, in themselves, create it. It seems necessary to make this rather obvious statement since there are many managers or psychologists who hold, or appear to hold, the opposite view. We constantly read, for example, that increasing illumination by x per cent raised production by y per cent, or, to take a specific instance, that wearing earplugs in a noisy weaving factory increased production by 3 per cent. (Weston and Adams, *Effects of Noise on the Performance of Weavers,* Industrial Health Research Board, No. 65, 1932.) The validity of the figures given is not in doubt, but *what* it was that caused production to be raised or absenteeism lowered is quite another matter.

It may be accepted as proved beyond doubt that there are optimum conditions of heating and lighting, hours of work, and so on. Indeed, minute regulations have been laid down by the Ministry of Labour regarding factory lighting under certain conditions, and other bodies, such as the Illuminating Engineering Society and the Industrial Health Research Board, have given details concerning optimum conditions of light and temperature, not to mention air flow, relative humidity, and other factors. Noting this impressive array of figures, one cannot help wondering whether the investigators have always kept in mind (1) the wide range of individual preferences, and (2) the fact, clearly demonstrated by the Hawthorne research, that it is impossible to carry out experiments on any group of people without influencing them emotionally. For example, although we are told (*Emergency Report No. 1* of the Industrial Health Research Board, 1940) that suitable temperatures for winter when work is moderately heavy, range from 60 to 65 degrees Fahrenheit, Dr May Smith points out that in an actual inquiry it was found that somebody was comfortable or uncomfortable at each recorded temperature from 54 to 76 degrees Fahrenheit. Regarding illumination, 65 per cent of the subjects of one study judged intensities of anything between ten and thirty foot-candles the most comfortable for reading, while the rest were often considerably above or below this range. Few investigations into the influence of environmental factors on working capacity give any indication that an attempt has been made to decide how much of the effect observed is due to direct physical influence (e.g. clearer vision from better lighting), how much to individual preferences for dim or bright light, how much to increased cheerfulness in the appearance of the workshop after changed lighting, and how much to better morale from the awareness that management had taken an interest in the conditions of work. The Hawthorne experiment in which production went up even when the light was so dim that its intensity was that of bright moonlight demonstrated the fallacy of supposing that the psychological state of the workers remains unaffected by the conditions of an experiment. Under other circumstances, the investigators might well have deduced from the investigation that dim illumination was best suited for this type of work. Many industrial psychologists fail to see that unless the rise in output or decrease in absenteeism observed in their experiments can be shown to have been the *direct* result of the improved lighting, temperature control, or diminished noise, so that the same result would be obtained wherever and whenever their recommendations were carried out, they become almost valueless. They tell us nothing except that in a specific factory on a given date certain vaguely specified conditions produced certain measurable effects; for a scientific experiment is only valid when all the variables but the one under investigation are kept constant. Since in the vast majority of cases this has not been done (the emotional factor having been left out), many of the results are seriously in doubt.

It follows that great caution is required in interpreting the results of psychological experiments on human beings. Man's most serious drawback from the point of view of the scientist is that he tends to respond to his environment not *as it is*, but *as he sees it*. He is constantly interpreting events and looking for the significance which he assumes to lie behind them, with the result that what appears to be a response to an environmental change may in fact be a response to the assumed intentions of those who are manipulating the environment, or, perhaps, to some other factor unwittingly introduced by the experimenter. It has frequently been pointed out by psychologists that time and motion studies are likely to lead to successful results only insofar as they are accepted by the workers as having been initiated for the general good – if it is supposed that the motive behind them is exploitation by management, the results may be worse than if they had never been attempted. Two further examples will demonstrate the difficulty of excluding the emotional factor from psychological research. The first relates, not to an actual piece of research, but to an observation made by the writer and others in a London factory which gave permission for a Blood Transfusion Unit to come and collect blood from volunteers of managerial, clerical, and labouring staff. During the session, several people were having blood removed at the same time and after it had been collected they were expected to lie on couches in the rest room until they had recovered, management and employees being mixed up indiscriminately. In the following weeks, morale was noted to be high, production went up, and everyone was noticeably more friendly. The mechanically-minded observer might have deduced from this 'experiment' that the removal of blood was good for the health and raised production, but the results were evidently due to the fact that management had shared this experience with the workers – they had behaved 'like the rest of us'. Management stock had gone up and remained high for some time afterwards. The second example is taken from an investigation into the properties of alleged 'cold-prevention' tablets, which had been tested out in several factories, and it has been shown that, when the employees were divided into two groups one of which was given the tablets and the other not, the former group showed an appreciably lower incidence of colds. But when a less credulous medical officer repeated the experiment the employees were divided into *three* groups, one being given no tablets, the second being given the 'cold-prevention' tablets, and the third tablets similar in appearance but containing only sodium bicarbonate and colouring matter. The result of the second experiment showed that all those who had been given tablets were more free from colds than those who had been given none – but those who had been given the dummy tablets were just as free from colds as those who had taken the genuine ones. In other words, the apparent effect of the tablets was simply due to suggestion, and they had no curative properties at all. (A similar experiment was carried out during the last war by a Government Department which decided to investigate the alleged 'tonic' effect of sunlight lamps on its employees. All those who were given sun-baths felt much better than those who had been given none – but those who had been exposed to a lamp with an invisible screen cutting out all the 'health-giving' ultra-violet rays felt just as well as those who had been given the genuine article. Here, again, the feeling of well-being was due to suggestion.) All modern work demonstrates that human beings, whether individually or collectively, react with greater sensitivity to changes in psychological atmosphere, to intentions, implications, and suggestions, than they do to any of the ordinary changes in physical environment. A misplaced word, a misinterpreted phrase, will lower morale or efficiency to a much greater degree than considerable rises or falls in temperature, humidity, or lighting intensity. Gordon Rattray Taylor tells of a case in which a strike was called although the management had offered to submit the dispute to arbitration. It was later discovered that the men had thought that the word 'arbitration' meant 'surrender'. In yet another company, the management decided on its own initiative to double the monthly pension it gave its employees. But those concerned, instead of welcoming the concession without negotiation of what had always been one of its main claims, threatened to bring charges of unfair practice against the company for having increased pensions without consulting their trade union. Many employers would do well to learn and put into effect the words of the popular song: 'It's not what you do, it's the way that you do it.' In general, workers complain about working conditions, not because they are objectively bad, but because they are worse than they need be in the circumstances. If it is in the nature of a job to be dirty or unpleasant very few complaints may be received, but if the job is avoidably dirty or unpleasant there will be justifiable resentment at the lack of good intentions which this implies. For these reasons, recent work in industrial psychology, while admitting the great importance of good working conditions in the physical environment, is more concerned with investigating motives, intentions, and attitudes. What it is necessary to know is why people want, or do not want, to work, what their feelings are, and why.

A final example of the difficulty in separating the relatively objective from the purely subjective is provided by the problem of noise. That noise is to be avoided if possible is obvious, but whether it is objectively harmful, and, indeed, what different people consider to be 'noise' is quite another matter. Dr May Smith makes this point very clearly and wittily in her *Introduction to Industrial Psychology*: 'No one can avoid knowing how much some people dislike noise. Before the war at regular intervals a spate of letters appeared in the Press emphasizing with lurid detail the appalling effects of being subjected to the noise of machinery, of our streets, and railway stations. If the writer was physiologically minded, he explained exactly what he thought was the effect on the brain and nerves, and usually concluded with a dissertation on the increase of nervous disorders (not very clearly defined) due to noise, particularly of the kind of noise most distasteful to himself. If he were commercially minded and desirous of making financial shudders run down our spines, he told us exactly how many millions of money were lost through preventable noise. One writer, unfortunately he does not give us the details of the calculation, thought that it could be over one million pounds a week.' Dr Smith goes on to point out that a 'golden age' is frequently described in which noise was unknown, yet a glance into the past shows that when people were not grumbling about the outrageous noise of motor cars and mechanized traffic they were writing to *The Times* objecting to the impossibility of hearing oneself speak in Piccadilly owing to the noise of the iron tyres of horse-drawn cabs and carts. Still earlier

Schopenhauer was complaining of the cracking whips of tradesmen and carters: 'The sudden, sharp crack which paralyses the
brain, destroys all meditation and murders thought, must cause
pain to anyone who has anything like an idea in his head.' But,
of course, what is noise to one person is music to another – at
least within a very wide range of sounds – and a great deal
depends on the subjective significance attached to the sound.
Dr Millais Culpin has said of the effect of the noise of passing
motor-cycles on the sleeper: 'If every pop should mean a shilling
in my bank balance I could sleep happily beside a continued
procession of motor-cycles, and only wake up when the noise
ceased.' Similarly, the noise of a pneumatic drill is much more
irritating to the person who has to listen passively than it is to the
man who operates it. It is well known that amongst boiler-
makers, riveters, and operators of automatic stamping machines,
deafness may result in the range of tones of the same pitch as the
noise, whilst normal hearing is retained over other parts of the
scale. But this is an extreme result of excessive noise which has
little relevance to the sort of thing discussed by the type of person
referred to above. So far as nervous disorders are concerned,
undue sensitivity to noise is a symptom of neurosis and not its
cause. (The comedian W. C. Fields once complained that he
was unable to take an effervescent drink to relieve the effects of
excessive alcoholic indulgence, because he 'just couldn't tolerate
the noise'.)

An incentive is an objective goal which is capable of satisfying
what we are aware of subjectively as a need, drive, or desire.
Some needs, as we have seen elsewhere, are innate, but the vast
majority are acquired in the process of social interaction and
from everyday experience. For practical purposes it does not
matter whether Freud was right in assuming that all acquired
needs are ultimately based on, and derive their energy from, the
innate drives, or Allport who assumes that acquired needs may
become functionally autonomous. What is clear is that acquired
needs are, for the most part, culturally defined, and even the
innate drive of hunger appears in the culturally approved form of
a wish for roast beef and Yorkshire pudding at 12.30 p.m. on
Sundays. We have taken the view in this book that certain needs,

whether or not they are what the psychologist would ordinarily describe as acquired, are virtually universal since they derive, not from the peculiarities of any single culture, but from certain features which are universal to all societies everywhere. Such needs as the desire for status, for appreciation, or for emotional security come into this category, whereas the desire of a boy for a bicycle like that of the boy next door is based on his experience as an individual in a particular society, although it may be utilized to gain status amongst his comrades. Acquired needs may be just as real and intense to the person experiencing them as his innate drives, and, since they are derived from experience, it follows that people define their needs in terms of the time and place in which they live. This statement may seem to be a truism, but it is quite obviously not understood by those who express the opinion that, since the workers of today are much better off than their counterparts of a century ago, they should be satisfied with their lot and stop grumbling. As Maier has said, the answer to this observation is that, since men had fewer acquired needs a hundred years ago, the same conditions which now represent deprivation did not do so then, If, to take an extreme example, 90 per cent of families in Britain had television sets, the 10 per cent who had not might feel just as frustrated at their lack as the Egyptian peasant who is starving for lack of bread. Frustration is not wholly related to the objective circumstances of the individual but rather to what he feels himself entitled to. An important point which those whose idea of 'welfare' is giving people free gifts fail to notice is that such gifts never continue to give the same degree of satisfaction – the object which was a source of delight when it was first received soon comes to be regarded either as a commonplace necessity or a useless piece of bric-à-brac. Trying to satisfy people with material gifts is, in the long run, like trying to fill a bottomless pit. When certain psychological needs are satisfied, however, they continue to give pleasure: emotional security, a status which gives the holder self-respect, satisfying relationships at work and at home, pride of craftsmanship, and appreciation from seniors, are all satisfactions of this nature. It follows, then, that workers who are placed in a comfortable and attractive new workshop may like it at first, but this attitude will soon give way to acceptance, to the feeling that such surroundings are 'natural', and even a slight lowering in the standard of the surroundings will cause more grumbling than if they had never been experienced. When their emotional needs are satisfied, this 'law of diminishing returns' does not apply. Of course, physical standards of comfort, both in relation to hygiene and in the aesthetic sense, should always be as high as possible. We are only pointing out that the attempt to keep people quiet with gifts, fussing, and unnecessary 'improvements' while ignoring their self-respect and other psychological needs leads to a situation rather like that of the traveller pursued by wolves who has to cut loose one of the horses drawing his sledge every now and then in order momentarily to satisfy the wolves and gain himself some respite from the chase.

Many attempts have been made to investigate, with a view to utilizing them as incentives, the needs which workers consider it most important that their jobs should be able to satisfy. As might be expected, there were found to be certain divergences of opinion, depending on sex, age, class and the particular problems of the individual firm. Women tended to attach greater importance to good working conditions than men, and men usually attached more importance to opportunity for promotion than women. If the firm had a boss who was disliked, the need for a good boss was naturally higher up the list than in a factory in which no such problem existed. However, what is really surprising about the results of the investigations so far carried out has been the large measure of agreement as to what workers believe to be the most important factors in their employment. When, in a British factory, 325 women workers were asked to arrange ten items in order of importance, steady work came first on the list, good working conditions (in both the physical and psychological senses) second, and high pay sixth. (Wyatt, Sangdon, and Stock, *Fatigue and Boredom in Repetitive Work:* Industrial Health Research Board, Report 77, 1937.) Another study of 100 department-store employees and 150 miscellaneous workers showed that good pay came sixth and seventh respectively on a list of twelve; opportunity for advancement came first and steady work second in both groups. (Chant, 'Measuring the

Factors that Make a Job Interesting', *Personnel Journal*, 1932, 11.)
J. D. Houser found that employees in a trading organization
placed good pay twenty-first on a list of twenty-eight items
('What People Want from Business') and the 17,000 employees
of Joseph Lucas Ltd placed security first and high earnings
fourth of seven items. Concerning incentives in general, the
following facts are significant:

(1) There is no one ideal incentive. Incentives vary from one
culture to another, from one firm to another, and from one
individual to another (e.g. one man may value money whereas
another may find greater leisure or opportunity for promotion
a more powerful stimulus).

(2) The law of diminishing returns applies to all material
incentives – that is to say, as the reward increases the desire for
further reward decreases until it reaches vanishing point (e.g. as
G. R. Taylor points out, the miners, on getting higher rates of
pay, increased their rate of absence, because the point had been
reached at which the need for more money had become secondary
to the need for more leisure).

(3) Incentives may conflict with other motives (e.g. a worker
may ignore financial incentives if he fears that his rate may be
cut or that he may work himself out of a job).

(4) Without exception, all industrial psychologists are agreed
that money is of much less significance than has hitherto been
supposed. Except under conditions when wages are very low or
during periods of inflation, money is one of the least powerful
incentives.

(5) On the other hand, we must remember that in our own
culture, as Taylor has noted, motives tend to become 'monet-
ized'. 'People have been taught that money is the key to satisfaction, so when they feel that something is wrong with their
lives they naturally ask for more money. A demand for money
undoubtedly indicates that they want *something*, but it does not
tell us what.' Professor Viteles similarly observes that '*if money
is all that a man gets for his work*, he will take any means possible
to get all that he can.' Constant demands for more money (when
wages are already adequate) indicate either that the workers feel
vague dissatisfaction without quite knowing why, and think of

money as the obvious solution, or else that they are aware of the causes of their discontent and are taking the attitude 'If you won't give us what we really need, you must pay us in the only way you seem to understand.' It is easily noted that, in the firm with poor morale, the workers continue to ask for more money even when the wage rates are much higher than in most factories in the area. In other words, they feel that when conditions are unsatisfactory they deserve extra incentives to offset the disadvantages of their employment.

We shall now go on to consider certain social factors in industry which have the power to act as incentives or disincentives as the case may be. In doing so, it is useful to classify them under the headings used by E. W. Bakke in discussing those bonds which provide cohesion between members of the working group. (Bakke, 'Teamwork in Industry', *Scientific Monthly*, March 1948.) These are (A) job specifications and requirements, (B) the communication system, (C) the status system, (D) the system of rewards and punishments, (E) the organizational charter.

(A) *Job specifications and requirements*

These relate both to the job itself and to its circumstances. The worker must know specifically what his job is and how it is related to other jobs; preferably there should be an area within which he is free to use his own inventiveness and initiative. The job must be suited to the abilities of the worker, and this depends either on the common sense of the supervisor or on the use of suitable tests by the personnel department. The worker must have reasonable security – a term which includes not only physical and economic security, but also the need to avoid threats to status and prestige, the need to have the backing of the group, to know who is who and what is what, and to feel that he is unlikely to lose his job. In the space available, it is only possible to discuss two aspects of this problem: firstly, the problem of change, and secondly the problem of craftsmanship in modern industry. As Dr May Smith and others have pointed out, the success of the technical organization of a factory depends to a large extent on change – machines must sometimes be redesigned, the technical layout of the job altered, and piece-rates reset. But while to the management all this seems quite natural and inevitable, to the worker it may appear that he is constantly at the mercy of technicians. Changes occur which he can neither control nor initiate, his work routine is altered, his friends shifted elsewhere, and his rate of pay may go up or down in a manner which he completely fails to understand. Even when the changes may be, objectively speaking, in his own interest, this is no ground for satisfaction if they have never been explained and he does not understand their full implications. Under such circumstances, the worker tends to become conservative, to keep his output constant, acting on the principle that if it is too high or too low management might *do* something. When changes are made they are likely to be resisted because nobody except the management (who usually do not tell) knows where they might lead. In point of fact, workers have ample grounds for anxiety in such situations. More efficient machinery and over-production *have* in the past led to loss of employment, and when workers have earned above a certain amount rates *have* been cut. So-called restrictive practices are described by S. B. Mathewson in the paper from which we have already quoted as 'self-protective resistance against wage incentive plans, piece-rate cuts, and lay-offs'. Fear was obviously the main, although not the only factor at work in these cases, and the workers themselves gave such reasons as, rate-cutting, fear of unemployment, excessive speeding-up, and resentment at management. Such practices are recognized by the trade unions, and the journal of the Amalgamated Engineering Union (May 1948) expressed the official view of the unions as follows: 'Restrictive practices are defined as safeguards affecting the skilled crafts, dilution of labour, overtime, wage scales, the position of trainees, demarcation problems, the performance of skilled operations by unskilled or semi-skilled and also female labour.' Since this problem has a long history it will obviously take time to overcome the fears of the workers, but, quite apart from fears of rate-cutting and unemployment, there are many restrictive practices which relate solely to conditions within the individual factory. The workers do not want their groups broken up, they do not want to be 'messed about' or to give up a job in a department to which they have become accustomed for one in another part of the factory. From these observations two conclusions may be drawn. Firstly, that when changes are made it is essential that this should be done with the least possible disturbance of the group life of those concerned. 'The successful management of any human enterprise depends largely on the ability to introduce more efficient methods without disrupting in the process the social foundations on which collaboration is based.' (*Fatigue of Workers and its Relation to Industrial Problems*, National Research Council, New York, 1941.) Secondly, that all changes should be thoroughly discussed with those concerned before being initiated. Mathewson concludes his survey with the observation that 'the worker has not been brought to feel that he can freely give his best efforts without incurring penalties in place of rewards. Regardless of how much the individual may desire to contribute a full day's work, his actual experiences often turn him away from good working habits.' By engaging in restrictive practices the workers are behaving in a manner which, under the circumstances, is perfectly natural, and until the situation is altered so that good work no longer leads to what are seen as penalties, they are unlikely to stop. Since managements also from time to time make use of restrictive practices, they should find it all the easier to understand their employees.

Most people would agree that one of the most basic satisfactions to be obtained from work is the feeling of pride and achievement at having accomplished something, or, as it is usually called, the instinct of craftsmanship. It seems unlikely that there is any innate drive corresponding to this so-called instinct, although many psychologists have supposed that man has a natural urge to 'mould and adapt his environment'. What seems clear is that such manipulative behaviour is closely related to the individual's desire to obtain status and recognition within the limits permitted by his society. When he has done a piece of work well and produced something unique, his self-respect is thereby increased. It is characteristic of the attitude of the craftsman that, although the work may be carried out for some practical end, it is also to some extent done for its own sake.

Earlier in this chapter we have suggested that there are three types of motive for working, each related in varying degrees to the work itself:

(1) The work may be done as an end in itself (i.e. as a craft).

(2) It may be carried out willingly for motives other than (1), but directly associated with the work situation (e.g. comradeship, status, power, and so on).

(3) It may be carried out for genuinely extrinsic motives (e.g. for money to be used for a hobby, for the family, or for a chance of getting out of that particular job and setting up in business on one's own).

Evidently (1) is the most satisfactory reason for working, (2) although less satisfactory is a quite adequate motive, and (3) is the least satisfactory. The question naturally arises whether under modern conditions it is possible to expect people to work for the first reason and to like their work as such. If we find that, in most cases, this cannot reasonably be expected of the worker, then the most sensible thing to do would be to increase the social satisfactions of the job so that, at the very least, the worker may take pleasure in his employment from motives directly related to it. Only as a last resort should the extrinsic motives be made primary, since to do so would be a confession of failure.

When the word 'craftsmanship' is mentioned, one's first reaction is to think immediately of the situation in primitive communities or during the Middle Ages, when, it is often supposed, all work was a form of craftsmanship. But it is by no means certain that this belief is based on historical fact, and the truth seems to be that craftsmanship has never been so common as the more romantic historians have thought. A great deal of man's work has always been, from an objective point of view, drudgery. But it was not regarded as such, since it was possible at most times to see the work in its social context. Washing clothes in the river is, one supposes, dull work in the objective sense, but it is not experienced as dull firstly because the woman realizes to what end she is doing the work, and secondly, because she is doing it in the company of other women with whom she can talk and exchange gossip. Boredom is not something attached to the work in itself, but depends rather on the circumstances surrounding the work and its social context. What is found to be most intolerable about certain types of industrial work is (a) that it is meaningless to the worker, and (b) that it is often carried out under circumstances which make talking and gossip impossible. Professor M. Viteles writes that 'the individual whose attention becomes either entirely absorbed in the task or entirely dissociated as a result of its mechanization is free from the feeling of boredom in work.' That is to say, when a worker does a job which requires concentration and skill, he may (other things being equal) perform it as a craft, and he is not bored. But what is even more important, because less obvious, is that when a worker does a job which is almost entirely automatic, boredom will not arise provided that the situation permits day-dreaming, conversation, and social distractions to take place. When a job of this type is properly arranged so that the worker realizes its significance, feels that the job is valuable, and can also engage in conversation with his or her comrades, the situation is in no respects different from that of the primitive farmer planting his crops, pulling out weeds, or the woman washing the family laundry in the river. What is frustrating is to have to do work which does not make sense whilst separated by noise or space from other workers, or to perform a task which is semi-automatic so that there is just enough distraction to keep one from day-dreaming or talking and not enough to make the job interesting. Other problems of industrial fatigue and boredom will be dealt with later, but the points we have just made are immensely important in the present context, since they show that a good deal of nonsense is spoken about the dangers of mass-production in destroying the creative impulses of the worker. In all probability the converse is true: that in modern society there is far greater scope for skill and craftsmanship than in any previous society, and that far more people are in a position to use such skills.

Two other points are of significance in relation to the alleged 'decline of craftsmanship'. In the first place, what is called craftsmanship may refer not only to the manipulation of materials but also to the process of dealing with people. In this sense the supervisor or manager is a craftsman, and, at the best, a very skilled one. So, too, is the charge-hand or the shop-steward of the union. There is an increasing need for what Mayo has described as 'social skills' which require for their success the highest manifestations of craftsmanship. In the second place, the nature of industry is changing so that the type of worker needed is decreasingly the sort of individual satirized by Charlie Chaplin in the film 'Modern Times' and more the sort of person who has the knowledge and skill to control the machine. This change in modern technology is seen most clearly in the army, where the unskilled infantryman known to Kipling has been replaced by the skilled technician who knows about tanks, motor engines, wireless, electricity, and radar. Another point brought out by M. M. Lewis in his *Language in Society* is that the social organization of the worker in relation to his job has altered. Lewis observes that there are three stages in the development of group organization in industry: the stage of division of labour and specialization, the stage of automatization, and, finally, the ebbing of this automatization in favour of the growing awareness of the group of its own techniques. 'Division of labour', a phrase devised by Adam Smith, is found even in the most primitive societies, but the division of labour characteristic of the early paleotechnic period shows not only an increase of specialization and a greater degree of breaking-up the various processes of a job – it introduces machines to replace the individual. In this way, a stage of automatization commences in which the skilled craftsman becomes not only unnecessary but a positive nuisance. Andrew Ure, an early apologist of the factory system, wrote in the first quarter of the nineteenth century that: 'By the infirmity of human nature it happens that the more skilful the workman, the more self-willed and intractable he is apt to become, and, of course, the less fit a component of a mechanical system, in which by occasional irregularities he may do great damage to the whole. The grand object of the modern manufacturer is, through the union of capital and science, to reduce the task of his workpeople to the exercise of vigilance and dexterity.' In short, we come to the stage of F. W. Taylor's 'trained gorilla', in which the less skilful the worker the better he is suited to industrial techniques. So far as communication is concerned, 'consciousness is withdrawn from the individual members of the group to a few centres of direction – the overseers and the managers, so that in extreme cases some of the workers may cease to exercise any conscious guidance even of their specific tasks.' But, as processes become more complex, the illiterate and isolated worker who behaves like an automaton can no longer deal with the situation. A third stage comes into being in which 'there is a growing demand for an extension of technical education for everyone engaged in industry, the demand that each worker, however limited and automatic the task he performs, shall command literacy over a field wider than this task alone. It is seen now that the full integration of a group technique in industry demands some awareness in the group of the task of the group. There must be a technique of communication throughout the group commensurate in range and complexity with the industrial techniques of the group.' (M. M. Lewis.) What is of particular interest about this statement is its realization that concern with the working group, with social psychology, morale, and improved communication in the factory, is not merely due to the necessity of solving the problems mentioned in Chapter 1, of getting people to work in the absence of the threat of unemployment. It is also due to the fact that modern techniques are so delicate and complex that they can only be entrusted to workers who are educated, co-operative with their mates, fully-informed as to all that is going on, and who not only accept their job but do it willingly.

(B) *Communications*

Certain defects which may arise within the communication system have already been mentioned. For example, those in charge may become so obsessed with the purely technical aspects of the factory processes that workers' suggestions, grievances, and feelings on day-to-day matters come to be ignored. This leads not only to resentment on the part of employees, but ultimately reacts on the technical efficiency of the plant. To ignore the human factor in industry is to be lacking in humanity, but it is also a sign of gross incompetence in the technical field. Secondly, the communication line may be so long that information is more or less distorted before it reaches those who are in a position to take action. Thirdly, when morale is bad and management is not trusted, the communications may not be believed. As representative of certain common problems of communication in the factory we shall discuss the question of honesty on the part of management and the question of what the psychologist describes as 'knowledge of results'.

Whether for reasons of cowardice or because they pride themselves on being gifted with subtlety and cunning, many managers are a good deal less honest towards their employees than the latter have a right to expect. For example, when a firm is engaging new supervisors or junior managers, it often happens that either in the advertisements or in reply to the queries of the applicants it is implied that 'for a good man in our firm the sky is the limit'. In many cases this is a lie told for the peculiar reason that it is believed that the best type of men will be attracted in this way. Since the chances of promotion in most firms are strictly limited, one result of this lie is the rather pathetic figure of the junior manager who has done his best (and may even have ruined his family life by neglect in the process) always with this carrot being dangled in front of his nose. At the age of forty, or thereabouts, he begins to realize that the chances of further promotion no longer exist. What is he to do? He must either submit with resentment to the old situation or in middle age tear up his roots and go to a smaller firm where the chances of promotion appear to be more favourable. One of the grave defects of modern industry, and, indeed, of modern industrial society, is this intense stimulation of desires and the limitations imposed on satisfying them. As Ogburn has said 'to widen the gap between what people want and what they actually have or can reasonably expect to have is to make for widespread discontent and nervousness.' (*A Handbook of Sociology*.) An even worse example of dishonesty is seen in the type of manager whose desire is to have peace at any price. Such men often attempt to deal with subordinates who have rendered useful services or who are proving difficult to handle by making rash promises of later promotion which they have not the faintest intention of carrying out. This is, it would seem, one of the commonest ways of 'shutting people up', and many so-called agitators and trouble-makers are men who have been dealt with in this way. Paradoxically, it appears that this attitude may be partly due to the modern emphasis on 'good personnel relations' within the factory; for, whereas the old-fashioned manager could afford to tell the truth (often in a rather harsh and blunt manner), the modern manager tends to adopt a more Machiavellian approach. When confronted by a dispute between two of his subordinates, for example, he will not see them together but will rather talk to them separately. To Mr A. he will say, 'Ah yes, Mr A., you needn't worry any further – I have spoken to Mr B., and, of course, we realize that he is at fault – but you know as well as I do what Mr B. is like'. To Mr B. he will tell the same story, and so, although nothing has been settled, peace has been maintained and the manager need no longer look anxiously towards *his* superior who might have disagreed with him had he made a clear decision or might have been annoyed had the trouble been brought to his notice. Of course, both Mr A. and Mr B. will have created certain impressions in the mind of their manager and sooner or later one or other will be wondering what has happened to his promotion or his salary increases. Many firms, and especially the larger ones, seem to be imbued with this unpleasant attitude of desiring peace at any price, which is (quite wrongly) supposed by some to be a 'psychological approach'. Employees are likely to be regarded rather in terms of whether or not they cause trouble – wittingly or unwittingly – than in terms of the objective situation. The supervisor or the manager feels that he must preserve at all costs the appearance of tranquillity and industry in his department, and any embarrassing question or any suggestion that all is not well will cause him to look up anxiously to his superior and downwards resentfully to the man who has brought the trouble to his notice. Here, once more, the observer can only note the immeasurably superior methods of the army which provides mechanisms whereby those engaged in a dispute are entitled to be confronted with each other and have their complaints settled in a definite and clear-cut manner, and which make it increasingly possible for capable individuals to reach the top through Officers' Selection Boards.

Another source of frustration relating to defective communication which is to be found in many firms is the failure to let the employee know how he stands with respect to his job. Psychologists have shown beyond any shadow of doubt that, when a person is engaged on a piece of work, informing him of his performance as he proceeds will act as an incentive. When K. of R. (knowledge of results) is given following performance without K. of R. the per cent gain was found in one series of experiments to be about 12 to 15 per cent. Douglas H. Fryer concludes that 'knowledge of results increases personal efficiency generally, and in degrees according to the completeness, exactness, and clearness with which the K. of R. is related in intention to the details of the performance.' ('Individual Mental Efficiency', in *Fields of Psychology, Basic and Applied*, edited by Professor J. P. Guildford.) This important incentive is withheld in many factories, and there seems to be a general belief that keeping people in the dark as to their progress may act in some unspecified way as a spur to further effort. The writer has frequently seen employees, especially in office departments, asking for a transfer as they feel that they are getting nowhere in their jobs and are failing to make a success of it, who when their record card is examined are discovered to be regarded as amongst the best workers in their department. Miller and Form tell of a large chain of grocery stores which stimulated each manager to improve his position. He was told that promotion depended on his rating in relation to that of the managers of other stores, but was never told where he really stood. If he did badly, he was informed of this, but he was never allowed to know how 'good' he was. A higher executive told the investigator that 'if a man knows that he is on top, he will not continue to improve. If he doesn't know how he stands he will try to improve continually.' In fact, all that happened was that local managers were discouraged and many went to other organizations where they would be told how they were getting on. Others got together informally to compare their performances. The policy of higher management had simply promoted a conspiracy among their employees.

From the above and the preceding paragraph we may make the general statement that every worker should be entitled to know exactly how he stands in relation to his firm, what his progress has been, and what his prospects are. Should he become involved in a dispute, he should be entitled to have it judged fairly and be told of the decision. If he disagrees with the decision, it should be possible to take the dispute to a higher authority without risk of later victimization.

(C) *Status*

The status system has been fairly fully discussed already, and we have noted that the system should be *clear* so that each worker knows to whom he must look for guidance and formal approval, it must be *fair* so that both in its formal and informal aspects it is accepted by the employees, and, finally, it must not be so autocratic that all sense of importance is denied except to those at the top. Men have a need to run their own lives and tackle their own jobs (within reasonable limits) as seems best to themselves. This desire for self-determination is not in opposition to the equally strong desire to be accepted as a member of the group. What it means is that each individual wants 'freedom to decide on all matters in which he feels competent and guidance or leadership in all situations which make him feel insecure.' (Gordon Rattray Taylor.) For example, in many factories workers will be seen doing a particular job in what is obviously a stupid and wasteful manner, and when asked about this they will shrug their shoulders and say: 'We all know it's stupid, but they won't listen to us.' Although it is impossible to allow everyone to do his own work in his own way, it should be quite feasible to combine technical efficiency with a certain amount of freedom. Time and motion study is often misused when it attempts to eliminate all variety and the personal peculiarities of the operator. William Foote White has suggested that a solution to this state of affairs in which people are too closely overlooked would be to give each supervisor more men or women than he can readily observe. The orthodox principle of administration known as the 'span of control' states that the number of men who can be closely supervised by one individual is strictly limited. In this form, the principle is a truism. But the conclusion usually drawn – that the number supervised should be kept at a minimum – does not follow at all. This conclusion only follows if it is assumed that the employees should be *closely* supervised, and Dr White denies that this is true. He proposes that the ratio of supervised to supervisor should be high enough to give each individual a certain amount of freedom to tackle his work in his own way. The worker may then make mistakes, but he will develop a higher sense of responsibility and a greater satisfaction at having mastered the job. It is often forgotten by managements who complain that their employees have no sense of responsibility that it is impossible to show responsibility unless one has already been given it. There are many senior executives who cannot believe that any of their subordinates are capable of managing their own departments or doing their own jobs and completely fail to see that if their belief is true the fault lies with their own incompetence in choosing or training the wrong men. If, on the other hand, their belief is mistaken they are simply making nuisances of themselves when they make a practice of interfering at all levels of the organization. The senior executive who believes that he is indispensable is ignoring the obvious fact that a firm of any size cannot, or should not, be regarded as a one-man business – it is an organization which should be largely independent of the personality of any one individual. Subordinates should be selected because they are competent within their own field, and, once chosen, they should be left alone and held responsible for their own departments. Furthermore, the status and function of each individual and his place in the line organization should be clearly delineated and not left vague and indefinite as is so often the case. A refusal to inform employees as to their duties and the exact scope of their authority is sometimes a deliberate policy on the part of power-loving executives, since they are thereby enabled to take credit to themselves when things go well and put the blame on their subordinates when they go badly. Since nobody is quite clear as to who is responsible for what, this rather unpleasant trick is made so much the easier. While executives of this type really believe themselves to be indispensable, there are other unfortunates in subordinate positions who, realizing that they are not indispensable, are terrified lest they should be found out. The industrial medical officer knows all too well the junior manager who works himself into a state of collapse and is desperately afraid lest, should he take a holiday, some senior official might discover that the department works equally well without him. There is an all-pervading sense of insecurity in some firms which leads to such forms of behaviour as this, often combined with childish self-advertising, taking credit for the good work done by others, putting blame on someone else when things go wrong, and pretending to work hard all the time even when there is nothing to do. Many junior managers realizing that appearances are all stay late at 'work' and come into the factory at all hours of the day or night, not because the job necessitates this but because it must appear to do so. From the above we may make the second generalization that all firms should see to it that authority is delegated so that no one person becomes indispensable, that each individual's sphere of responsibility should be made clearly known, and that within that sphere he should not be interfered with without adequate cause. The individual should be able to feel secure that, provided he does his job reasonably well, his position is safe and he will be free to use his own judgement as to how the job may best be done. Time spent at work should ordinarily be limited to reasonable hours (for both managers and workers), and it should not be necessary to use deception in order to get on.

(D) *The System of Rewards and Punishments*

This is one of the most important factors in determining good human relations within the factory. Like all the other systems we have dealt with, the system of rewards and punishments must not only be fair – it must be recognized as such. It should be capable of being clearly understood; for example, it is a mistake to introduce systems of paying employees which are so elaborate that only a financial genius is capable of comprehending all their details. Nor should they work in such a way as to induce conflict by rivalry between individual workers at the expense of group co-operation. (Competition is a very valuable thing, but those who advocate it often fail to see that there is all the difference in the world between competition within the framework of the group – as in a football team – and the ruthless all-out struggle for purely selfish ends which was part of the ideology of the paleotechnic period.) Finally, the system should not emphasize purely economic rewards at the expense of the desire of the workers for self-respect and social recognition; no amount of money will make up for the failure to treat people as human beings.

One of the most neglected incentives in industry is the need of the individual for approval, both from his equals and from those in authority over him. Morton, in his *Introduction to Foremanship*, gives it as his opinion that failure to give praise when praise is due is one of the outstanding drawbacks in British industry, and Gordon Rattray Taylor notes that, at a foremen's meeting, it was discovered that eighteen foremen had reprimanded, and only two praised, someone in the course of a day. A large number of experimental studies have been made on the differential effects of praise and reprimand on the work of people engaged on various tasks, both in respect of quality and quantity. In all cases it has been shown that praise is many times more effective in improving results than reprimand. Thus, in one series of experiments, praise led to improvement in 87.5 per cent of instances, while public reprimand caused improvement in 11.9 per cent of instances and poorer results in 10.7 per cent. In general, it has been found that there is only one form of disapproval which does slightly more good than harm, and that is private reprimand. All other methods motivate people to do worse and lead to worse results in proportion as they injure the individual's self-esteem. Reprimand, ridicule, and sarcasm injure self-esteem in increasing degree and produce bad results in that order. When done in public, the results are correspondingly worse. Another obvious drawback about disapproval is that it not only wounds but tells people what they should *not* do rather than what they should.

Punishment is what psychologists describe as a negative incentive. That is to say, whilst a positive incentive may be said to draw a man in the desired direction, a negative incentive pushes him away from the wrong direction. The significant difference is that, whereas reward clearly guides a person to the desired behaviour, punishment never exerts complete control. As Maier says, it invariably leaves open other possibilities and its action is rather like that of a man who tries to control a toy clockwork car by pushing it away from all directions except one. If, in a factory workshop, a supervisor offers positive incentives to his men, they are likely (if the incentives are adequate) to do the work required of them willingly. But if he threatens or abuses them, they may stop loafing (or whatever specific form the undesirable behaviour has taken), and instead damage equipment, pretend to be busy, or steal supplies. In other words, it is possible by offering suitable rewards to make a person *want* to do something, but no amount of punishment will make him do it other than unwillingly. Also, punishment and threats lead to resentment which may take a long time to die down and even one resentful person in a department where morale is rather low may do a great deal to destroy discipline. 'It is quite characteristic', writes Maier, 'that once punishment and restriction of freedom are begun, the need for extending them increases and the situation gets worse rather than better.'

(E) *The Organizational Charter*

This term is used by Bakke to refer to the picture that employees have of the firm as a whole. The importance of acquainting employees with some sort of outline of their firm (what it does, how the individual's job fits into the whole, how the firm fits into the national economy) has already been discussed, and little more need be said. Pearl Jephcott who worked as a factory hand in a British factory described her impressions in a most interesting article in the *New Statesman and Nation* of 11 September 1948. Hours and pay were good, and the surroundings light, airy, and gaily painted. 'We have all the standard facilities – a first-rate canteen; nurses; hot water; music while you work; pension schemes. We see notices about cricket and tennis, but the only voluntary activity which has touched my mate or me was the Derby sweep.' Miss Jephcott continues: 'Here are my mate and I, grown women, with the firm for three months, and we know less of the how and why than any visitor who gapes round of an afternoon. We know nothing of its history, war record, personalities, triumphs – the human story which, to quote our magazines, would touch our little womanly hearts. Profits, losses, experiments, difficulties – where the raw materials come from, where our two thousand boxes each day go off to – who knows? And, of course, we know nothing whatever of our firm's part in the production drive. Are we hitting the target? Have we got a target?

'We shouldn't care if we did know? My hunch is that such an assumption underestimates our goodwill and our wits. If that's how management assesses us, I'd say it's too witless itself to realize what social and economic reforms, plus a couple of wars, have done to raise the level of the traditional female factory hand. I've another hunch, that we women are incurably altruistic. We've a passion to be useful – to a person. And some of us would extend this feminine vice from our private life to our job if we realized that anyone's well-being depended on us in the national economic crisis or even in (this) unintelligible concern.'

Surely it is time that managements came to realize that hiring men and women to work in complete ignorance of what they are doing, why they are doing it, and for whom they are doing it, is a preposterous anachronism, and that, although people may be induced to *join* a firm by promises of high wages, good working conditions, pension schemes, and all the usual paraphernalia of 'welfare', they will only *stay* with the firm when it is able to satisfy their needs as human beings.

8

LEADERS AND LEADERSHIP

IT has already been made clear that it is meaningless to talk of 'leadership' as if it were a psychological trait, something within the individual, which some people have and others do not or have in only a negligible degree. The word makes sense only when we specify to what end and in what circumstances the leader will be expected to act. Yet most books on industrial psychology will be found to give longer or shorter lists of leadership qualities which tell us, for example, that the leader must have intelligence and good judgement, insight and imagination, ability to accept responsibility, a sense of humour, a well-balanced personality, and a sense of justice. The foregoing list is that provided by Dr May Smith, who apparently is concerned with the personality of the leader as a more or less isolated individual. Puckey, on the other hand, supplies us with a list which has the advantage that it takes into consideration the relationship between the leader and those who are led. He includes such qualities as power to co-ordinate, power to express the common aim, impartiality, power to delegate, power to reflect the progress of the group, and so on. Tredgold justly remarks in his *Human Relations in Modern Industry*, that 'certain of these qualities did not exist in some of the most successful, or temporarily successful leaders in history', and that 'the longer and more comprehensive the list of qualities, the more obvious it must be that their possessor would be of no use as a junior leader in industry, for he would inevitably be in demand elsewhere as a Prime Minister, or maybe as an archangel.' When we consider such men as Hitler, Napoleon, the Wesleys, John Knox, and Oliver Cromwell, or such women as Mary Baker Eddy, Queen Elizabeth, and Mrs Pankhurst, it becomes absurd to say that a leader should be well-balanced, possess a sense of humour, or a sense of justice. Some of the most successful leaders in history have been neurotic,

219

insane, epileptic, humourless, narrow-minded, unjust, and authoritarian; there have been religious leaders with a pathological sense of guilt, political leaders with delusions of omnipotence, and military dictators with delusions of persecution. If the objection is made that we are concerned with industry and not with religion, politics, or military affairs, it is easy to show that the great 'captains of industry' have been equally lacking in the qualities recommended by the psychologists: such men as Hearst, Ford, Carnegie, and Morgan were by no means paragons either of virtue or normality. Looking at the problem historically, we have good reasons for supposing that mental abnormality is no drawback in a leader and, indeed, may be an advantage, so long as he is insane in the appropriate direction. Hitler with his paranoia and Hearst and Ford with their obsessional neuroses were successful precisely because they had these defects and the defects happened to be in some sense appropriate to the existing situation.

Investigations into the problems of leadership have followed three general types of procedure. Firstly, the traits of those who have been acknowledged as great leaders either in the past or the present have been analysed in order to discover what it is that they have in common. Secondly, experimental groups have been formed, asked to nominate members for the position of leadership, and the nominees have then been studied as in the first case. Thirdly, it is to be feared that a great many lists of leadership qualities are purely subjective creations which represent nothing but the writer's concept of what constitutes 'The Great Leader'.

One of the most comprehensive surveys of the literature on leadership is that of W. Jenkins who in his 'Review of Leadership Studies with Particular Reference to Military Problems' (*Psych. Bull.* 44: 1947) summarizes the whole field over a period of thirty years. The conclusions he comes to are that:

(1) Leadership is specific to the particular situation under investigation. Who becomes the leader of a given group engaging in a particular activity and what the leadership characteristics are in the given cases are a function of the specific situation including the measuring instruments employed. Related to this conclusion is the general finding of wide variations in the

characters of leaders who become leaders in similar situations, and even greater divergence in leadership behaviour in different situations.

(2) In practically every study leaders showed some superiority over the members of their group in at least one of a wide variety of abilities. The only common factor appeared to be that leaders in a particular field need and tend to possess superior technical competence or knowledge in that area. La Piere in his *Collective Behaviour* comes to similar conclusions. In a study of different types of group: rebellious, conversational, rioting, revelling, and so on, he shows clearly that what makes for good leadership in one situation may actually militate against it in another.

There are many classifications of leadership, for example those of W. M. Conway (the crowd-compeller, the crowd-exponent, and the crowd-representative), F. C. Bartlett (the institutional, the dominant, and the persuasive), and A. B. Wolfe (the radical, the conservative, and the scientific). But these seem to be of little help when we are considering industrial leadership. It is essential, however, to distinguish between what Kimball Young calls 'leadership' and what he describes as 'headship'. The former is that form of dominance which is based on a compelling personality, the acceptance of the group, or special knowledge in a given situation. It is essentially informal in nature and is related to the needs of the group at a particular place or time. The latter is a word referring to formal power which is culturally transmitted. A king, a lord, or a tribal chief each possess power which is relatively independent of their characteristics as individuals – a king is a king and his power stems from the acceptance of the principle of kingship by the society over which he rules. As was noted in the chapter on formal organization, it is an accepted belief that the power of management is of this nature, it is presumed to be institutional in nature and need not be related to personalities. We obey the chairman of the company because he is the chairman, the supervisor because he is supervisor, and nothing more need be said. But we have seen that, whether or not in the legalistic sense this supposition is valid, it is clear that management can no longer be regarded as a purely formal hierarchy of headship. We are concerned with good or bad leadership which produces good or bad results both in terms of industrial efficiency and in terms of human happiness. 'Measured financially, reduced output, high labour turnover, and high sickness absence are uneconomic; measured in terms of human unhappiness, the person in authority who is not suited as a human being to his work is a tragedy.' (Dr May Smith, *An Introduction to Industrial Psychology*.)

When we look at the problem from this point of view, it is seen in a totally different light, and the leadership studies which have already been discussed will be noted to have the following defects:

(a) They often fail to distinguish between 'leadership' and 'headship' (i.e. between leaders who have been freely chosen by the group and those who lead by virtue of formal power).

(b) They tend to assess the leader in terms of material achievement – production of goods or wealth in the case of industry, military conquest in the case of the general or dictator, and party power in the case of the politician. What influence they have had, for better or worse, on the physical and psychological well-being of their followers is often ignored.

(c) They fail to note that, even when the leader is genuinely elected or put into power by the group, this does not necessarily mean that he is, in any objective sense, the man who is best suited to the circumstances. He is certainly the man who most closely reflects the feelings of the group, but it has to be recognized that *a sick group will inevitably select a sick leader*. For example, the sick society of post-war Germany put into power the sick man Hitler, who, while he genuinely represented popular feeling, led the society to its downfall, and the aggressively sick industrial group puts an agitator into power who, likewise, will not be able to solve its problems. So, although psychologically it is true to say that a group always selects the leader who seems best fitted to deal with the problems of the moment, the man whose personality is an epitome of the group attitudes of the moment, it is entirely wrong to conclude that this man is always the one who is objectively the best choice. Since the leader reflects the attitudes of the group in this way, only the healthy group can select the best type of leader in a given situation.

The leadership studies of the sociologists are, in the main, quite valid when we are considering what sort of people have *in fact* been selected as leaders by various groups in different circumstances, but they do not help us to decide what sort of person would be *in the best interests of the group* in the situations found most commonly in industry. Nor do the lists of traits supplied by the psychologists prove much more helpful. Qualities such as 'a sense of justice', 'a sense of humour', and 'ability to accept responsibility' are extremely complex and are not single traits which a person either has or has not, any more than 'laziness', 'shyness', and 'cowardice' are simple traits which belong to a given individual and appear in all the situations in which he acts. It is, of course, self-evident that the leader of a healthy group must be reasonably intelligent, reasonably well-balanced, and must not have the sort of rigid, self-centred personality which would make him insensitive to the feelings of the group. He must, in other words, be capable not only of *giving out* orders and instructions but also of *taking in* messages from his environment which will influence the orders and instructions that he gives. Low intelligence, emotional prejudices, and a self-centred outlook make a man unfit to be the democratic leader of a healthy group because they are likely to distort incoming messages from his environment and adversely influence his ability to control it. Mr Puckey, whose list of leadership qualities includes such qualities as the power to co-ordinate, the power to express the common aim, the power to reflect the progress of the group, and so on, has understood this, yet these qualities are not to be found within the leader but in the total situation of the leader-in-the-group. Such power as Mr Puckey describes are not 'in' any man, although he may have such basic traits as intelligence, a well-balanced personality, and emotional sensitivity to the feelings of others which will enable him (other things being equal) to bring them about in the situation of group-interaction. Provided that a man possesses these essential basic traits, it is likely that he may be instructed in the technique of bringing about group co-operation.

In order to make this thesis clearer, we may take an analogy from the sphere of technology. The earliest types of machine were, for the most part, of such a nature that, once started, they went on carrying out certain actions with mechanical precision until the man controlling them stopped the engine or until they ran out of fuel. Left to themselves, they would grind on whether they were being fed with work or not. But to an increasing degree the modern machine is self-regulating and its work is controlled by such devices as the photo-electric cell which regulates the machine by passing on to the controls messages from the environment. As a very simple example, the ordinary electric heater when turned on will go on giving out exactly the same amount of heat regardless of the temperature of the room. At most times this may be quite satisfactory, but in very cold weather its heat may not be enough and in very hot weather it may be too great. The most modern heating system, however, is controlled by a thermostat, so that in very cold weather the system regulates itself to give out more heat, and in warm weather it gives out less. Whatever the weather, the temperature of the room will remain reasonably constant because the system is controlled by messages from the outer environment. The inefficient leader is like the old-fashioned machine. His personality is rigid and fixed, he receives no messages from the environment, and his leadership is only effectual when the emotional climate of the group happens to coincide with his own peculiarities. Hitler, for example, or the industrial agitator could only make effective leaders when they were in charge of suspicious or resentful groups of people; in any other situation they are seen as pathetic misfits or dangerous lunatics. Such men may be intelligent, but they are men of emotionally prejudiced minds with rigid personalities and fixed ideas. On the other hand, the effective leader is like the thermostatically-controlled heating system. He is receptive and his power is under the control of the incoming messages which inform him of the changing emotional climates of his group. This does not mean to imply that his role is purely passive, or that he is a chameleon who changes his opinions with every swing of emotional climate. On the contrary, while being receptive to such swings, he will endeavour to act like a human thermostat in keeping the climate constant at a healthy level. Nor does it mean that he is capable of handling all possible situations.

He is not a superman. But he will certainly be able to deal with a much wider range of situations than the prejudiced man with fixed ideas. In short, his function is to keep the emotional climate constant through many changing situations, to keep the situations which seem to demand the dictator or the agitator from arising.

Two statements on the nature of leadership may clarify these points. The first is by C. I. Barnard, a leading authority on management, from an essay on 'The Nature of Leadership' in the book *Human Factors in Management*, edited by S. D. Hoslett. Dr Barnard writes that the good leader in industry may sometimes give the impression that he is 'a rather stupid fellow, an arbitrary functionary, a mere channel of communication, and a filcher of ideas. In a measure this is correct. He has to be stupid enough to listen a great deal, he certainly must arbitrate to maintain order and he has to be at times a mere centre of communication. If he used only his own ideas he would be somewhat like a one-man orchestra, rather than a good conductor, who is a very high type of leader.' The difficulty, says Barnard, is to find people who have these qualities, who are 'properly' stupid, effective channels of communication, and capable of stealing the right ideas. The second statement consists of two quotations from the *Tao-Te-King*, the Taoist scripture of China which dates from about five or six hundred years before Christ:

'The best soldier is not soldierly;
The best fighter is not ferocious;
The best conqueror does not take part in war;
The best employer of men keeps himself below them.
This is called the virtue of not contending;
This is called the ability of using men.'

'The great rulers – the people do not notice their existence;
The lesser ones – they attach to and praise them;
The still lesser ones – they fear them;
The still lesser ones – they despise them.'

The leader who is, in effect, a one-man orchestra is what we shall describe as an *autocrat*. The autocratic ruler shows the following characteristics: he gives orders which he insists shall be obeyed, he determines policies for the group without consulting them, he gives no detailed information about future plans but simply tells the group what immediate steps they must take, he gives personal praise or criticism to each member on his own initiative, and remains aloof from the group for the greater part of the time. In other words, like the old-fashioned heating system, he gives out energy without regard for the emotional climate which surrounds him. Contrasted with this type of leader is the *democrat* who gives orders only after consulting the group, sees to it that policies are worked out in group discussion and with the acceptance of the group, never asks people to do things without sketching out the long-term plans on which they are working, makes it clear that praise or blame is a matter for the group, and participates in the group as a member. Of a third type of leader, the *laissez-faire* type, little need be said, except that he does not lead, leaves the group entirely to itself, and does not participate. These types may be sub-divided, and anyone who is at all acquainted with industry will be able to name examples of each of the following types of leader in the various factories he has had occasion to visit:

A. *Autocratic leaders*
   (1) Strict autocrat
   (2) Benevolent autocrat
   (3) Incompetent autocrat
B. *Democratic leaders*
   (1) Genuine democrat
   (2) Pseudo-democrat
C. *Laissez-faire leaders*

These terms are largely self-explanatory. The strict autocrat is stern, strict but just according to his principles. He does not delegate authority, and his factory is a one-man show. Although not necessarily unkind in himself, he acts on the principle that 'business is business', and is fond of such phrases as 'time is money', 'if a man shall not work, neither shall he eat', 'what they want is more money', 'a little dose of unemployment is what we need', and so on. He usually has Conservative leanings, is a (nominal) member of some Church – probably the Church of England, a violent patriot, an upholder of the master-and-man theory, strongly anti-socialist or -communist, and, possibly, anti-feminist and anti-semitic in a mild sort of way. He can be quite 'decent' to his men, provided that they 'know their place', and even generous towards members of the rapidly dying-out species known as 'faithful servants of the firm'. The benevolent autocrat resembles the foregoing in many respects, but is afflicted by a nonconformist conscience. He is probably a Presbyterian, a Methodist, or a Quaker, and is burdened by the thought that he has a moral responsibility towards his employees in addition to seeing that they turn out the goods. He wants to do people good – not in terms of what they want, but rather in terms of what he thinks they should have. No improvements in the material sense are too good or too expensive for his employees, but they have to take what they get, and like it. If he is strongly religious, he may take a considerable interest in the beliefs and even the morals of his employees – an interest which is not always appreciated. Whilst these two types, whatever their faults, are logical and consistent in their outlook, the incompetent autocrat corresponds to what Dr May Smith describes as the 'baby' in management. The 'baby' has plenty of energy, but is domineering and erratic. His praise and blame depend entirely on his own feelings of the moment. He wishes to be powerful, but is desperately insecure. 'Hence he tends to promote, in the absence of effective safeguards, weak rather than strong people, and then complains fretfully that nobody can take any responsibility. He also believes in the all-powerfulness of his wishes, so that when he gives an order he fails to envisage the means that often demand much work and time, with the result that he harasses his subordinates with fractious and querulous inquiries as to whether the work is done yet.' Unlike the other types of autocrat, who are usually honest according to their own lights, the incompetent autocrat is completely unscrupulous, and lies, bribes, and bullies or takes any measures which he feels will help him to attain his goal.

The genuine democrat has already been described. He is the conductor of an orchestra rather than a one-man band, and he realizes that his job is to co-ordinate the willing work of his employees. He realizes, too, that a firm should be something beyond individual personalities, and that it is the sign of good leadership that things will go quite smoothly when he is temporarily absent. His employees know what they are doing and why, and they do not have to pretend in order to get on. Authority is delegated all down the line, and all levels of management feel sufficiently secure to consider the well-being of their subordinates instead of constantly looking up the line to make sure that they are being approved. The pseudo-democrat may aspire to be this sort of man, but he is too insecure to make a success of it, and ends up by being not very different from the 'baby' autocrat. The only difference is that, in his more penitent, sentimental, or convivial moments, he tends to adopt an attitude to his subordinates which says: 'We're all boys together,' or, if he is an American, 'We're just one big happy family.'

The *laissez-faire* leader is represented by the chairman of the board who does not manage, but leaves all responsibility and most of the work to his subordinates. Probably a large part of his day is spent in being hospitable to visitors and dispensing drinks – he is, in fact, a sort of host on behalf of the firm (unless the firm is a very small one, this may be the best sort of chairman to have, especially if, by his personality, he acts as a sort of figure-head who is ornamental without being a nuisance). But, at the lower levels, where leaders have to be more than mere figure-heads, the *laissez-faire* leader is less successful. He may be a man who has been given his position on grounds of technical knowledge, and who is quite incapable of assuming any sort of authority or control over his subordinates or of getting them to co-operate. So they just muddle on, virtually leaderless.

These various types of leader exist, with minor differences, at all levels of management. The strict autocrat is the ruthless foreman whose sole concern is keeping his job and seeing that his men produce the goods. The benevolent autocrat may be the decent sergeant-major type of foreman who is known to be 'all right' when the men do their job, but 'gives them hell' when they do not. So far as industry is concerned, it has long been the practice to measure the efficiency of leadership in a group in terms of its productivity, and, as we have seen, such a criterion gives some indication not only of the technical efficiency of the group but also of its mental well-being or morale. Of recent years, however, it has become increasingly possible to measure the effects of good or bad leadership or good or bad methods of leading in purely human terms. In other words, it has become possible accurately to measure the efficiency of leadership by observing its effects on those who are led. Some of these effects were demonstrated by Lewin, Lippit, and White of the University of Iowa in a series of experiments designed to find out what effect, if any, was produced on group members by various types of social structure. Schoolboys of about ten years old were asked to volunteer to attend an after-school club at which they would be able to carry out various handicrafts such as model-making, carving, designing toy aeroplanes, and so on. They were divided up into groups, some of which were autocratic, some democratic, and some *laissez-faire*. These groups were in charge of adults, who, so to speak, created the atmosphere desired. In the democratic groups, the leader gathered the children together and discussed with them what should be done. Various suggestions were given to the boys, and the leader offered to give them any further information they desired, but the final decision was always left to them. The boys decided what they would do, worked out a complete plan, and arranged which members should work together. The leader throughout acted as a member of the group. The autocratic leaders imposed the decisions made in the democratic groups on their own autocratic ones, so that both groups were doing the same work, the first from choice and by general agreement, the second by orders from above. The autocratic leader told the boys what they were to do, revealing only one step of the operation at a time, and he assigned boys to work together regardless of their own preferences. Apart from directing them, he remained aloof from the group and was friendly but impersonal. Unlike the democratic leader, he gave no reasons for praise or blame. Finally, the *laissez-faire* groups were allowed to do just as they pleased. The boys were supplied with material for their model-making and were told that they could ask if they wished any information. The leader offered no help, did not participate unless asked to do so, and neither praised nor blamed anyone. He was, in fact, rarely asked for information and still more rarely to participate.

Thus, while in the democratic groups the leader acted as a catalyst which speeded up the natural processes of the group and helped it to attain the structure which was the most suitable one in the circumstances, the autocratic leader imposed a structure on the group which reflected his own wishes rather than those of the members, and the *laissez-faire* leader was not a leader at all. As will be noted, the methods of the autocratic leader closely approximated to those generally used in industry: the director devised the plan without consulting the group; he enforced it on them without even revealing what the whole plan was; he ordered them what to do at each step (you're not paid to think – do what you're damn well told); and, finally, he arranged the individuals without regard for what they preferred to do or with whom they preferred to work. The results of this arrangement were equally typical of what is frequently seen in industrial concerns. It was found that autocratic leadership produced two different types of behaviour within the groups: in some instances there was a marked increase of aggressiveness (towards the leader, other members, and even inanimate objects), while in other cases the general response was apathy.

The groups which became aggressive were resentful of their leader because he restrained them, but they were also afraid of him and showed their resentment by means of indirect forms of aggression. They would pretend that they had not heard when they were spoken to, they would break rules 'by mistake', leave before time was up, and damage materials. Once they threatened to go on strike and frequently asked their school-teacher to intervene. When the teacher refused to intervene and suggested that they go to the leader directly, the proposed strike broke up. A significant feature of these groups was that the boys were not only aggressive towards their leader, but were equally aggressive towards other members. Group members disparaged each other's work ('Your model is no good, mine is much better'), refused to co-operate, and on one occasion the whole group picked on a single boy who was treated in such a hostile manner that he left the group on a medical excuse. ('The doctor says that my eyes are so bad that I must play outdoors in the open air instead of coming to club meetings'). This boy was clearly a scapegoat, who, by the process of displacement, was attacked in place of the leader. When at the end of a meeting the members were told that they could keep the models they had made, many of the boys proceeded to destroy the models on which they had been working for many weeks. The apathetic group under an auto-cratic leader were just as resentful as the other, and the members during interviews disclosed the same dislikes and hatreds. But they did not voice them either openly against the leader or dis-place them against scapegoats or other objects. The boys were tense, dull, submissive, and apathetic; they did not smile, joke, or play freely together. But, when the leader left the room, they dropped their work, ran about, shouted, and showed all the signs of released tension. The analogy between the behaviour of these groups and the behaviour of similar groups in industry is quite striking: the negativism, the destructiveness, the scapegoating, the making mistakes intentionally, the threat of stoppages and the sabotage, are all typical.

The *laissez-faire* groups were chaotic. The members showed a great deal of aggressiveness, but without the tension which was manifest in the authoritarian groups. Practically no work was done, and they were completely uncontrolled whether or not the leader was present.

In contrast, the boys in the democratic groups behaved entirely differently. They thought highly of their leader who was des-cribed as 'a good sort who works along with us and thinks about things just as we do'; it was said that 'he never tried to be boss, but we always had plenty to do'. They looked forward to the meetings and worked well together, proving more constructive than any of the other groups. The work was always described as 'our models', and they referred to 'our' group and what 'we' do. The work of the more skilful members was looked on with admiration rather than jealousy as was the case in the other groups since the skilful workers were considered to be a group asset. Criticism of each other's work was objective and fair, and when, at the end of the session, they were told that they might keep the models they had made, many presented them to their leader. When the leader left the room, work went on just as before. The actual work was better done, both in quality and quantity, than that of any of the other groups. As a control experiment, the group members were changed about; those who had been in an autocratic group being placed in a democratic or *laissez-faire* group and vice versa. But the results proved to be quite independent of personalities. Each group produced behaviour which was dependent on its structure rather than on who was in it, or who was its leader.

These experiments, which have been repeated many times with the same results, seem to show:

(1) The superiority of democratic control (i.e., democratic in the sense used here, which is not necessarily related to the behaviour of any of the political groups which describe themselves as being 'democratic').

(2) That, while discipline is always necessary, there is a great deal of difference between the self-imposed discipline of the 'we' group and the externally-imposed discipline of the autocratic group.

(3) That the analogy between the behaviour of members of an experimental autocratic group and the behaviour complained of by managements in many industrial groups is very close.

(4) That democratic methods of control can be taught to any well-balanced, intelligent individual who does not suffer from any of the defects already mentioned (i.e., low intelligence, self-centred personality, or emotional prejudice).

Of course, as Professor W. J. H. Sprott points out in his *Social Psychology*, it has to be remembered that the general background of the children in these experiments was the American way of life. 'Whether the results would have been the same with children brought up under different cultural conditions is a matter of doubt. Furthermore some of the boys preferred the autocratic to the democratic order. This was particularly the case of the son of an army officer who placed a high value upon strict discipline. We are reminded of Peak's study of Nazi membership in the course of which he observes: "Persons reared in the authoritative family, which is common in Germany, typically find greatest security and satisfaction where they are dominated by superior authority on the one hand and where they can, on the other, lord it over someone else of lower status."' This is a perfectly valid criticism, but on the other hand it has to be remembered that, like the Americans, we in fact live in a democracy and therefore people in this country are likely to respond to democratic methods. Secondly, that democracy in industry is not being recommended for abstract reasons but rather because certain changes which we have already discussed seem to make it necessary. Finally, it may be observed that a democratic group is, in at least one respect, superior to an authoritarian one since it is able to pool the information and wisdom of all its members rather than rely on those of one.

In 1941, Sidney Hillman of the United States Division of Labour asked the National Research Council's Committee on Work in Industry to devise methods of improving supervision at the work level. The result was the Training Within Industry scheme, or T.W.I., which has been utilized both in America and Britain to provide practice in dealing with human relations in industry. The ten-hour training course called 'Job Relations Training' taught supervisors that 'good supervision means that the supervisor gets the people in his department to do *what* he wants done, *when* it should be done, and the *way* he wants it done, because they want to do it.' As an indication of the approach recommended, the following instructions from the *Job Relations Manual* will show what has been taught to supervisors and others in many thousands of factories: 'a supervisor gets results through people'; 'people must be treated as individuals'; 'let each worker know how he is getting along'; 'give credit when due'; 'tell people in advance about changes that will affect them'; 'make best use of each person's ability'. It will be noted that T.W.I. emphasizes control by co-operation, and the same may be said of the more detailed Supervisors' Courses run by Unilever Ltd and many other large concerns.

Lewin has pointed out that, in autocracy, responsibility resides in the leader; in democracy it resides in the group; and in *laissez-faire* situations, it is distributed amongst the members as separate entities. One type of group shades into the other. 'Both democracy and autocracy have lines leading to the *laissez-faire* condition,

233

representing tendencies in the direction of complete freedom or chaos. There may be benevolent despots and paternalists who respect many individual freedoms, and there may be loose democracies which are controlled only in part by group action. Similarly, one may have strict despots and strict democracies. It is also apparent that a democracy may be more disciplined and strict than an autocracy. In the strict democracy, the group *will* dominates, and social pressure forces the individuals in line; whereas in strict autocracies, the leader must exert control and wield the force.' (Maier, *Psychology in Industry*.) It is rather strange that industrial leaders have been, in the main, put out by the very mention of the words 'democracy in industry', whereas army leaders, who are usually pictured as being highly reactionary, have frequently used democratic methods with considerable success. Lord Montgomery, as Commander of the Eighth Army, made it a rule that the plan of campaign should be made known to every soldier in the Army, and it was fully discussed by groups of men at all levels, but the average factory manager would consider such a proposition as completely absurd, utopian, and dangerously revolutionary. Even as early as the 1914–18 war, the British Army provided a brilliant example of democratic control in the manner in which it dealt with the problem of the Labour Battalions in France. A. D. Lindsay (later Lord Lindsay), in an article in the *Economic Journal* for March 1924, describes how men in these battalions were, in general, the dullest and least promising material to be found in the whole Army. They had to do all the 'dirty jobs' such as digging trenches, loading and unloading ammunition, and so on. Initially, their morale was bad. Groups were constantly being broken up, the team spirit was ignored, and the men were simply regarded as tools for carrying out the dull but necessary duties required by the other services. Finally, some steps had to be taken to deal with their poor morale, and the following suggestions of the labour directorate were put into effect:

(1) The men were treated as members of their team. Companies were kept together, and groups were no longer permitted to be broken up indiscriminately.

(2) Records of the work done were kept and displayed, so that efficient companies began to take special pride in their skill and achievements.

(3) Each company was given a definite job, allowed to take its own time over it, and permitted to go back to camp whenever the work was done. Army pay was poor, but in this way the incentive of more leisure was utilized.

(4) Instead of giving detailed orders, the technical services were asked to state simply what they wanted done. The responsibility for the work, and the decision as to how it could most efficiently be done, was left entirely to the labour company.

The result of these new methods was that 'production was increased, and friction between the men and those directing them was removed. Monotonous routine was turned into an opportunity for thought, contrivance, initiative, and experiment. The men found scope for decision on matters they understood and passed from the category of living tools to that of co-operators. Their labour was used economically, and they were relatively happy in the new status of partners in production.' (*Personnel Management, its Scope and Practice*, by C. H. Northcott.)

Compare this reasoned approach with that of the departmental head of a transport department in a large organization, as quoted by Dr May Smith, who insisted on having the vehicles put into the garage in a certain way which the drivers considered made extra work. 'When asked if he had explained to the men why he did so, he replied, "No, why should I?" In that "why should I?" lies the key to the difficulty. That attitude is the cause of endless trouble in industrial and even other relations. In this connexion a letter appeared in *The Times* of Monday, 19 October 1942, about a Tyneside shipyard strike. The writer complained that numbers of the workers were not consulted about an increase in their hours of work, and that they were expected to work under conditions imposed by agreements made without their knowledge or consent.' Nobody who is at all acquainted with industry will suppose that this sort of attitude is unusual. On the contrary, taking all firms into consideration, it is probably more common than the attitude of consultation and co-operation.

There is a great deal of misunderstanding as to the meaning of the term 'democracy in industry', which many people seem to assume carries the implication that the factory is treated like one of the 'free expression' schools where children, it is supposed, do as they please. Of course, there are different degrees of democracy, but its essentials are those already given: the leader does not think that he is a special kind of man, but rather that he is one of the group; he never gives orders without explaining why they are necessary; he discusses problems with the group and treats his men as co-workers rather than instruments; he keeps them informed about future plans, so that they know *what* they are doing and *why* they are doing it; he delegates authority and sees to it that nobody is indispensable; he provides an atmosphere of emotional security in which people can afford to be honest. Democracy does *not* mean that discipline is ignored – on the contrary, as we have noted, discipline may be much more strict in a democratic group than in an autocratic one. It does *not* mean loss of power by the leader – on the contrary, he becomes more powerful since he has the group behind him. It does *not* mean mere majority rule, since (a) 'a skilled leader functions to crystallize the thought and goes beyond the point of obtaining a mere majority opinion' (Maier), and (b) 'it does not deny that some problems must be solved by experts . . . a distinction, therefore, must be made between problems which hinge on differences in attitudes and tastes and problems which require factual knowledge.' (Maier.) But although 'some problems must be solved by experts', it must be remembered that many workers in industry have a much greater knowledge of their job than many people suppose. Gillespie tells how, as an industrial consultant, he found in a certain factory that the men in the tool-room were in the habit of ordering their own material and pricing their own work without supervision. Expecting to find inefficiency and thinking that he might be able to effect substantial savings, he proceeded to fix the prices for them, only to find that their rates were considerably below what he himself would have proposed. Many managers vastly underrate the honesty, helpfulness, and common sense, of their fellow-men, and, admittedly, what one sees of them in the factory is rather depressing; but they forget that, as has been pointed out in Chapter 1, it is the social surroundings of the factory which, in large measure, make them as they are. Outside the factory, they are not irresponsible, lazy, stupid, and destructive – they are ordinary citizens who look after their children, vote for members of parliament, fill in income-tax forms, and, whatever their faults happen to be, members of the most politically adult and literate democracy the world has so far known. If the incidents so frequently reported in the daily papers often make it appear that industrial workers behave in childish and irresponsible ways, it should be realized that, firstly, these incidents have been torn out of their context (nobody has ever gone on strike solely because of the trivial reasons often given), and secondly, that there is no behaviour on the part of workers which is not exactly paralleled by that of management. Workers make a great deal of fuss about status, and so do managers; workers engage in restrictive practices, and so do managers; workers steal, and so do managers when, as often happens, they take home raw materials or goods produced by the firm (they make the practice even worse by doing it openly); workers demand higher wages, managers higher salaries; some workers engage in sabotage, so do some managers; and so on. Finally, it is generally forgotten that, in modern industry, compulsion has to be replaced by co-operation, both because the un-co-operative worker is a danger under modern conditions in which sabotage may do a great deal of damage, and because there is simply no others means of getting people to work. We have a right to ask of the man who rejects the demo-cratic solution: 'All right – but what would you do?' Under full employment people cannot be compelled or bought – they must be asked to co-operate. That this is the case, every supervisor knows all too well. He realizes that, under existing conditions, the orders he gives are lacking any sort of sanction since his employees no longer fear the sack. Virtually, if he uses an authoritarian technique, he is bluffing, and when any worker calls his bluff he is without an answer. The democratic supervisor, on the other hand, has the power of the group behind him, and the threat of expulsion from the group is not bluff. It would make an immense difference to industrial morale throughout the country if even the mildly democratic suggestions of T.W.I. were generally applied. That the leaders of industry should have less enterprise and initiative than those who lead the army is an extraordinary situation, but there are many people who have experienced both and believe that this is so. Co-operation cannot be produced by force, and the factory manager is liable to forget that, while as the representative of formal authority in the factory he may exert some control by reason of his power to appoint or dismiss his employees, the workers by reason of their informal authority have the much greater power of accepting or rejecting co-operation with the formal hierarchy. '*Of the two*,' writes Barnard, '*the informal authority is fundamental and controlling*. It lies in or consists of the willingness and ability of followers to follow. To many who have struggled and worried regarding appointments or dismissals of leaders, and to whom the maintenance of formal authority is the very keystone of co-operation, order, and efficiency, what I say may seem absurd or even subversive. But we have all many times proved it correct. For has not our first question always been in effect "Can he lead and will they follow?" If our answer were "No!" would we not appoint at the peril of our own leadership? And when there has been a failure of followers to follow, writhe as we would, were not our only resources to change the leader or possibly to change the followers?'

The belief in the 'Führer', the 'Great Leader', and other figures admired by those with autocratic tendencies fails to take into account the obvious fact that the most powerful leader who ever lived can only produce from the group which he leads what is already there and what they choose to give. No agitator can produce industrial unrest. 'Unrest may be utilized by a potential leader, but the causes of unrest lie in the frustrations which are already there. No leader can organize a mass of well-adjusted people into an aggressive movement.' (Maier.) Similarly no leader can increase productivity, raise morale, or improve social conditions in the factory without the co-operation of others. The supposition that the leader is someone with a 'powerful personality', a 'magnetic eye', a 'commanding voice', and so on, is a dangerous fallacy. In fact, there are good reasons why self-centred and power-loving individuals should not be placed in positions of responsibility; for the power-loving man is a sick man who seeks to compensate for his own inadequacies by gaining control over others. As Alex Comfort has noted in his book *Authority and Delinquency in the Modern State*, power-loving and delinquency are closely related. 'The chief factor which makes any overt act "delinquent" is the assertion in it of the right of the actor to behave without regard for others. He may do so by burglary or murder, and take the consequences, or he may find a place in the social pattern which licenses him, within certain limits, to make his assertion unchallenged. *The opportunities for this kind of accepted and acceptable delinquency lie almost entirely within the pattern of power.*' It follows that the policy in competitive societies of giving power to those who succeed in pushing themselves to the front can no longer be accepted as a wholly valid means of providing leaders. So far from it being true to say that those who thrust themselves forward for a task are the best fitted to carry it out, the truth is almost the direct opposite. Many years ago Alfred Adler pointed out that people have a strange tendency to compensate for their real or imagined deficiencies by striving to attain superiority in the very field in which they are inferior, and, while in some cases their adjustment may be satisfactory, it is more often the case that such compensatory behaviour will show up the sort of defects one would expect from its origin. For example, the politician, as Ranyard West says in his book in the Pelican series entitled *Psychology and World Order*, is often a man who is trying to live down his own failures of adjustment: 'Political power offers superb platforms to the unconscious play-actor from childhood – to shout defiance at erstwhile school-fellows whose hands are no longer able to reach out and twist his arm, to prove the prizeman in yet one more test, to hurl yet more fiends down to hell before the final reckoning comes, to scoff at still more nannies and greybeards.' We have seen, too, that childhood conflicts and resentments against the father often show in later life as a hatred of all authority, or a hatred of what the father has supported. It is no coincidence that fervent Christians often have atheistic sons, and atheistic fathers Catholic ones. One does not need to be a practising psychologist to note the frequency with which men with homosexual tendencies are motivated (in all sincerity) to become leaders in boys' clubs, doctors with chronic skin diseases to become skin specialists, men with unconscious sadistic attitudes towards women to specialize in gynaecological surgery, chronic neurotics to become psychiatrists, and those with some physical or mental trait which makes them feel inferior to become 'big bosses'. Now compensation for such defects is a healthy thing in itself, but when the inferiority has been deeply felt, the individual is likely to overcompensate. The homosexual is more likely in a boys' club to get into trouble, the unconsciously sadistic surgeon to operate unnecessarily, the neurotic psychiatrist to project his own mental peculiarities on to his patients, and the leader who seeks power because he has a basic sense of inferiority to victimize those whom he has to lead. When, during the war, volunteers were asked for to do dangerous tasks – for example, to become commandos – it was easily seen that only a small minority of those who put themselves forward were genuinely suitable. The rest were a mixed bag of love-sick youths who wanted to show their girls that they had been driven to doing the equivalent of joining the Foreign Legion, sadistic psychopaths, mental defectives, and chronic neurotics. In other words, some were criminals, some histrionic, some stupid, and some pathetically trying to prove that they were not afraid; only a few were responsible men who knew the risks involved and felt that they were worth taking. Yet it is this same method of selection upon which we depend for the most part when seeking leaders in the fields of politics, industry, medicine, and the law. H. von Hentig says of delinquency amongst those whose job it is to enforce the law that 'The police force and the ranks of prison officers attract many aberrant characters because they afford legal channels for pain-inflicting, power-wielding behaviour, and because these very positions confer upon their holders a large degree of immunity; this in turn causes psychopathic dispositions to grow more and more disorganized . . . It is wrong to limit the group (of moral imbeciles) to the criminal. It is often forgotten that many of our legitimate vocations require a lack of emotional sensibility. Prototypes are the executioner, or the officer who applies the lash to a prisoner. Yet these are only the crassest instances, those which cannot be smoothly concealed behind the screen of means justified by the end.' (*The Criminal and His Victim.*)

It is impossible not to see that, in industry, there have been and still are men in positions of power who were quite unfitted to hold authority over others. Certainly they may have been men who 'got things done' and were 'efficient' – but at what cost to the health and happiness (and even lives) of others? The quotation from Drucker's *The Future of Industrial Man* already mentioned more than once is relevant in this connexion: 'In itself functional efficiency is nothing unless we know the answer to the question: efficiency to what purpose and at what price?' Dr May Smith in Chapter 3 of her *Introduction to Industrial Psychology* gives many examples which show that the industrial leader, no matter how efficient he may be in the technical sense, who is inefficient in the sphere of human relations, is a menace to the well-being of the factory, both in the material and the psychological aspects. Such a man may, by his influence, lower production, raise absenteeism and labour turnover, increase neurosis and sickness, lead to frustration, strikes, and aggressiveness. There can be little doubt that the problem of selecting suitable leaders, both in industry and in other fields of society, is one of the most urgent matters facing us today.

The layman is rightly suspicious of any means of selection which is based on the assumption that experts or specialists should carry out selection based on criteria of their own which may be incomprehensible to the non-specialist. He will reasonably ask: 'But who is to select the selectors?' Bad as the older methods may be, they at least may seem to have a sort of rough common sense and justice about them. But the prejudiced chairman of the board is no better than the prejudiced expert. Every man has a natural tendency to suppose that those who most resemble himself are the most superior specimens of the human race, and the 'rough common sense' method of selecting management trainees often results in numbers of men being accepted into the firm who bear a suspicious resemblance to the 'old man' who chose them. The factory comes to have a sort of collective personality from which the visitor who has got no further than the main entrance might accurately forecast the character of the chairman. It was an acute observer of men who wrote in the book of Ecclesiasticus that: 'As the judge of the people is himself, so are his officers: and what manner of man the ruler of a city is, such are they that dwell within.' A method of selection which has none of the drawbacks of the two mentioned is that which was used during the war in the W.O.S.B.s (War Office Selection Boards), and led to strikingly successful results capable of subsequent validation in terms of the later careers of those selected. This method is fully described by Dr Henry Harris in his book *The Group Approach to Leadership-testing* in the preface to which Brigadier A. Torrie has suggested that the method might well be applied to the selection of industrial leaders. This, in fact, has now been done, and the method is in use, not only in the Civil Service, but also in such large privately-run concerns as Unilever Ltd.

It is impossible in the space available here to give any sort of detailed account of the group method of selection. The postulates upon which it is based may be illustrated by the following quotations from Dr Harris' book: 'Leadership is a collective function: collective in the sense that it is the integrated synergized expression of a group's efforts: it can only arise in relation to a group problem or purpose; it is not the sum of individual dominances and contributions, it is their relationship. In so far as a man contributes to the collective leadership function . . . he will realize that the ultimate authority and true sanction for leadership, at every point where it is exercised, resides – not in the individual, however dominant, strong or efficient he may be – but in the "total situation" and in the demands of that situation. It is the situation that creates the imperative, not the individual. To the extent that the individual is aware of that imperative, is able to make others aware of it, is able to make them willing to serve it: to the extent that he is able to release collective capacities and emotional attitudes that may be related fruitfully to the solution of the group's problems: to that extent he is exercising leadership.'

'What seems to emerge is that every man should be capable of some degree of leadership – influencing others towards a satisfying participation in collective effort; and being sensitive to the influence of others – on his own level and in his own field of activity: and one might regard it as a basic sign of mental and social health that he show some degree of effective, happy, and spontaneous leadership on that level.' Since some degree of ability for leadership is a basic sign of mental and social health, it follows that neurosis is a barrier to good leadership or a sign of lack of group effectiveness. 'Leadership then may be regarded as the expression of a man's adequately realized group-effectiveness on his own natural level: neurosis, as the indication and result of an inadequately realized group-effectiveness, of some impediment (be it external, internal or both) in the realization of his potential group-effectiveness, natural leadership, and capacity for zestful living.'

The W.O.S.B.s submitted candidates to various problems and social stresses in an experimental micro-community of about eight members. The group was expected to perform tasks of different types, such as group discussions, physical and outdoor or indoor situations which necessitated some degree of collective planning. No leader was appointed, since the intention was that the group should throw up its own natural leaders. In addition to these communal tasks, the members were thoroughly examined medically (i.e., by a psychiatrist, in order to discover any emotional or intellectual abnormality), and psychologically, by means of psychological tests (both intelligence tests and personality tests, in order to discover the level of intelligence and gain some insight into the character of members). The work of the specialists was not to select suitable leaders – that was done in effect by the group – but rather to give confirmatory evidence of normality or abnormality. When we say that the group selected its leaders, we do not mean to imply that this was done by a show of hands or in any formal sense; the group was kept under observation while the collective tasks were being carried out and it was noted which men were spontaneously followed by the group in the varying situations which it had to face. As Dr Harris puts it: 'From observation of the man's group-effectiveness in several different activities under varying degrees of stress it (the W.O.S.B.) gains a balanced impression of his general group-effectiveness which it checks and co-ordinates with tests of him as an individual either *apart* from the group or in charge of it. Co-ordinating group tests with individual tests is an important technical device in W.O.S.B. By varying in this way the field of activity and the degree of stress in the group task, one may draw conclusions about the man's ability in various fields, his "contact" with people, and the amount of stress he can tolerate without serious deterioration of his effectiveness.' When selecting leaders in other than military fields, the type of task given to the group has, of course, to be altered, but the principle remains the same.*

It is important to remember, however, that suitable candidates as management trainees or those who are already leaders in industry may, provided they have none of the defects already mentioned elsewhere, have their efficiency considerably improved by training in handling men. Many large concerns run courses for managers and supervisors which attempt to give this sort of training. But the mistake is commonly made of supposing that such training may be adequately carried out solely by means of lectures and reading. This is quite incorrect. It is no more possible to train men in adequate leadership technique by lectures and books than it is possible to learn to play golf or to swim in the same way. Alex Bavelas has made this point in an article on 'Morale and the Training of Leaders' in *Civilian Morale*, edited by G. Watson, and Norman Maier writes that: 'Practice under supervision has been found to be highly important in training leaders. A man may not know when he is being sarcastic, unreasonable, or impatient. He may not know when he is talking over a man's head or frightening him . . . By practice and criticism the foreman can learn to detect his own weaknesses and become aware of the way his methods influence his men. In addition he learns to take criticism and advice. Becoming sensitized to the reactions of the members of one's group is one of the most important benefits to be gained from leadership training.' (*Psychology in Industry*.)

* See, however, Dr H. J. Eysenck's *Uses and Abuses of Psychology* (Penguin Books, 1953), Chapter 5, for some criticism of this approach.

9

FRUSTRATION

SOONER or later, every individual is confronted by situations in which his knowledge, innate intelligence, and experience fail to produce the results he desires. When a person is motivated towards a goal and something interferes with his progress towards it, he is said to be frustrated. In such a situation the appropriate type of behaviour is what Maier has described as problem-solving behaviour, in which the habitual modes of response are replaced by new responses of a creative nature which are well-adapted to the solving of the problem with which he is confronted. But when, for one reason or another, the problem cannot be solved and the goal is not attained, a greater or less degree of frustration is likely to result. If the motives are relatively minor ones, the person may simply accept the situation and go on his way. Sometimes he may be satisfied with a substitute, as when he fails to obtain his favourite brand of cigarettes and has to be contented with another brand. But if the motives are strong and the goals are important to him, more or less emotion is aroused, the energy output is increased, and activity is re-directed. What forms this redirected energy may take will be the subject of the present chapter; for, although reactions to frustration are variable and highly personal, there are certain patterns of reaction which are so common that it is important that they should be recognized.

The degree of frustration produced depends on many factors: on the individual's tolerance, his previous history (both immediate and in early life) of frustration, his interpretation of the situation, and the pressure under which he is functioning. It is possible that some individuals are temperamentally more liable to frustration than others, and it is certain that childhood experiences play a considerable part in determining what kind of situation is experienced as frustrating and in influencing the general degree of security felt in later life. For example, a bullying supervisor is likely to be a source of frustration to all the workers in his department, but to the worker who has been bullied by his father in childhood the situation may be felt as intolerable. Recent experiences are also likely to influence the response to a given situation, so that the man who has been severely frustrated at work will tend to 'fly off the handle' when confronted by relatively trivial sources of frustration at home. Above all, people are influenced by the way in which the situation is subjectively experienced, by their attitudes and expectations. The workers who felt angry when they saw two supervisors talking together were influenced by an attitude of suspicion which caused them to interpret what they saw in terms of the supposition that the supervisors were discussing them unfavourably, and the Egyptian peasant who accepts hunger as an everyday experience is often less frustrated at the possibility that he may not be able to get enough bread than is the British worker who finds that he is unable to buy a bicycle or a television set. Maier has also pointed out that we are more likely to be frustrated by interference caused by another person than by interference caused by inanimate objects, since we are liable to experience people as sources of deliberate intent to irritate rather than as impersonal problems. The young child who does not make this distinction is just as likely to be frustrated by his toys as by his mother. Finally, although many frustrations are based upon conflict between the individual and his environment, it is frequently the case that the individual frustrates himself. Conflicting desires within the mind may lead to frustration as readily as desires which conflict with the surrounding environment. Thus self-consciousness may be in conflict with ambition, hate with love of the same person, and the desire to have a restful life at home with the desire to achieve success at work.

There are four major characteristics of frustrated behaviour, each of which may be readily observed and is capable of being experimentally produced in the laboratory. These are, aggression, regression, fixation, and resignation, and they are so important in understanding certain types of behaviour found in industry, and, of course, elsewhere, that it is necessary to consider them in greater detail. Before doing so, however, something must be said about the nature of aggression and frustration, their relationship to each other, and their physiological basis.

Aggression is frequently discussed as if it were a specific desire to be cruel, to inflict pain, or to destroy the object against which it is directed, and certain writers, including Freud, have supposed that such desires are innate in mankind. The implication is that people are 'naturally' cruel and sadistic and that it is only by repression or by the sublimating influence of civilization that these primitive desires may sometimes be controlled. This belief seems to rest on the sort of verbal misunderstanding which is so often at the root of divergent opinions in the social sciences. 'Aggression' in one sense of the word is indeed innate, but it cannot be equated with a tendency to sadism or deliberate cruelty – in its essence aggression is simply the need to do something about painful or unpleasant circumstances either by avoidance or by mastering them. Psychologically speaking, so far from being, as Freud supposed, a drive towards death and destruction, aggression in the primary sense is one aspect of the need to keep alive, since living necessitates both the approach towards sources of satisfaction and the avoidance or overcoming of obstacles to satisfaction. As Gordon Rattray Taylor rightly points out, 'since all man's actions are directed towards modifying the environment, physical or psychical, in the face of various difficulties it follows that they could all strictly be described as aggressive. In other words, aggression is not a specific mode of activity which can, by careful management, be eliminated.' (*Conditions of Happiness.*) What we describe as anger and hatred ('aggression' in the second sense of the word) are the results of frustration of the drive to overcome difficulties with which the individual has been faced; they represent accumulations of stored-up energy which has been blocked in its attempt to find expression. Sadism, which is not, as some people seem to suppose, identical with anger and hatred, is a definitely pathological combination of aggression (in the second sense) and sexuality. Briefly, then, the organism is constantly being driven by the need to maintain itself into situations in which it tends to move towards objects which it regards as desirable or away from what it regards as unpleasant or harmful. When these processes are proving successful, the individual experiences a subjective sensation which is described as satisfaction or relief, and the energies which had previously been mustered to this end are dissipated by his efforts and revert to the normal level. But when barriers to satisfaction or avoidance are present which are difficult to surmount, energy continues to build up in an attempt to overcome the barrier and a subjective feeling of anger or displeasure is experienced. When the situation is felt to be a real threat to the integrity of the individual (mentally or physically), the feelings may be anger mingled with fear and anxiety. In other words, fear, anxiety, and rage are only experienced when the organism's attempts at adjustment fail, or appear to be about to fail, to achieve results.

At the physiological level, the two basic emotional states – the avoiding reactions (fear and rage) and the approach responses (love and desire) – are represented by the two components of the primitive autonomic nervous system which is controlled by a centre in the base of the brain known as the hypothalamus. In the higher vertebrate animals, this part of the nervous system may be observed as a nerve chain with ganglia (i.e., groups or clumps of nerve-cells) at intervals lying on either side of the spinal cord at the back of the abdomen and thorax. One of the main ganglia of this chain, the solar plexus, is familiar by name to the layman. The function of the autonomic system is to prepare the organism for emergencies or to allow it to relax when no emergency exists. It is, in fact, the source of those energies which we have described as being mustered in order to overcome barriers to satisfaction or escape. If we observe an animal or human being in a state of fear or rage, we can note various changes of a physiological nature: the pupils are dilated, the heart beats faster, the blood leaves the skin and internal organs and accumulates in the muscles, the blood pressure is raised, and the stomach and intestines are in a state of muscular spasm. These changes serve the function of preparing the organism to fight back, to master the obstacle, or to run away, and are produced by the so-called sympathetic component of the autonomic nervous system. The pallor, the palpitation, the dilated pupils, and sometimes the diarrhoea or frequency of urination, noted in states of anger or anxiety are the external signs of these changes. The other component, the parasympathetic system, has the opposite effect. Under its influence, the pupils contract, the heart slows down, the blood accumulates in the skin and internal organs, the blood-pressure is lowered, and the stomach and intestines relax. In this case, the external signs are the flushed skin, the slow breathing and pulse-rate, and the general reduction of tension which may be noted following satisfied desire, most obviously following the satisfaction of hunger or sexual desires. The body is being prepared for relaxation. At a later stage, we shall see the significance of these physiological changes.

Rage is one of the most obvious signs of frustration, and Freud was one of the first to demonstrate that the rage following frustrating experiences may be dealt with by the individual in a variety of different ways. Firstly, and perhaps most frequently, it may be directed against the object or person which is experienced as being the source of the frustration. This may lead to various forms of more or less direct attack. The angry worker may strike his supervisor, or, by attacking him in a more disguised form, may impugn his reputation or instigate malicious gossip about him. But situations frequently arise in which this direct attack cannot be made. The source of frustration may be an impersonal one which cannot be attributed readily to any one individual (e.g., in the case of unemployment or the sort of vague dissatisfaction felt in many factories), or the actual source of frustration may be known but also feared (e.g., the tough supervisor, or the boss who holds one's fate in his hands). Under these circumstances, the mechanism known as displacement or 'scapegoating' may be utilized, and the resentment turned against another, and safer, object. The resentful worker may pick a quarrel with his wife, kick the cat, beat his children, or, more constructively, work off his feelings by chopping wood, by cursing and swearing, or engaging in violent exercise or horse-play of an aggressive nature. Often the weaker, less popular, 'queer', or unsociable workers in a department may be 'picked on' (as we saw in the case of the Lewin experiment on group structure) and made to suffer for the sins of an objectionable supervisor or a frustrating factory atmosphere. The frustrated worker may develop into the type of man who has, as we say, a 'chip on his shoulder'. Frustrated groups show an unusual amount of malicious gossip, quarrelling, and destructiveness towards equipment. Possibly the resentment may, in the interests of peace within the group, be directed towards the out-groups. Thus the Germans retained their internal solidarity in the face of frustration by hating the Jews and Bolsheviks, and in the factory frustrations within one shift or department may find expression in the form of irrational hatred of another shift or department which, objectively speaking, has little to do with their frustrations. H. K. Smith in his *Last Train from Berlin* describes how the German people, as their frustrations increased and no other scapegoats were available (the Jews having mostly been imprisoned or murdered, and the 'Bolsheviks' temporarily turned into friends by the Hitler-Stalin pact), became abusive towards each other on the subways. The slightest incident would cause a whole coachful of passengers to take sides and participate in the argument. Unable to attack the sources of their frustrations or the former scapegoats they relieved themselves on substitute objects. Ordinarily, in a world in which frustration is the inevitable lot of most people, it is found that there is an inverse relationship between the amount of aggression within a society and the amount directed outwards beyond its frontiers. When a nation is at peace, resentments arise between managements and employees which, in wartime, are forgotten as they come to be directed against an external enemy. Warfare between states is one of the surest ways of obtaining peace within the national boundaries – hence the good spirit and comradeship in this country during the war when all hatreds could be directed against Germany. But, of course, a much safer way of reducing hatred is by reducing the amount of frustration, as has been done in such small and peaceable communities as the Arapesh. Frustration, then, influences the attitudes of group members so that they may interpret compliments as insults, are continually on the defensive, and tend to be unusually suspicious. When the frustration is of a minor degree or applies to only a few members, the resulting resentment may be fairly constructive and directed more or less rationally against the sources of the grievances. But when it is more severe and affects a larger number of people, it is liable to become generalized, wholly irrational, and directed against quite innocent individuals. The existence of a frustrating atmosphere in a factory may easily be diagnosed by the presence of such symptoms as excessive criticism of management, malicious gossip, the voicing of superficial grievances, damaging of equipment, militant political attitudes, absenteeism, and neurosis. Productivity, of course, is also low. Such symptoms should always be regarded as an indication that something is far wrong and that constructive steps must be taken at once to set it right. Unfortunately, as we have seen elsewhere, the commonest response on the part of management is to become alarmed, attempt to enforce stricter discipline, impose severer penalties, and to vent its spite on both the workers and their unions. This leads to further frustration, more resentment, more destructiveness, and merely aggravates the situation. If carried far enough, the workers may be cowed into submission, and the final result will be a smouldering hatred which is like to poison management-worker relations for a long time to come, or, perhaps, the workers may go on strike.

A final method of dealing with resentment described by Freud is more of a pathological entity, although, perhaps, it might be partially equated with what other psychologists have described as 'resignation' or apathy. This is the process of introjection in which, for various reasons, the hatred fails to find an external outlet and is turned against the individual himself, resulting in self-hatred or depression. Introjection may result from three general situations. Firstly, it may be the case that all external outlets are barred and the individual cannot get rid of his resentment. In effect, he 'stews in his own juice'. Secondly, it may be impossible to attack the source of frustration because it is also loved – a combination of love and hatred, or what the psychiatrist would describe as 'ambivalence', is felt for a single object. Thirdly, in certain individuals, who have been brought up to believe that any form of aggressiveness is wrong, this fear of their own aggression may also lead to introjection with consequent severe depression. The second and third situations are those which lead to abnormal states of depression and often end with the individual committing suicide. They are, except in mild forms, pathological, but it is important for managers to realize the part which industry may play in inducing them in predisposed individuals. The man who has always been regarded as the 'faithful servant' of an authoritarian firm is often one who has been so browbeaten throughout his life that he fears to assert himself (this, of course, is precisely why he is appreciated). But a time may come when the accumulated frustrations of years produce a complete breakdown, which may take the form of psychotic depression, attempted suicide, or a psychosomatic disease such as high blood-pressure. It is one of the ironies of life that these conditions occur almost invariably in the conscientious, hard-working, over-controlled, type of man or woman. Such people, just because they appear to be willing, may easily be driven too far, with serious results. The careful manager should always be on the look-out for signs of approaching break-down in his 'good servants'. It is not healthy to be too 'good'.

The second characteristic of frustrated behaviour is regression. Frustrated people tend to give up constructive attempts at solving their problems and regress to more primitive and childish behaviour. The most extreme examples of this process are to be seen in the neuroses and psychoses which are caused by prolonged frustration, whether intrapsychic or due to external factors, both predisposed to by childhood experiences (in the case of the neuroses), or a combination of childhood experiences and organic factors (in the case of the psychoses). But normal people also show regressive behaviour when they are confronted by a situation to which no solution can be found. The man who fails to start his car and proceeds to kick it is demonstrating the process of regression, and so is the manager or supervisor who indulges in temper tantrums when he is frustrated. Barker, Dembo, and Lewin have demonstrated experimentally that mild frustration in children may lead to a drop in mental age of two years or more. In other words, their play became temporarily less constructive and resembled that of a child two years younger. An increase of aggressiveness also occurred. Similar results were noted in Lewin's experiments on group structure already described. Frustrated people show regression in that they are more suggestible and less critical. They readily believe what they are told – provided, of course, that it fits in with what they wish to believe – and throw reason to the winds. They regard the past with favour and the future with anxiety, longing to return to 'the good old days'. In industry, the main symptoms of regression are lack of emotional control, responsiveness to rumours, inadequate social organization, and blind loyalties towards certain people or organizations. Foolish destructiveness is also a symptom of regression. On the side of management, hypersensitivity, refusal to delegate authority, inability to distinguish between reasonable and unreasonable requests, and stupid generalizations on the subjects of labour or political questions, may also be evidence of regression. The inability to make fine distinctions, without which good management becomes impossible, is a sign of either regression or low intelligence.

A third characteristic of frustrated behaviour is fixation, which may be defined as the compulsion to continue with a type of action which has no adaptive value. The same action is repeated again and again although experience has shown that it can accomplish nothing. One of the effects of frustration is to freeze old and habitual responses and prevent the use of new and more effectual ones. Unlike pure regression, the behaviour of the fixated individual may have all the outward appearance of normal habit, but the real difference lies in its rigidity. Maier has shown that, whereas habits are normally broken when they fail to bring satisfaction or lead to punishment, a fixation actually becomes stronger under such circumstances. (*Frustration – a Study of Behaviour without a Goal*, Norman Maier.) It is, in fact, possible to transform a normal habit into a fixation by too much punishment. This is often seen in children who, when severely punished for some act, may have the compulsion to carry on doing it blindly. Maier concludes that punishment may have two quite different effects on the individual. Either it may have an effect opposite to that of reward and, as such, discourage the repetition of the act, or, by functioning as a frustrating agent, it may lead to fixation and the other symptoms of frustration as well. It follows that punishment is a dangerous tool, since it often has effects which are entirely the opposite of those desired. In industry, common symptoms of fixation are the inability to accept change, the blind and stubborn refusal to accept new facts when experience has shown the old ones to be untenable, and the type of behaviour exemplified by the manager who continues to increase penalties when he sees that they are only making conditions worse. The tendency to go on insisting that money is the most powerful incentive when everyday experience shows the wrongness of such a belief is an example of fixation. Most frustrated behaviour in industry shows a combination of aggressiveness, regression, and fixation: 'To pass along the rumour that a prominent person is insane is aggressive action; to believe it shows suggestibility and lack of critical attitude, indicating regressive tendencies; to persist in the opinion, despite evidence to the contrary, shows fixation.' (*Psychology in Industry*.) An interesting phenomenon which may be related to fixation, and which most psychologists have failed to notice, is what Snygg and Combs have described as 'tunnel vision'. (*Individual Behaviour*.) These two writers note that, under threat, the individual's field of attention tends to shrink and he prepares to defend himself, so that, as we have seen already, he is less rather than more likely to change his views. When, for example, we attack a man's religious or political views, his ability to judge them with an open mind becomes less, his field of vision becomes narrowed, and he holds the beliefs more strongly than before. In a sense, they become fixated.

Finally, in certain circumstances, prolonged frustration may lead to apathy or resignation. As has already been suggested, this mechanism may be partly based on the introjection of aggression, but it seems likely that there is also a quite separate process in which there is a genuine apathy, a 'giving-up' of all attempts at adaptation without any introjection having taken place. 'This general way of handling frustration can be either temporary or permanent; it can mark itself upon the face and posture of the "man with the hoe", or the defeated soul who has no outlet, no escape, and whose only protection against renewed stress is the maintenance of shallowness.' (Gardner Murphy, *Personality –*

a Biosocial Approach.) The most striking examples of apathy and resignation have been noted among the refugees from Nazi Germany (Allport, Bruner, and Jandorf in an essay in Kluckhohn and Murray's *Personality in Nature, Society, and Culture*), and among unemployed workers (P. F. Lazarsfeld and Zawadzki.) Lazarsfeld and Zawadzki in their essay 'The Psychological Consequences of Unemployment' (*Journal of Social Psychology*, 1936, 6), have described the resignation of the unemployed in great detail. In the economically disintegrated Austrian village in which their study was made, they noted that men no longer busied themselves in trying to find work or even in amusing themselves with their hobbies. Like hibernating animals, they merely existed in a state of suspended animation. One carpenter, about thirty years old, married, and on the dole, described how, following dismissal, he was at first furiously resentful, anxious, and depressed. For a time he tried desperately to find work, but, after many fruitless attempts, he finally became indifferent: 'I decided not to go anywhere any more. And for months, lying in the sunshine, I wait quietly for the day when my wife will tell me that she has spent the last money and that the grocer does not want to give us credit. But it lasts very long, and I ask myself how fate will finally decide.' M. Lazarsfeld and P. Eisenberg in an essay, 'The Psychological Effects of Unemployments' (*Psychological Bulletin*, 1938, 35), describe a similar picture. They write that 'the last stage of unemployment consists of a general narrowing of activities as well as of outlook on life. There is also a narrowing of wants and needs. Yet there is a limit beyond which this narrowing cannot go; otherwise a collapse occurs.'

Dr Hilde Himmelweit in a review of recent experimental work on frustration included in Professor T. H. Pear's *Psychological Factors of Peace and War* gives a list of certain types of situation which have been shown experimentally to be extremely frustrating. These include: the arbitrary withdrawal of desirable objects; preventing subjects from completing a task; inducing in subjects a sense of failure and a distrust of their own abilities; curbing an individual's drives towards self-expression and self-assertion through interference from outside; frustration due to satiation; frustration due to a discrepancy between desire and ability to solve a task; unsatisfactory leadership. It will be noted how many of these conditions may readily be found in the average factory.

The industrial fields which most clearly reflect the existence of attitudes of frustration are the following:

A. *Output:* quality, quantity, and economy
B. *Accidents and Industrial Diseases*
C. *Absence and Strikes*
D. *Neurosis, Sickness, and Industrial Fatigue*
E. *Labour turnover*

Some of these items have already been discussed and need not be dealt with here. In the space available, it would be impossible to consider in any detail all the possible effects of frustration, and we shall, therefore, only refer to those coming under the headings of accidents, fatigue, and sickness.

Accidents in the factory are related to many factors. General health, age and experience, fatigue, atmospheric conditions, and temperature have all been shown to be relevant in their causation in the individual worker. A survey in the Birmingham area has indicated that, in the average light engineering factory, 7 to 10 per cent of the workers injure themselves daily. In the year, about 3 per cent of the factory workers have injuries causing them to be absent from work for more than three days, the mean loss of time from injury being 24 to 31 days. (See Dr J. P. Bull, 'Industrial Injuries': *British Medical Bulletin*, 1950, 7, 69.) Here however, we shall say nothing further about the physiological factors or factors in the physical environment which influence the accident rate, since these are adequately dealt with in most books on industrial psychology. Instead, we shall deal with the psychological and social factors which determine what is generally known as accident-proneness. In 1939 there were 193,475 accidents in British factories which involved the loss of three or more days. 1,104 of these were fatal, so it is obviously important to discover, not only what conditions in the environment predispose to a higher accident rate, but also what psychological conditions within the individual have this effect. In other words, we wish to know whether some people are more likely to have accidents than others, and, if so, how such people may be discovered and helped.

When we consider the distribution of accidents in a given population, it is clear that they might be distributed according to one or other of four general principles:

(1) The distribution might be completely random – i.e., with everybody equally subject to accidents.

(2) There might be a 'just' distribution, according to which the man who has had an accident will be relatively unlikely to have another for some time.

(3) It might be the case that, contrary to (2), the man who has recently had an accident is so upset that he is more likely to have further ones.

(4) A final possibility is that some individuals are so constituted that, whether for psychological or biological reasons, they are more likely to have accidents than others.

These possibilities can readily be tested out by observing the accident records of various people over a period of time, or over two separate periods of time. If (1) is a valid principle, then distribution will be completely at random; if (2), we should find that a high accident rate in one period is followed by a low accident rate in the second period; if (3), a high rate of accidents in one period will be followed by an even higher rate in the next; finally, if (4) is correct, certain individuals will tend to have a consistently high rate in all periods. M. Greenwood and H. M. Woods, working for the Industrial Fatigue Research Board in 1919, observed that (4) is the correct hypothesis, so that, in the group under study, 80 per cent of the accidents happened to only 20 per cent of the workers. This ratio has been confirmed by numerous studies both of industrial accidents and road accidents. Dr Ronald MacKeith, in an article entitled 'Accident Proneness' (*New Biology*, 11, 1951), gives statistics from an American insurance company which analysed a series of industrial accidents. This company found that mechanical hazards caused less than 9 per cent of accidents, physical and mental defects about 3 per cent, and lack of skill less than 8 per cent. The remaining 80 per cent were due to personality defects in the form of accident proneness. Dr Flanders Dunbar has made a special study of patients who have had accidents and her work showed:

(1) That 80 per cent of those who have had one serious accident tend to have others and have a particular personality. The remaining 20 per cent are more or less normal, have no special personality type, and do not tend to have further accidents.

(2) People with a history of numerous minor accidents are more likely to have a serious accident. When compared with a group of patients with heart disease, 76 per cent of the total illness in their previous history was the result of accidents compared with only 2 per cent for the heart cases.

(3) Accident-prone people have unusually good health records, and are especially free from colds and indigestion.

(4) They are neither clumsy nor dull, but tend to be quick-witted men of action rather than deliberation.

(5) Accident-prone people are generally impulsive individuals who concentrate upon daily pleasures and have little interest in long-term goals. They are often resentful of authority, and Dunbar found that their personality-type closely approximated to that of the juvenile delinquent with the exception that one broke laws and the other his own bones. Recent workers have found a strong positive correlation between accident proneness and voluntary absenteeism.

It might be thought that an obvious means of preventing accidents is to make all machinery as fool-proof as possible, and, of course, this should invariably be done. But Farmer quotes H. M. Chief Inspector of Factories as saying that 'however well machinery is guarded, we cannot look for more than 10 per cent reduction in accident rate.' However, Dunbar quotes the case of a public utility company which reduced its accident rate by four-fifths by the simple expedient of shifting men with bad records to other work. It was found that the same men, instead of smashing up public vehicles, were injuring themselves at home. Although accident-proneness has hitherto been regarded as a neurosis which has developed long before the individual has reached the factory, recent work (e.g., that of Dr T. T. Paterson of Glasgow University) has increasingly tended to show the significance of social and cultural factors. Thus coal miners, from the same villages, working the same seam in two different mines, may have accident rates three times higher in one mine than the other. Such differences can only be attributed to variations in morale. Dr Paterson has also shown how collective frustration in an R.A.F. squadron led to an increase in the number of crashes of aircraft, which were materially reduced in frequency by the removal of the sources of frustration.

The breakdown of the mechanistic hypothesis which took the view that man is a machine has had important repercussions in the field of medicine which, in turn, must influence the practice, not only of industrial medicine, but also of management and industrial psychology. Physicians are giving up the idea that in every patient there must be some single localized fault or disease which is the 'cause' of his illness, that treatment means 'tinkering with the machine', and that disease is a fortuituous event for which the patient is no more responsible than if a slate had fallen from a roof on to his unwitting head during a storm. The relationship between 'body' and 'mind', whatever these words may signify, is so intimate that the individual can only be thought of as a unitary organism in action. Disease, using that word in its widest sense which implies lack of ease or failure of adjustment, is the total reaction of the individual to threats directed against his physical and mental integrity. What we know as symptoms are, in large measure, the defensive reactions of the organism when faced by such specific threats as: (a) infections by bacteria, viruses, and fungi, (b) insect infestations, (c) poisons, (d) mechanical damage, (e) dietary deficiencies, excesses, and imbalances, (f) extremes of heat and cold, exposure and the like, (g) allergens, (h) fatigue, (i) emotional stress, with its physiological concomitants fear, rage, anxiety, and so on. 'Emotional stress in which there is no actual damage to the organism can produce physiologic responses which lead to actual structural damage, and this structural damage can even be so severe as to cause death.' (Dr L. J. Saul, *The Bases of Human Behaviour*.)*

Emotional stress produces its effects on the organism through the mediation of the autonomic nervous system. Perhaps the simplest way of explaining this relationship is to say that the psychosomatic disorders (i.e., those predominantly emotional in origin, since all medicine is, or should be 'psychosomatic') are emergency responses which have become fixed or frozen into the body structure. The temporarily anxious man may have difficulty in digesting his food, but the chronically anxious man develops, on the basis of a hereditary and developmental foundation, a duodenal ulcer. The angry man has a high blood-pressure, but the chronically resentful man has a high blood-pressure which remains high and may one day kill him. Among the disorders caused by emotional stress, we may enumerate duodenal and gastric ulcer, mucous colitis, essential hypertension, angina pectoris, coronary thrombosis, many cases of cerebral thrombosis and haemorrhage, asthma, hay-fever, migraine, and other allergic diseases, many gynaecological diseases of women, rheumatoid arthritis, 'fibrositis', exophthalmic goitre, many cases of diabetes and obesity, alopecia areata (a type of baldness), the vast majority of skin diseases other than those due to infection, most industrial dermatitis, and many cases of lumbago, neuritis, and sciatica. Other diseases, although due to infections and various organic causes, have a large psychological element: for example, venereal disease is an infection, but the person who puts himself in the position to get such a disease may be suffering from a neurosis. Psychological factors may predispose to tuberculosis. (See Wittkower, *A Psychiatrist Looks at Tuberculosis*.)†

* Professor Hans Selye of Montreal has produced arteriosclerosis, arthritis, and hypertension in rats by exposing them to long periods of fear induced by noise (bells and sirens) and flashing lights.

† In a sense (and here I hope my medical colleagues will not take me too literally) we are returning to the old view that disease is due to 'sin'. For it is true to say that the more specifically psychosomatic disorders: (a) are not fortuitous and are brought upon the individual by himself because of the way in which he reacts to his environment; (b) are closely related to his personality traits; and (c) are caused by the 'bad' emotions of guilt, anxiety, fear, and hate or resentment. The patient is ill partly because he has met the circumstances he has, but largely because he is the sort of person he is.

The present interest in the psychosomatic and psychological aspects of disease is not merely a result of the reduced frequency of the more serious epidemic infections; it is unfortunately the case that psychological disorders are on the increase. Thus, in the first fifteen months of the First World War, discharges from the army due to gastritis and gastric ulcer were 709, while in the first twenty-seven months of World War II discharges due to peptic ulcer alone numbered 23,574. Between 1911 and 1936, the death-rate from exophthalmic goitre in England rose by 400 per cent in males and 230 per cent in females – in spite of improved methods of treatment. In 1924, it was estimated that about 140,000 people in the United States died of high blood-pressure, but in 1940 the figure had risen to 375,000. From the United States it is further reported that every second bed in hospitals is occupied by a mental patient; that one in every six men rejected by the army is turned down on grounds of mental disorder; that 600,000 people are in institutions for chronic alcoholics with an estimated two million heavy drinkers outside. In Scotland between the years 1931 and 1936 (a period when unemployment was at its height), statistics show that gastric ulcer increased by 130 to 140 per cent, 'nervous debility' by 90 to 100 per cent, and gastritis by 110 to 120 per cent. I am not unaware of the various fallacies involved in these figures. But, whether or not the *figures* be accurate, the *fact* of the increase in stress diseases is beyond doubt. The psychological and psychosomatic disorders are diseases of stress, and their increase has occurred predominantly in Britain, the United States, and the industrial countries of Western Europe. They are rare in primitive non-industrialized communities and in the rural parts of Britain. On the other hand, as Halliday points out, they have begun to appear in such countries as India and West Africa with the introduction of industrialism. Not only is the incidence of such diseases increasing quantitatively; the maximum frequency of onset is shifting towards the younger age-groups as more and more individuals are adversely conditioned in childhood. Our present position is that, while the physical health of the community is improving each year as measured by a decline in the general death rate, the infant mortality rate, and the incidence of such diseases as rickets, typhoid fever, and rheumatic fever, mental health, as measured by the incidence of suicide, neurosis, gastric ulcer, infertility, exophthalmic goitre, and hypertension, is getting steadily worse.

A report by R. Doll and F. Avery Jones on *Occupational Factors in the Aetiology of Gastric and Duodenal Ulcers* was published by H. M. Stationery Office in 1951. These workers draw attention to the facts that of just over 4,000 general medical and surgical beds 9 per cent were occupied by cases of peptic ulcer; that 10 per cent of patients in out-patient clinics are dyspeptic cases; and that in a consecutive series of autopsies 9.55 per cent of the cases showed an active ulcer or the scar of a healed one. But cases were not spread at random throughout the population and certain occupations showed a much higher incidence than others. Occupations with high incidences were found in doctors, foremen, and business executives – the latter two groups being those who hold the most responsible positions in industry. An exceptionally low incidence was found amongst agricultural workers. The research showed that the duodenal ulcer subject is almost invariably the over-conscientious, hard-working, and ambitious individual, and it is of particular interest to note that the anxiety giving rise to the ulcer appeared to be that relating to work. No association was found between duodenal ulcer and home worries. Clearly, then, peptic ulcer has assumed almost epidemic proportions in this country, is related to work in industry, and picks out the over-conscientious worker who is situated at points of social tension within the industrial system.

A similar state of affairs is revealed in the frequency with which those who have to bear the stress of industry become ill and die with cardio-vascular diseases. G. W. Gray writes that 'the death toll of busy men of affairs who succumb to heart disease in their forties and fifties is startling.' The main psychosomatic disorders coming into this category are high blood-pressure, angina pectoris, and coronary thrombosis – all of which are frequent causes of death. Indeed, this problem has become so serious that many of the larger concerns insist on yearly medical examinations of their senior executives in order that these conditions may be diagnosed at an early stage. Coronary disease, says Dr James Halliday, is found in those in whom unremitting work is 'associated with the need to attempt to attain, or to maintain, a subjectively evaluated rôle of authority or being on top' (*Psychosocial Medicine*), whilst high blood-pressure is found in those who have constantly to repress their resentments. As in the case of duodenal ulcer, the incidence of these disorders falls most heavily upon both executives and supervisors, but tends to select the former. Another serious problem is that of industrial dermatitis, which Dr J. H. Twiston Davies in an article on 'Skin Disease in Industry' bluntly describes as 'a disorder of the personality'. (*The British Journal of Physical Medicine*.) Although there can be no doubt that there are some substances used in industry – the so-called primary irritants – which might produce damage to the skin in anyone who came into contact with them, the vast majority (probably 95 per cent or more) of cases of industrial dermatitis are purely and simply a form of neurosis produced by poor morale at work or worries at home and aggravated by official policy. It is believed that there are more than 40,000 dermatitis claims each year for skin conditions allegedly caused by 'dust, liquids, or vapour encountered in industry', to use the official definition. Now, as another dermatologist, Dr Mark Hewitt, has pointed out, the untoward effects on the skin of the ordinary primary irritants rapidly disappear when the individual is removed from contact with them, but it is typical of the average case of so-called industrial dermatitis that it may go on for weeks or months after the patient has stopped handling any irritant substance. In short, whatever the immediate excuse for the condition, and whatever constitutional factors may be present, the basic cause of industrial dermatitis *other than the 5 per cent or so of cases due to primary irritants* is emotional. 'Persons who have too high or too low an ability or intelligence for the job in which they find themselves, sub-consciously rebel against their status. The ambitious workman with no prospect of advancement may not have the strength of will to leave his present job and kindly employer. His sub-conscious mind, however, through the development of minor eczematous lesions on the hands, may come to his rescue and enable him to achieve his object. Promotion of younger and what may seem to be less efficient colleagues may lead to irritation, dissatisfaction, aggression, and cutaneous breakdown. Often it is the man with poor ability and inadequate training, with a record of many changes of work, but who feels he should be in a supervising post, who tends to break down . . . Much depends on the attitude of the worker and his incentive to work – for he is influenced by unsatisfactory and tactless management or even incited to rebel as a result of inequalities shown by foremen who have no command over their workmen.' ('Social and Emotional Aspects of Industrial Dermatitis', by Mark Hewitt, M.B., M.R.C.P., *British Journal of Physical Medicine*, September 1951.)

Official policy, so far from discouraging 'industrial dermatitis', often plays a large part in creating it. Dr J. H. Twiston Davies points out that 'in their anxiety to show their solicitude for the welfare of the very few workmen who have developed a skin disease as the result of encountering an irritant at work, the authorities have overdone their propaganda and are now creating sickness at a greater rate than we can possibly hope to cope with. The character and wording of posters displayed in factories for the ostensible purpose of acquainting workers with their legal rights, and the film entitled "Industrial Dermatitis" issued last year by the M.O.I., are examples of a propaganda calculated to promote fear, aggravate introspection, and even to interfere with the sort of rational treatment that might assist recovery.' (*Psychosomatic Factors in Dermatology*.) 'Industrial dermatitis' may arise in those who handle the most innocuous substances – e.g. cold cream, cosmetics, soap, or vegetables – and in such cases (as contrasted with cases due to the handling of primary irritants), a high incidence is almost invariably found to be related to factors of morale and general discontent in the workshop. Unfortunately, the authorities have never been able to understand that the neuroses are basically different from other diseases in that they tend to show what psychiatrists have described as 'a desire for secondary gain'. That is to say, the neurotic, who is fundamentally afraid of life, has a strong tendency to stay ill in the more primitive form of adjustment which he has reached. Giving him pensions or compensations will have the effect of discouraging him from making a more effectual adjustment. In effect, we are saying: 'Don't worry, so long as you stay in your present state of maladjustment everything will be all right and you will be paid – but, of course, if you are so stupid as to get well, you will get no more money.' The huge part played by poor morale and 'compensationitis' in accident neurosis is nowhere seen more clearly than in the case of head injuries. It is well-known that serious neurotic sequelae following head-injuries are almost unknown when these occur on the hunting-field or during sports (i.e., in situations in which no question of resentment or secondary gain arises), whereas following industrial injuries such neuroses are the rule rather than the exception. The better the morale in the factory, the fewer will be the number of accident neuroses.

G. R. Hargreaves in an article in the magazine *Progress*, published by Unilever Ltd, has noted that in the British Army it was found that neurotic breakdown and psychosomatic disorders occurred most frequently among reinforcements to a battalion and during the recruiting period – that is to say, at times when (a) the soldier was faced by new stresses, and (b) he had not as yet been accepted into the group. Dr D. S. F. Robertson has commented on these observations of Hargreaves that, on the basis of his experience in industry, his own opinion has been that 'it is during the period of adaptation after starting work in a new job or under new supervision, accepting new responsibilities after promotion or returning to work after a long absence (whatever the cause of the absence), that the individual is found with the greatest problem of psychological adaptation and consequently is most likely to succumb to psychological breakdown.' ('Some Human Relations Problems in Industry', *Transactions of the Association of Industrial Medical Officers*.)

One of the most important studies of the incidence and causation of neurosis in industry was carried out by Russell Fraser (*The Incidence of Neurosis Among Factory Workers*, 1947) on a sample of light and medium engineering workers in or near Birmingham. The sample consisted of 3,000 workers, and it was found that over a period of six months about 10 per cent of these workers suffered from disabling neurosis, about 20 per cent more from minor neurotic complaints, and, finally, that neurosis was responsible for between one quarter and one third of the total sickness absence. These figures are confirmed by Halliday, who has reported that of 1,000 insured workers who were receiving sickness benefit under certification as unfit for work, 33 per cent were incapacitated as a result of neurosis (*Psychosocial Medicine*), and by Wyatt who found that 'nervous debility and fatigue' accounted for 21.2 per cent of sickness absence among 30,000 women workers in munition factories (*A Study of Certified Sickness Absence among Women in Industry*, Industrial Health Research Board Report No. 86). Neurosis showed a significant increase amongst workers who operated under the following circumstances:

(a) Worked for more than seventy-five hours per week.
(b) Had frequent recent changes of work.
(c) Lived alone or were overcrowded.
(d) Had been separated or widowed.
(e) Had heavy domestic responsibilities or stress.
(f) Had poor social contacts.
(g) Who disliked their job or found it boring.
(h) Who were doing jobs too high or too low for their intelligence.

It will be noted that the majority of these conditions relate to defects of social adjustment and the failure to 'belong' or fit into any group. (The objection may be made that such defects are not the cause of neurosis, but merely its symptoms. But this objection misses the point, which is that 'defects of social adjustment' and 'neurosis' are synonymous terms.* All experience shows that neurosis increases with social disintegration and decreases as individuals come to be re-integrated into primary groups. The healing effect of group life is, in fact, utilized by the psychiatrist in the form of group psycho-therapy in order to treat the neuroses.)

Industrial fatigue has always been an object of study for the psychologist or doctor in industry. Its cardinal signs, according

* 'Neurosis is the indication and result of an inadequately realized group-effectiveness.' Dr Henry Harris: *The Group Approach to Leadership Testing.*

to Dr Howard E. Collier, are that, 'the fatigued worker first experiences a lessening of interest in his work; this is followed by active disinterest, or boredom. Later, if the same occupation is persisted in, the worker experiences increasing annoyance and irritation as he struggles to continue. It is at this stage that industrial fatigue tends to produce industrial unrest. Finally, if the task is still persisted in, the utmost exertion of the will and the strongest concentration of the attention are not sufficient to keep the worker at his task.' (*Outlines of Industrial Medical Practice.*) Production is, of course, reduced, but even more important is the fact that industrial fatigue predisposes to illness. It is, says Dr Collier, a transition state between health and disease in which the individual becomes more susceptible to infections, accidents, and neurosis.

As we have elsewhere mentioned, it was long supposed that such fatigue was due to a physico-chemical condition of the body produced in the same way as the physical fatigue following extreme muscular exercise. The symptoms were attributed to the accumulation of toxic products from the muscles, or, if the work were mental, it was supposed by analogy that some sort of poisons were accumulating in the nerve cells. Of course, in heavy muscular exercise such products do, in fact, accumulate and produce fatigue, but, except in a small minority of cases, such factors have no bearing whatever on the problem of industrial fatigue. Bock and Dill in their *Physiology of Muscular Exercise* point out that: 'There are two types of fatigue, one originating entirely within the central nervous system, the other arising partly in the nervous system and partly within the active muscles. The former is of common occurrence, whereas the latter occurs comparatively infrequently. Industrial fatigue is usually of the first type.' This type of fatigue is entirely psychological in origin, since there is no known condition in which the brain-cells become exhausted. 'Many unsuccessful attempts have been made to produce experimentally, a condition of "neural" fatigue of the brain cells. It has been shown that many hours can be spent in adding columns of figures, in reading, in copying, in doing intelligence-tests or in performing other kinds of essentially mental work without the occurrence of manifest fatigue. In these experiments fatigue was produced as soon as interest in the task was lost and whenever boredom supervened.' (H. E. Collier, *op. cit.*) What this means is that nearly all so-called industrial fatigue, with the exception of a very few cases of physical exhaustion due to prolonged heavy physical work, is produced by purely psychological states of boredom, anxiety, and resentment.

While bad environmental conditions, long hours of work, bad spacing of rest-periods, and defects associated with the speed, rhythm, or intensity of work, are all relevant factors in producing industrial fatigue, the main factors relate to the psychological conditions of the job. Of these, Dr Collier gives the following as being the most important:

(1) Monotony.
(2) Absence of discipline and faulty supervision.
(3) Insecurity in employment.
(4) Absence of social or group-harmony.
(5) Incorrect work-incentives.
(6) Incorrect methods of personnel selection and promotion.

From what we have already said, three important conclusions emerge. Firstly, there is the importance of the primary group in the factory and elsewhere in maintaining physical and mental health, discipline, and happiness. Secondly, the serious implications of psychosomatic disorders in industry, since these conditions (or the more serious of them) tend to occur most frequently in the key-men of the factory, especially amongst managers and supervisors. Both these groups show a considerably higher rate of peptic ulcer, coronary thrombosis, angina pectoris, and high blood-pressure than any others either in or out of industry. Thirdly, there is the implication that industrial health is a much wider concept than has formerly been supposed. We have reached a state of affairs in which it is possible to measure not only the economic and technical efficiency of an organization but also its social efficiency. Low social efficiency means bad physical and mental health, and the physician cannot be indifferent when bad leadership and ineffectual organization are causing both misery *and disease*. We can now see the factory as a web of social interrelationships with certain areas of tension which cause those situated at such points to become sick. To be even more explicit, we can see that the neurotic supervisor or factory manager or senior executive may spread disease amongst his associates just as surely as if he had typhoid fever or smallpox. He will not, as in the case of typhoid or smallpox, spread the same disease in each case – to one of his associates he may give a neurosis, to another a peptic ulcer, to another death from cardio-vascular disease, to another simply misery, depending in each case on the personality type of the recipient. 'There are', writes Dr L. G. Brown in his *Social Pathology*, 'a great many carriers of mental ill-health in society. These individuals are not insane or likely to be. Frequently they are persons holding important positions and places of advantage in society. Because of their position they can play with the self-respect of their subordinates. They help to create psychopathic personalities, problem individuals, persons with feelings of insecurity, attitudes of self-pity, fears, doubts, obsessions, delusions, and serious compensatory distortions. These include parents, teachers, executives, ministers, lawyers, doctors, statesmen, relatives, social workers, nursemaids, and a whole host of others in positions of authority.'

That mental sickness is not found solely in the obviously neurotic or psychotic individual was realized long ago by Spinoza when he wrote: 'Many people are seized by one and the same affect with great consistency. All his senses are so strongly affected by one object that he believes this object to be present even when it is not. If this happens while the person is awake, the person is believed to be insane. But if the *greedy* person thinks only of money and possessions, the *ambitious* one only of fame, one does not think of them as being insane, but only as annoying; generally one has contempt for them. But *factually* greediness, ambition, and so forth are forms of insanity, although usually one does not think of them as illness.' It is for this reason that leadership selection is one of the most important problems in the society of today.

Of course, the stresses of the single individual or of the single factory are merely a reflexion of the general stresses of the whole society. Every personal problem is also a social one, and the future approach to health is likely to be primarily in terms of the sick society rather than the sick individual. Furthermore, we must think of health in terms not only of formal illness, but also in terms of such social sicknesses as crime, delinquency, discontent, psychosomatic diseases, neurosis, and so on. Dr L. K. Frank in an article in the *American Journal of Sociology* ('Society as the Patient', 1936, 42), writes of this new approach: 'Instead of thinking in terms of a multiplicity of so-called social problems, each demanding special attention and a different remedy, we can view all of them as different symptoms of the same disease. If, for example, we would regard crime, mental disorders, family disorganization, juvenile delinquency, prostitution and sex offences, and much that now passes as the result of pathological processes (for example, gastric ulcer) as evidence not of individual wickedness, incompetence, perversity, or pathology, but as human reactions to cultural disintegration, a forward step would be taken.'

The concept of cultural disintegration cannot be discussed in any detail here, but the following features of our society give some indication of how it influences the individual:

(1) More than any previous society it stimulates people's desires without being able to satisfy them.

(2) More than any previous society it is based on conflicting ideals which the individual finds it impossible to reconcile.

(3) More than any previous society, as Ortega y Gasset points out in his *Revolt of the Masses*, ours is a mob or mass society. The old primary groupings have been broken up – the family, the working group, the village council – and replaced by huge anonymous bodies in relation to which status, function, and personal significance are lost.

Since the primary group is the basic instrument of social control, of ethical norms, a mass society in which these groups have begun to disintegrate is a society lacking in moral standards. The other reason for moral deterioration is, of course, the fact that we are today in a transitional phase between paleotechnic and neotechnic phases. The old standards have gone and new ones have not yet arisen.

Behind all these factors lies the rapidity of technical change to which it becomes increasingly difficult to adapt. We have roads built for horse-traffic on which cars capable of moving at a hundred miles an hour attempt to travel, the free enterprise concept which was not inappropriate in a society of small businesses is applied in a society of huge competing concerns the collapse of which would disrupt our economy, certain religious bodies and nations encourage population increase and forbid birth-control at a time when uncontrolled population increase may come to be the most serious problem man has ever had to face, and so on.

Robert and Helen Lynd in their famous book *Middletown*, a social survey of an American Middle Western town (in fact, Muncie, Indiana) have demonstrated some of the ethical conflicts which face the members of modern industrial societies. The citizens of Middletown shared some or all of the following beliefs: that economic conditions are the result of natural order and cannot be changed by man-made laws; that men will not work unless compelled to; that any man willing to work can get a job; that human nature cannot be altered; that the individual must fend for himself and in the end gets what he deserves. (These are recognizable as based on the 'rabble hypothesis'.) Yet these same people would go to Church on Sundays and learn that one must love one's neighbour as oneself; that 'blessed are the meek'; that one must not 'count the wealth of this world as valuable'; and that brotherly love should rule the earth. On the one hand brotherly love and unselfishness are stressed, on the other attitudes of intense competition and 'business is business'. It is often said that competition is a law of life, but the type of competition typical of the paleotechnic period differed from that of most other periods and cultures in that (a) it was between single isolated individuals rather than between rival groups of co-operating members, and (b) it was all-out competition unlimited by moral or social considerations. Within the framework of the primary group competition may take place (as in the case of the football team) in which the winner adds to the repute of the team, as a whole and the losers are not shamed, but this type of behaviour cannot be compared with the devil-take-the-hindmost attitude of industrial society. 'A result of such (all-out) competition is the growth of hostility between individuals; another is fear lest one fail. The latter may be particularly pronounced, since the chances of failing are much greater than the chances of succeeding. The fear of failure, moreover, is intensified by our false ideology; if an individual fails, we are apt to say it was his own fault, a sign of some inadequancy on his part. The rôles of luck, exploitation, and circumstances are largely ignored. The belief that one has failed leads to lowered self-esteem and a sense of isolation from others that is painful.' (Ogburn and Nimkoff, *A Handbook of Sociology*.) The rise of capitalism with its intense competitive spirit led to great advances both in the fields of science and industry. But the other side of the picture was the increasing mental disorganization of those who fell by the wayside.

Two interesting investigations have shown the relationship between mental health and social conditions. Robert E. L. Faris and H. Warren Dunham made an investigation of the distribution of mental disorders in Chicago which is described in their *Mental Disorders in Urban Areas*. They calculated the number of cases of mental disorder in the various neighbourhoods of that city and found that the district with the greatest proportion of such cases had more than ten times the ratio of the district with the lowest proportion. The lowest rates occurred in the residential areas of the well-to-do, while the highest rates were in the areas of lodging houses, slum districts, and some of the Negro areas. High rates of poverty, crime and delinquency, unemployment, infantile mortality, and general diseases were also found in the areas with a high rate of mental disorder. The conclusion was that mental and social disorganization were associated. But it is incorrect to suppose, as is frequently done, that such symptoms of disorganization as crime, delinquency, neurosis, and insanity are caused by poverty and bad environmental conditions in themselves. Clifford Shaw, whose *Delinquency Areas* is a further study of social conditions in Chicago, points out that: 'It has been quite common in discussions of delinquency to attribute causal significance to such conditions as poor housing, overcrowding, low living standards, low educational standards and so on. But these conditions themselves probably reflect a type of community life. By treating them one treats only symptoms of more basic processes . . . In short, with the process of growth of the city, the invasion of residential communities by business and industry causes a disintegration of the community as a unit of social control. This disorganization is intensified by the influx of foreign national and racial groups whose old cultural and social controls break down in the new cultural and racial situation of the city.' The fact is that the individual's sense of security, his psychological satisfactions, and his moral standards come mainly from his primary groups, and when these disintegrate he is left insecure, anonymous, and a potential victim of mob psychology or individual eccentricity and psychopathy.

Mandel Sherman and Thomas R. Henry describe in the book *Hollow Folk* an investigation of settlements in the hollows of the Blue Ridge Mountains of Virginia. The first settlement, Briarsville, was near the main road – that is to say, in close touch with civilization – whereas the other settlements extended progressively further back into the mountains, each further away from contact with the outside world. Thus while Briarsville had cars, radio sets, newspapers, and all the amenities of modern life, Colvin Hollow, the furthest-away settlement, was illiterate, and its inhabitants lived in mud-plastered single-room huts, and ate mainly cabbage and maize. But in Colvin Hollow neuroses were practically unknown, and as one came nearer and nearer to civilization they steadily increased. Ogburn comments: 'The investigators asked the children in the five hollows what they would like to have. The only two wants expressed in Colvin Hollow were for chewing tobacco and money, but the children had little idea of the value of the latter. The list of things desired (and not possessed) grew as the questioners moved out towards the periphery. And, as already indicated, so did the amount of mental anguish. These communities would seem almost to have been made to order for the purpose of showing the close connexion between the state of culture and the amount of mental disorder in a society.' (*A Handbook of Sociology.*)

What we have said here concerning the causes of neurosis and psychosomatic disease has been inevitably over-simplified, and it should not be supposed that industry is being held solely responsible for the high incidence of these conditions, or even that they depend upon social factors alone. It is likely that heredity, upbringing, and contemporary factors in the patient's life-history (which may, or may not, arise in the industrial situation) play approximately equal parts in bringing such diseases about. What is, however, clear, is that any hereditary factor which may be present is rarely effective in the absence of the others, and that even heredity plus defects of upbringing does not necessarily lead to breakdown in the absence of contemporary stress. It is also certain that industrial communities have a much higher incidence of neurosis and psychosomatic disease than primitive or agricultural communities, that the incidence in industrial communities is increasing, and that the neurotic mind is a microcosm which demonstrates in an exaggerated form the stresses of the society in which it functions. As Karen Horney has said: 'It seems that the person who is likely to become neurotic is one who has experienced the culturally determined difficulties in an accentuated form.' (*The Neurotic Personality of Our Time*.) Finally, it appears that neurosis and psychosomatic disease are not ordinarily caused by a single emotion such as anxiety or fear, but rather by the battle between conflicting emotions. War, for example, does not necessarily lead to an increase of neurosis in the civilian population, and the suicide rate is even lowered in wartime. If Horney is correct, these conflicting emotions arise mostly in our own culture from such tensions as the following: (1) between competition and success on the one hand, and brotherly love on the other; (2) between stimulation of our needs and our factual frustrations in satisfying them; (3) between alleged freedom of the individual and all his factual limitations.

A traditional civilization which is in the process of disintegration or of rapid transition into a new society experiences a breakdown of its old system of values which conduces to mental disorders. H. D. Lamson observes in his *Social Pathology in China* that the transition between the old family pattern and the new Western one has led to serious difficulties and in Peking hospitals there were numerous cases in which this was the pre-cipitating cause. Margaret Mead has demonstrated the same effects amongst Red Indians (*The Changing Culture of an Indian Tribe*), and, conversely, Frankwood Williams has observed a tremendous decrease in the incidence of neurosis in the Soviet Union which he attributes, rightly or wrongly, to the reduction of 'anxiety pressures'. The present writer inclines to the view that a major part of the troubles of the modern world arises from the lack of any adequate philosophy of life, of what Erich Fromm describes as a 'frame of devotion and orientation'. Beyond all reasonable doubt human beings need to possess an overall philosophy of life (be it religious or political) in the framework of which their individual acts 'make sense'. Medieval Catholicism and Protestant capitalism both worked in their time, but they are dead or dying and no adequate system has replaced them. In short, we are situated between a dying world and one powerless to be born. This, however, will be discussed more fully in the last chapter.

IO

SUMMARY AND CONCLUSIONS

IN this final chapter it is proposed to summarize the argument, to answer some of the criticisms which may be levelled against it, and to discuss the problem of social change in industry.

First of all, it was suggested that we cannot understand the attitudes of either management or workers unless they are seen in their historical context, and unless we realize that much that has been regarded as due to 'human nature' is, in fact, purely the product of a particular culture at a particular stage of its development. The beliefs that work is an unpleasant necessity, that the individual is basically self-interested, basically lazy, and basically competitive, that society consists of a mass of unorganized individuals, each at war with the other; that the human body is a machine to which a mind is somehow attached; that fear of starvation is the main negative incentive and money the main positive one – all these are products of a certain type of society at a certain stage in its development. They correspond to no fundamental human traits, and, even when they were most generally accepted, were never true of more than a minority of the members of industrial society. Unfortunately, these assumptions were made the basis, not only of management practice, but of most work in industrial psychology. Starting with the efficiency engineers Taylor and Gilbreth and the early industrial psychologists Münsterberg and Myers, the approved approach was a thoroughly atomistic and mechanistic one which took no account of psychological motives or social factors. Nigel Balchin, in an article on 'Satisfactions in Work' (*Occupational Psychology*, July 1947), suggests that, although in the early days of industrialism the struggle was hard, the worker at least had the possibility of feeling a sort of grim satisfaction with his lot. 'In that struggle to wrest even a bare living from the world there was still something, at least, of the early workers' satisfaction in wresting a living from nature – of taking on something enormously powerful, and if not defeating it, refusing to surrender to it. I hold no brief for those days. But we are talking about satisfactions, not justice or equity. Nobody who has met survivors from the bad old days of industry can doubt the pride and satisfaction that come from the mere process of survival, in the days when survival was not easy. Moreover (and this is vitally important) those were days of deep and simple religious conviction. To many people, this life was simply a short period of preparation for eternity. There was not that desperate sense of the flight of time and opportunity that we have today. Happiness – real happiness – was a thing which was to come; not today or next week, but when this world had been left behind.' But, as time went on, and management became more enlightened (although often in the wrong direction), this irrational satisfaction in the struggle against a hostile world was taken away. Under more modern conditions the worker faced a new situation. His religious beliefs had been largely destroyed and he wanted pleasure here and now. What was he offered? 'The size of the incentive he is offered is not survival but the capacity to buy a new radio set. Apart from that it is all negatives. It shall all be quite easy and not very unpleasant and anyhow there shall only be forty hours of it a week, and if he does get dirty, he shall have a nice bath after it . . . and so on. We say, in effect. "Look, we know this is a lousy job and that you don't want to do it. But we'll do our best to make it as tolerable as we can."'

So the psychologists got to work and talked about 'industrial fatigue', and the influence of temperature, lighting, noise, and humidity on industrial productivity. Everything, in fact, except people. The result was a compound of platitudinous statements and sheer nonsense which it is almost incredible that any human being could possibly have supposed to lead to 'good working conditions'. Balchin writes: 'I have been in a factory workroom containing five hundred young girls – most of them under thirty. There they were, under "perfect working conditions", light, warm, clean, comfortable. The conditions were so perfect that it might have been a model cow-house. Perfect working conditions – but what appalling living conditions! They were young girls and outside their jobs they lived for colour and excitement and drama and change – for emotion. Yet there they sat, for eight hours a day, in that sterile place, from which everything they really cared for had been left out. I often wonder whether our factories and offices – even the best of them – are not organized by people who hate the human race, and deliberately set out to make people's working lives as deadly dull as possible.'

Wherever we go in this modern world we see examples of this curiously perverted hedonism – the belief that what people want is more money, more pills, more radios, more things – the more material objects they are able to collect or get for nothing, the happier they will be. And, of course, if people want these things, there is no reason why they should not have them. But it is a serious mistake to attempt to satisfy men and women with what are merely adjuncts to happiness whilst ignoring their more fundamental needs, and it is an even greater mistake to give them things for which they have to give nothing in return. An object is valued according to what the individual has sacrificed in order to get it, and when he has given nothing it will mean little to him. Human beings are not, or should not be, like captive penguins standing with their beaks passively opened for the keeper to fill them. They need to struggle, to have a cause, to meet some resistance which they can overcome. Georg Brochmann, a Norwegian engineer, has criticized this hedonistic attitude to life in his excellent book *Humanity and Happiness*. When we enter a modern house, he says, we find that: 'Everything, to be sure, seems as good as it can possibly be; there is nothing to do here but sit down in a perfect functional chair, and wish you have never been born. What is there to live for in a home where you can't drive a nail into the wall or undertake the tiniest improvement?'

The manager and the industrial psychologist have passed from the stage of ruthless exploitation, the carrot and the stick, and a mechanistic attitude to work, to a new stage of fussing, perverted 'welfare', and the same old mechanistic attitude. And, to the worker, the new era is not much better than the old so far as real satisfactions are concerned. No self-respecting individual wishes to be treated like a child or a cow in a model dairy – if he is offered something for nothing he will, of course, take it, but he will not like the purveyor of goods any better. A worker in the Michelin factories in France, which are noted for their social schemes, expressed himself thus concerning their 'welfare': 'I was born into Michelin baby-linen and fed with a Michelin bottle in a Michelin house. Of course I played in a Michelin nursery, then as a Michelin apprentice and operative I had my meals in the canteen and went to the Michelin cinema and Michelin entertainments. If I don't get out of this joint directly I shall soon be buried in a Michelin coffin.' (Jacques Chapuis, 'Je fais du social', *Chefs*, No. 4, April 1945.) Hyacinthe Dubreuil, the author of the book *A Chance for Everybody*, and himself a worker, has remarked of the modern tendency: 'If it goes on like this, every workman will soon have a social worker by his side.' Dr Franziska Baumgarten, a Swiss industrial psychologist, from whose book *Die Psychologie der Menschenbehandlung im Betriebe* the above quotations are taken, comments on such 'welfare' schemes: 'In the long run all these measures involve interference with the worker's private life. Taken together they constitute a kind of "paternalism" – the carrying into effect of a tendency shared by a large number of Swiss industrial psychologists – which desires to "extend the idea of the family to the undertaking" and which is identified with "social conscience". If anyone is congratulating himself on having organized a large number of social schemes it will be necessary for him to beware lest he have a conception of "social conscience" that is far too narrow and is consequently false.'*

It has already been pointed out that the physical conditions of work do influence the individual, but that the prevalent concentration on these to the exclusion of other more important matters exemplifies a complete failure to see the wood whilst making a detailed study of the trees. The physical environment is a perfectly legitimate object of study, but we should put first

---

* Some large American corporations are becoming positively sinister in their interference with the private life of their employees - particularly executives. (See *Life* magazine, 7 January 1952, 'The Wife Problem'.) Whether or not the husband is promoted depends a great deal on whether his wife fits the 'pattern', and in the end the company conditions almost everything the wife does, from the books she reads to the companions she is permitted to meet.

things first. Furthermore, reasons have been given for supposing that many of these experiments are invalidated by reason of failure to control the situation properly so as to exclude other factors which may have produced the observed results. But the last word on this subject may be left to an official American publication *Fatigue of Workers: Its Relation to Industrial Production* compiled by the Committee on Work in Industry of the National Research Council. There it is stated that: 'The efficiency of workers is affected by certain physical conditions, *but these conditions are not very often encountered in ordinary work in industry.* The Western Electric researches, particularly the Relay Assembly Test Room, showed that changes in intensity of illumination, heat, humidity, hours of work, etc., affected workers far less than had been believed. The human organism seems to be able to maintain a state such that it makes unconscious and automatic compensation for these changes.' Welfare, too, is an excellent thing when it is kept within reasonable bounds and rightly conceived. Pensions, sickness benefit, free medical attention, and other schemes are of major importance, although the employee of the firm which provides them sometimes forgets what a vast difference they make and accepts them as part of the natural order of things. To have security in a job, to know that one can be ill without incurring loss of money or risk of dismissal, to have the assurance that the future is financially moderately safe – these are tremendously valuable benefits. But that they may exist in an atmosphere of dissatisfaction and poor morale is demonstrated by the suspicious frequency with which, in many firms, workers seem to develop illnesses which exactly fill the period of the time for which they are entitled to sickness benefit. Welfare becomes unreasonable when (a) it is done for ulterior motives and used specifically as an incentive, since it then becomes an example of 'the greatest treason – to do the right thing for the wrong reason,'* and (b) when it reaches the stage of managers racking their brains to find some new (and essentially useless) piece of 'welfare' to act as a stimulus to work and vie with anything supplied by other companies. Welfare should be regarded as a social act and not as an incentive to

* T.S. Eliot, *Murder in the Cathedral.*

increase production – which, in any case, it does not do; for the worker may be *attracted* to the firm with such schemes, but he will neither stay with it nor work hard for it unless he finds other satisfactions when he has settled down.

In the second place, we attempted to discover what psychology and sociology had to say concerning the essential nature of man, whether there was a basic substratum of genuine human nature beneath all the variations imposed by his cultures. Rightly or wrongly, the conclusion was reached that a man is born with a certain level of intelligence, a certain temperament (both of which may be modified within limits by the environment), and his organic drives of hunger, thirst, sex, and so on. Instincts, in the ordinary sense of the word, are not found in man, but certain needs, although not strictly speaking inborn, are universal since they arise from the nature of man's biological situation after birth. Being helpless, and incapable of feeding or looking after himself (i.e. of satisfying his organic drives), he needs love and emotional security. This is his most basic psychological need, a need which in adult life takes the form of the need for social status and function – the awareness that he 'belongs' within the scheme devised by his culture and has a part, however humble, to play in that scheme. *From the point of view of the social psychologist, the need of the individual for status and function is the most significant of his traits, and if this need remains unsatisfied nothing else can compensate for its lack.* Loss of status leads to social isolation, and is one of the commonest causes of neuroses. It is most likely to occur:

(1) In primitive societies, when the individual has broken some part of the social code and has been deliberately rejected by his society.

(2) When a culture begins to disintegrate so that its ideology no longer makes sense (e.g., the caste system of India under the impact of industrialism). If this happens, the status system based on the ideology becomes meaningless and the individual feels lost.

(3) In modern mass society, when the primary groups which confer intrinsic status have been broken up and no

ideology has as yet become generally accepted on which a system of derived status may be based.

In medieval times, formal status was based on an aristocracy of birth, but in modern times both formal and informal (derived and intrinsic) status are, to a considerable extent, based on work. We largely judge a person by what he does. It is therefore true to say with Burlinghame that: 'Work is the source of man's most basic satisfactions, it is his social catalyst – the purveyor *par excellence* of his status and prestige among his fellows.' This being the case, the real problem for the industrial psychologist is to discover what has happened to transform a basic need into a source of dissatisfaction and resentment. We have suggested that a major reason for this is the breaking-up of primary groups and the attempt to substitute for these, large, formalized, secondary groupings whose ideology conflicts with that of the worker, and which are, in any case, too large to arouse in him any real feeling of loyalty.

It is an important principle of social organization that the loyalties of the individual begin within his primary group and other more distant and secondary groupings only receive his loyalty insofar as their interests coincide with those of his primary groups. We saw that this was the case in the 'bank-wiring room' at the Hawthorne plant, when the workers, in their own interests, continued to restrict production in spite of the appeals and incentives offered by the firm. This principle is a universal one – not restricted to workers – which is evidently not understood by those who blame the miners for failing to produce more coal when the country badly needs it. Professor C. A. Mace has expressed this principle very clearly in an article on 'Satisfactions in Work' in *Occupational Psychology* for January 1948: 'For example, consider the case of a particular miner living in a particular mining village and working in a particular pit. At the present moment he is subject to the following, among other, forms of social pressure: (1) the pressure of what England expects of him in the current crisis of production, these expectations being voiced, for example, in the leading articles of the daily press; (2) the pressure of the expectations of high officials of the National Coal Board, of the Government, and of his Union; (3) the more local pressure of the expectations of the supervisory staff at his pit; and (4) the still more local expectations of his wife and family and of his immediate associates in his daily working life. Clearly, local pressures are much more potent than pressure propelled from a distance. One might almost say that the power of an expectation at any place varies inversely with the square of the social distance of that place from the point of emission. Local pressures, moreover, may act as a kind of insulating barrier against pressures more remote in origin. This is part of the explanation of the relative ineffectiveness of long-range propaganda. Hence the miner's response can be predicted only by those who are suitably placed to see what the more local forces are.' It follows, then, that for this reason amongst many others, management should do all within its power to preserve the informal groups within a firm, and they should see to it that the interests of these groupings correspond with those of the firm as a whole. 'To predict the behaviour of a plumber it is not enough to know the expectations of the man who holds the carrot or the stick. Nor is it only a matter of the expectations of the officials of the plumber's union. We must also know the expectations of the plumber's mate.' (C. A. Mace.)

Finally, we noted that a great deal of behaviour which has been supposed to emanate from within the individual, to be based on his fixed character traits, is, in fact, a function of the individual within his group. On the other hand, it was suggested that, in spite of the great variability of the individual's behaviour in different settings which has tended to be underestimated in the past, there is a basic substratum or core personality which is relatively fixed and contains personality traits which are 'really' part of the individual. Most people are suspicious only in a specific situation, but there are others who are suspicious in every situation, the person who has a craving for power may show his craving in widely different ways according to the situation he is facing but he does not cease to want power; and the obsessional or orderly person remains so unless his personality deteriorates seriously. Nevertheless, in industry (except when we are dealing with single individuals who are in positions of authority and are therefore capable of imposing their peculiarities on others) we are mainly dealing with behaviour which is peripheral in origin and is a function of the individual in a group setting. When dealing with this aspect of personality we have to realize that changes in the external environment of the group and changes in its social structure may make a tremendous difference to its emotional climate, either for better or worse.

But, although we must concentrate on the informal working groups, it is important to realize that in altering the social structure of a factory all levels must be considered, and, in particular, the management who are so largely instrumental in setting the scene. 'Although the smaller working groups must be the focus of attention, action needs to be taken on a broad front and at every level. The initiative rests with higher management since, in any "set-up", it is the function of leaders to lead. There can be no excuse for the leader who says, "The more *I* do, the less *they* do." This only shows that he is doing the wrong things.' (C. A. Mace, *op. cit.*) Lastly, it is necessary in attempting such changes to adopt a thoroughly objective and scientific approach. We must work on the hypothesis that all behaviour is caused, that no matter what a man does, he does it for good and sufficient reason. 'When we change the reason for, or the cause of, his behaviour, then, and only then, will his behaviour change.' (Norman Maier.)

There are two fundamental criticisms of this approach, both of which are adequately stated in the following quotation from Sir George Schuster's book *Christianity and Human Relations in Industry*. He writes: 'An idea which runs through much of the contemporary "social science" literature (and which has been propounded most clearly in books by the late Professor Elton Mayo, such as *The Social Problems of an Industrial Society*) is that the main cause of humanity's troubles today is the fact that men's "social skills" have not advanced equally with their scientific and technical skills. It is the emphasis on the word "skill" which alarms me. This is not merely a matter of skill. If, for example, we are to create the right human relations in industry, we need right moral attitudes more fundamentally than intellectual skill. Before studying psychology, we need to study *and accept* the principles of the New Testament. And for these principles there is no question of any need for "advance". They express eternal truths which cannot change. We do, indeed, as I have at all points insisted, need skill (based on hard intellectual effort and scientific study) in working out methods for the application of these principles among all the complexities which we have created for ourselves in modern industrial society; but, unless the exercise of such skill is guided by the principle of Christianity, unless our aims are regulated according to a true scale of values, the skill will not merely be as useless as a "sounding brass or a tinkling cymbal", but can become an instrument of devastating evil. Dostoievski's Grand Inquisitor in *The Brothers Karamazov* shows what this can mean. Hitler and Stalin have given examples of consummate skill in the manipulation of mass psychology.' Sir George then goes on to make the two specific criticisms of current 'social science' literature. Firstly, he says, 'there is the error of claiming for the concepts and generalizations of "social science" – especially those concerning the behaviour of human personalities – a validity of the same nature as can be established in the field of the physical sciences.' Secondly, there is a misconception of what any kind of scientific knowledge can do: 'If man is to take the right course at the present crucial moment in the history of humanity, then it is essential not to be misled by false ideas about what science can do. Science cannot solve man's moral problems. Science cannot explain for him the meaning of his existence. No scientific discovery can give him a scale of values or rules to regulate the dictates of his conscience.'

What these criticisms amount to are the two doubts, (1) whether the social sciences can claim a validity of the same nature as in the case of the physical sciences, and (2) whether knowledge in the field of psychology or sociology may not be misused unless it is based on moral principles such as those taught by the Christian Church.

The first problem is more easily answered than the second. It is based on the so-called 'Free will problem', and may be restated as follows: science, it is said, is based on the validity of the Law of Cause and Effect – but if we accept this law as applying to human behaviour we, by implication, deny the existence of free will, and if free will is a delusion we destroy the whole basis which makes science possible. A psychological theory can no longer be regarded as an expression of truth but simply as the end-result of an inevitable chain of cause and effect in the brain. If, on the other hand, free will *does* exist, psychology is still impossible; for if we all have complete freedom of choice there can be no laws of behaviour to study. This paradox, however, is an unreal one. In the first place, many modern philosophers agree that the free will question is not a problem at all, but merely a pseudo-problem based on the inadequate definition of words. But what is much more important is that the trend of opinion in modern physics is away from the rigidity of the Law of Cause and Effect as originally formulated. In 1927, the German physicist Heisenberg showed that every description of nature contains some essential and irremovable element of uncertainty. The consequences of what has come to be known as the Principle of Uncertainty have been brilliantly analysed by Dr J. Bronowski in his book *The Common Sense of Science*. Bronowski shows that the older concept of inevitable effect has been replaced by that of the probable trend. When, for example, a gas in a container is allowed to escape, most of the molecules composing it rush outwards away from the container. This does not mean to say that individual molecules may not move against the stream – they do – but, statistically speaking, by far the most probable trend is outwards and this fact leads to the observed result. This statistical approach applies equally to the problems of human behaviour in psychology, sociology, or in history. Human behaviour is, says Dr Bronowski, 'neither determined nor random. At any moment, it moves forward into an area whose general shape is known but whose boundaries are uncertain in a calculable way. A society moves under material pressure like a stream of gas, and on the average its individuals obey the pressure; but at any instant, any individual may, like an atom of the gas, be moving across or against the stream. The will on the one hand and the compulsion on the other exist and play within these boundaries.' For example, the technological revolution which brought about the paleotechnic period caused, as we have seen, ideas of the 'just price' and fixed inherited status to dissolve. This revolution was not brought about deliberately by any man, but the creation of new machines brought about a new situation to which he unconsciously proceeded to adapt himself, and soon the idea of the 'just price' began to seem 'wrong' and ideas of the 'market price' and a competitive society began to seem 'right'. There have always been those who protested against the paleotechnic ideology – they were quite free to do so – only no significant number of people listened to them. Their ideas did not fit the new society which had arisen.

The physicist of today, unlike those of the past, has no longer any good reason to regard the social sciences as less scientific than his own. Another of the difficulties of psychological experimentation already noted – that the very fact of observing people's behaviour may influence the results – applies with equal force to the behaviour of electrons. In fact, Dr Bronowski specifically aligns psychology and physics in this respect: 'Examples are often quoted from quantum physics to show that the act of observing itself affects the particles we are looking at, much as a rabbit scurries away from our headlights at night. In the same way, it is hard in the social sciences to take a poll of opinion and frame the question so that it does not bias the replies. And in psychology the method of asking oneself questions has now been shown to be most fallible: you cannot watch your own mind and pretend to yourself that you are not looking.'

Psychology, like all the other sciences, has as its main aim the prediction of future behaviour in the systems observed. That it can never predict in detail is irrelevant, since it is sufficient that we can predict probable trends. This, of course, is constantly being done even by those who are not psychologists. For example, it is assumed that an increase in the bank rate which causes those who wish to borrow money to pay a higher rate of interest will discourage business expansion. Every day we carry out actions which assume that others will respond in a more or less predictable way. The psychologist, then, aims to investigate human behaviour with a view to discovering its underlying causes; for it is only by dealing with causes that we can hope to influence future behaviour when and if this becomes necessary. We can no longer take the attitude that everybody has *complete* freedom to make of his life what he will, that if he does wrong it is entirely his own fault and he deserves to be punished. Thus those who advocate that the increasing number of divorces should be dealt with by 'a tightening up of the divorce laws' completely fail to see that this increase is not due to an increase in immorality, but to such social factors as the economic independence of women, housing shortages, and the disintegrating influence of the industrial revolution on family life which has been referred to elsewhere. It follows, then, that if we wish people to be 'good', we must, in the first place, be very sure that we know what *is* good in any given situation, and, in the second place, we must be sure that their circumstances are such that this form of goodness is possible for more than a small minority. There is nothing unethical or materialistic about this approach, which was, indeed, expressed centuries ago by the Chinese philosopher Mencius in his parable of the trees of the New mountain. These trees, Mencius says, were once beautiful – but, because they were situated on the borders of a large state, they were hewn down. When they again attempted to grow under the influence of rain and sun, the cattle and goats came and browsed on them. 'To these things is owing the bare and stript appearance of the mountain, which when people see, they think it was never finely wooded.' He then goes on to compare the situation of the trees with that of the man in an unfavourable environment and continues: 'The way in which a man loses his proper goodness of mind is like the way in which the trees are denuded by axes and bills. Hewn down day after day, can it – the mind – retain its beauty? But there is a development of its life day and night, and in the calm air of the morning, just between night and day, the mind feels in a degree those desires and aversions which are proper to humanity, but the feeling is not strong, and it is fettered and destroyed by what takes place during the day. This fettering taking place again and again, the restorative influence of the night is not sufficient to preserve the proper goodness of the mind; and when this proves insufficient for this purpose, the nature becomes not much different from that of the irrational animals, which when people see, they think that it never had those powers which I assert. But does this condition represent the feelings proper to humanity?'

The second criticism, that if we are to create the right human relations in industry we need 'right moral attitudes more fundamentally than intellectual skill' and 'need to study and accept the principles of the New Testament' which express 'eternal truths which cannot change' seems, to the present writer, to be based on several misunderstandings. To begin with, although it may be agreed that 'right moral attitudes' are essential, such attitudes cannot be created simply by talking about them – as has already been suggested, we must begin by creating an environment which favours their development. Nor is it so easy to misuse the principles of 'social engineering' as Sir George Schuster seems to imply. That 'social engineering' may be misused is not in doubt. See, for example, Chapter 5 of Robert Jungk's terrifying book *Tomorrow is Already Here.* What is denied is that Machiavellian individuals can pervert to their own ends any reasonably healthy society. So far as industry is concerned, all the methods we have discussed in this book pre-suppose a factory and a society in which worker-management relations have not broken down beyond repair, in which there is some desire, however weak, to co-operate. Industrial democracy as described here does not rely on the 'manipulation of mass psychology' or, indeed, upon any sort of manipulation at all – on the contrary, it relies upon freeing the workers from irrational controls and unnecessary irritations and injuries to their self-respect. It is believed that, when this has been done, the workers will respond by showing an increasing sense of responsibility, a greater interest in their work, and that the good employer will earn their freely-given trust and respect. The incompetent manager, on the other hand, will not be tolerated. Did Hitler, as Sir George Schuster suggests, manipulate the masses to his own end? Or is it not rather the truth, as was suggested elsewhere in this book, that the masses manipulated Hitler? (Here, of course, we have left the field of science and are discussing problems to which neither the writer, Sir George Schuster, nor anyone else knows the answers – they are, at any rate to some extent, matters of opinion.) Suppose, however, that we wished to pervert a group of people utterly by making use of the latest techniques of psychology, would it be easy or possible to do so? We know that the contented industrial group pays no attention to the political agitator, so why should we suppose that any other group could be influenced against its will? The sick group produces a sick leader, the healthy group a good leader. If Hitler had been in England instead of Sir Oswald Mosley would we all have become National Socialists? I do not think so; for a large society can only be perverted when the rot has already destroyed its foundations, and a small group can only remain perverted or spread its perversity widely within the boundaries of a rotten national society.

Sir George Schuster then mentions the principles of the New Testament which, he says we must first study and accept since they 'express eternal truths which cannot change'. But we must first ask ourselves exactly what these principles are, and, secondly, just how he proposes to get people to accept them. To be sure, the words and meaning of the New Testament are abundantly clear to the unprejudiced reader, but when or where in their simple nakedness have they ever been accepted? All history shows that, whether or not there exist eternal principles which cannot change, men have invariably adapted them, often beyond recognition, to the circumstances with which they were confronted. Christian principles were accepted by most people in the Europe of the Middle Ages when heresy often led to torture and death, they were accepted by the slave traders, by the owners of the 'dark satanic mills' who were often deeply religious men, and today they have been accepted by such various individuals and national groups as Salazar's Portugal, Franco's Spain, and Dr Malan's South Africa. Dr Malan, indeed, was once a minister of the Dutch Reformed Church and was, according to his rights, a fervent Christian; but this fact hardly benefited the coloured population of his country. It should not be thought that the writer, in stating these facts, is taking any sort of pleasure in them or criticizing the Christian religion. We may all have our own opinions about the rights or wrongs of Christianity, but these facts are sad things to have to say, and nobody, Christian or otherwise, should be able to extract any satisfaction from the contemplation of the uses to which the sayings of Christ have been put. Yet it is essential to realize that the use of moral exhortation, of whatever nature, will in itself accomplish nothing in the way of bettering society, nor can we appeal to 'eternal truths' which are capable of such widely divergent interpretations. It may be possible to get a man to change his brand of cigarettes or go to see a film or a play by the use of posters and other forms of propaganda, but it is quite another matter to attempt to change his way of life by such means. To say glibly that we must convert Britain once more to Christianity is exactly analogous to the attitude of those tiresome bores who appear to suppose that the present troubles of industry can be cured by articles in the Sunday newspapers which assert that 'we must all pull together' and that we must 'bring back the spirit of Dunkirk'. (With the significant difference that industry, whatever its failings, is still alive, while many of the Churches, if not dead, are very sick indeed.) As we have elsewhere tried to show, the possibilities of change in any given situation are strictly limited, and preaching and propaganda (that is to say, mere talking) can only bring about essentially superficial changes such as are compatible with existing social trends. Thus, at the individual level, the fervent Fascist or Communist may become a fervent Roman Catholic or vice versa, since all these forms of belief, however vast their differences in intellectual content, share a certain similarity of emotional background. All of them are likely to appeal to the individual who, in his basic personality, wishes to have his life regulated by external authority. Similarly, many of us have known Presbyterians who became atheists, but their lack of sense of humour, their rigidity, their narrow-mindedness, their failure to appreciate the aesthetic values of life, remained unchanged. Formerly they had worshipped an intellectual concept named 'God', afterwards they worshipped 'No-God' – that was all. Such changes in outlook may occur without any radical change in the underlying personality traits, and, however impressive they may appear, they are not really difficult to produce. On the other hand, to change a person of totalitarian or authoritarian outlook into a genuine liberal is quite another matter, which cannot be accomplished by preaching alone. In the political or social spheres, too, people are apt to talk as if *anything* were possible – as if we could by appropriate action convert Britain to anarchism, or an absolute monarchy, or a return to 'free-enterprise'. But, of course, this is not so; for at the level of social and technological development this country has reached, such changes are quite impossible. It is the beginning of political wisdom to realize that some changes are entirely outside the bounds of possibility in a given situation, some can be accomplished only by radical alterations in the social structure, and none but a few can be brought about by propaganda alone. For example, the attempt to impose prohibition in the United States was a complete failure – inevitably, since the social tensions which lead to drinking to excess had not been removed, nor had a substitute for alcohol been provided. The Weimar Constitution in pre-Hitler Germany attempted to impose democratic methods upon a people whose whole social structure from the family upwards is authoritarian, and likewise resulted in total failure. In Chapter 2 we noted what happens when social changes which do not fit the existing structure of a society are imposed upon it. Living as we do in a political democracy there is every reason to suppose that it should not be too difficult to alter the social structure of industry in a more democratic direction, but this change requires a great deal more than good intentions to bring it about, although good intentions are a useful beginning. On the other hand, we have noted that certain trends within our society seem to be making such changes inevitable in the long run. Full employment, a more educated and sophisticated people, the increasing political awareness of the workers, the failure of other methods to bring about the desired results, and, above all, changes in the nature of the technical processes used in industry are examples of such trends. However, to attempt to change matters by lecturing to people without doing anything is simply a waste of time. Trying to induce discontented workers to produce more by telling them of the serious economic plight of the country is like the action of a well-meaning teetotaller who hires the Albert Hall and lectures to a host of alcoholics on the evil effects produced by drinking to excess. Of course, nearly all alcoholics know of these evil effects already, and, although drunkards *have* been cured by a lecture, it was certainly not in any socially significant number; for the cure of this, or any other, ill can only be accomplished when the causes which lead to the observed symptoms have been removed, or when (as in the case of the headhunters quoted in Chapter 2) one symptom may be interchanged with another which, although emotionally equivalent, is thought to be more desirable socially. Drunkards, for example, have been cured by the Salvation Army or by the body known as Alcoholics Anonymous simply because these two groups supply an atmosphere which satisfies the same cravings in a more desirable way.

Therefore, although there is every reason to suppose that appropriate methods are capable of increasing both industrial production and the general well-being, such methods cannot be applied without a clear appreciation of what is *not* possible. There are certain changes, such as increasing state control and planning, increasing worker participation, and the increased use of mass-production methods, which we have every reason to suppose will continue to exist, and, in fact, to become more general. Whether or not the older concepts of 'free enterprise', craftsmanship, or paternalism were 'good' or 'bad', the plain fact is that they are not possible to any extent now. 'To insist upon keeping antiquated social institutions in operation when new institutions are necessary will not prevent new situations from coming. It will prevent them from being intelligently designed. They will come through acts of desperation and violence. Unless enough [people] are willing to invest their idealism in the project of remaking our social order into a positive means for utilizing our resources for the common good, it will not be long before there will be no idealism to invest.' (Max Otto: *Science and the Moral Life*.) The more tough-minded critic of the use of social science in industry will have an entirely different view from that of Sir George Schuster. He will say in effect: 'All this stuff about psychology, groups, morale surveys, and workers' attitudes is a sheer waste of time – what we need is more common sense and less theorizing' – and the present writer, for one, finds himself largely in agreement with this point of view.

We *do* need more common sense, and, if we had it, we should not need to talk about psychology, since managers would do the right thing without requiring to justify their actions with theories from books. But, unfortunately, 'common sense' is not so common as these critics suppose, and although even a little more would improve the condition of industry almost beyond recognition the truth is that some managements are almost unbelievably imbecilic. For example, in one factory during a hot summer day many women workers were fainting in the heat of a small workshop with a glass roof, yet all the windows were closed. The medical officer asked the supervisor to have the windows opened, but was told that this could not be done without the permission of the departmental manager, who, however, refused to do anything without the permission of the factory manager. The request went right up to the chairman of the firm, since nobody at any other level would accept the responsibility for carrying out even this simple and necessary action. When, at last, the chairman was asked, his reply was: 'Certainly not – you know these damn women as well as I do – no sooner will the windows be opened than they will want them shut again.' Now, such behaviour may not be general, but it is certainly not very uncommon, and one manager of this type in a few firms may do a vast amount of damage to morale in industry as a whole. There can be little doubt that the major problem in industry today is the problem of suitable leadership. There are far too many petty Hitlers in factories who are not only working off their own mental conflicts on others to the detriment of the psychological health of the community but are psychologically incapable of delegating authority and making industry more democratic. Indeed, one of the main drawbacks of the *laissez-faire* system is that those who rise to the top are not always the best qualified to be there. Bertrand Russell points out in his *Power: a New Social Analysis* that '. . . in a social system in which power is open to all, the posts which confer power will, as a rule, be occupied by men who differ from the average in being exceptionally power loving'.

'But', the tough-minded critic may continue, 'what about all this nonsense you tell us about frustration? Why, when I began work in a factory, we knew what frustration was . . .' and he will go on to tell us about conditions twenty years ago when he started work. How, he will want to know, can people be frustrated in any significant degree when conditions are so much better? This problem has already been discussed, but the error of thinking along such lines is so common that it is worth repeating the fundamental fact that frustration is not an absolute – a man or woman is frustrated for the most part when there is a gulf between what they have and what they have come to believe they are entitled to. Paradoxically, the degree of discontent is in inverse proportion to the distance of the goal desired, so that, the more attainable the goal appears to be, the greater is the discontent at not attaining it. In that brilliant little book *The True Believer*, Eric Hoffer writes: 'Misery does not automatically generate discontent, nor is the intensity of discontent directly proportionate to the degree of misery. Discontent is likely to be highest when misery is bearable; when conditions have so improved that an ideal state seems almost within reach.' The very poor and the utterly oppressed are not frustrated – they accept their condition and rationalize it, as we have already noted in the quotation from Nigel Balchin at the beginning of this chapter. Alexis de Tocqueville in his study of France before the revolution of 1789 noted that the condition of the common people had never improved more rapidly than in the twenty years before the revolution and yet 'the French found their position the more intolerable the better it became'. Clearly, we must accept the fact that what satisfied workers twenty years ago is far from satisfying them now, and that this is just as it should be. On the other hand, no small part of modern discontent with existing conditions has been indirectly created by the leaders of industry themselves who by modern advertising methods have striven to create the feeling that all sorts of superfluities and unnecessary gadgets are necessities of life. '. . . our culture uses numerous methods like high-pressure advertising and instalment buying to whet the human appetite for more goods and satisfactions, that is, for a higher standard of living. But it is much easier to create wants than to supply the means of satisfying them. To widen the gap between what people want and what they actually have or can reasonably expect to have is to make for widespread discontent and nervousness.' (Ogburn and Nimkoff: *A Handbook of Sociology*.) The factory manager who relies on spoon-fed welfare, and then complains that his employees are always asking for more amusements, services, and goods, forgets that this is, in effect, precisely what he has asked them to do. No matter what he says, his deeds tell the workers: 'Conditions must improve in this factory, but they must improve along the lines I have laid down – you cannot have more freedom to talk, more freedom to express your views, or more participation in the running of the firm, but you *can* have more money, more goods, and more services.' Under such circumstances, his employees have no choice but to press for the only type of 'progress' they are allowed to consider. This is a further example of the self-fulfilling prophecy.

When we come to the actual process of changing the 'bad' factory into a 'good' one, the questions of social structure and culture discussed in Chapter 2 become relevant. Unless the changes projected are quite superficial ones which will leave the actual social structure substantially unchanged, it is necessary to treat the factory as an integrated structure with all its parts interrelated. That is to say, it may be compared to a jig-saw puzzle composed of interlinked parts in which one part cannot be replaced by another without risking the disintegration of the whole structure. For example, consider the case already given of a factory with a strongly authoritarian management which wishes to improve the techniques of its supervisors and to this end sends them to a supervisors' course which teaches them (as most of such courses do) along the lines of T.W.I. to make use of a more democratic approach. When the supervisors return, they discover that what they have been taught cannot be applied in the situation in which they find themselves, with the result that they become disillusioned and their morale, so far from being improved, is likely to become worse. Or, to take an example from Dr May Smith's *Introduction to Industrial Psychology*, imagine what will happen to two factories, one in charge of a blustering egoist and the other of a 'persuasive man who knows what he wants and draws out the best work that the people can do', if their managers are changed around. Both will, in all probability, have the greatest difficulty in adjusting to their changed circumstances. 'In the first factory, as soon as discipline is relaxed there will be slacking, unpunctuality, slipshod work; in the latter there will be opposition, active or sullen.' The reason for this is, of course, that each factory had made suitable adjustments to enable it to deal with the type of manager it possessed, and when the managers were changed round this adaptation broke down, resulting in greater or less disintegration of the social system in each firm. One of the commonest examples of this failure to treat the factory as a social unit built up of interrelated parts is seen when an authoritarian firm attempts, perhaps under pressure from the government, to introduce Joint Consultation. To begin with, the workers are asked to elect their representatives, and, of course, nothing happens. The workers, having been given no responsibility in the past, show none when the opportunity is offered them. So the management, secretly pleased that their belief in the irresponsibility of the workers has been thus confirmed, proceed to nominate members for the council. But the council that has been formed in this way shows no trace of 'joint consultation' – nothing is discussed and the workers' representatives do little but produce minor and relatively safe grumbles of the sort already mentioned elsewhere. Joint Consultation can only work in an atmosphere of mutual trust – or, at least, in a situation in which management intentions are not entirely suspect. It follows, then, that the piecemeal approach to social change in industry does not work unless the factory situation as regards morale is reasonably good already.

There are two other methods of bringing about social change. Either one studies the organization from the standpoint of structure and attempts to change the structure in such a way as to improve communications and bring about co-operation between the various groupings within it, or one deals directly with the attitudes and intentions of the individuals and groups within the organization. As Gordon Rattray Taylor points out, one of the difficulties of the first approach (i.e., altering the structure of the firm) is that in many cases the real trouble lies with those in power. Unless these are got rid of, clearly little can be accomplished. For example, a firm with a bullying managing director, a man with inferiority feelings who has to work out his conflicts on his subordinates, can never be materially changed unless the managing director is removed, and this may be difficult or even impossible. Since the saying of Ecclesiasticus that 'as the judge of the people is himself, so are his officers: and what manner of man the ruler of a city is, such are they that dwell within', is substantially true, we are often presented with an almost insoluble problem. Of course, the fact that management have called in industrial consultants in the first place argues that their intentions are reasonably good, but, unfortunately, management, like the parents who take their child to a child-guidance clinic, are not always prepared to find that they themselves will be expected to accept a large share of the blame for bringing the undesirable situation about.

The second method of bringing about social change is to deal directly with the attitudes and intentions of those involved. While the first method has been most popular in America, where the tendency is to prefer a sociological approach, this second method has been utilized by some firms in Britain. Consultants with special training in psycho-analytic methods have, in effect, attempted to 'psycho-analyse' a whole factory in the course of group discussions. The reader will find this very elaborate and delicate technique discussed in a book by Elliot Jacques entitled *The Changing Culture of a Factory*. Dr Jacques, as a member of the Tavistock Institute of Human Relations, has, with Dr A. T. M. Wilson, carried out a great deal of work in this field, and his book describes his investigation of the Glacier Metal Company, a London engineering firm. This method, as we have indicated, requires great skill, and it seems likely that, as in the case of individual psycho-analysis, its main value will be in the field of research. Certainly it seems probable that the time and money involved will place it out of reach of more than a very few firms.

It has to be understood that any radical social change is bound to be difficult and almost always leads to resentment on the part of some members of the community. It is therefore foolish to expect sudden improvements and wise to expect that, for a time at least, things may even be worse than before. The new Joint Consultation Committee has to learn by painful experience a sense of social responsibility, the workers from an authoritarian factory may be perplexed and troubled when placed in a democratic one. They may misuse their new freedom to work off their old-standing resentments, and they may very well dislike the new responsibility which has been thrust upon them. Having no responsibilities has its satisfactions and people have to learn that democracy not only gives rights but also imposes obligations. Dr Erich Fromm has drawn attention to the 'fear of freedom' which causes many individuals to be drawn towards a totalitarian type of society; for democracy implies hard work. But there can be no doubt that, under existing conditions, industrial democracy is becoming a necessity. One of the difficulties in bringing about change in any society is the existence of 'vested interests' – although these are not necessarily of the economic type to which the term is usually applied. Clearly, any social change usually implies a change in the distribution of power, and the dispossessed are likely to feel resentful at their loss of authority. Thus when the management of a firm is changed, those who were important under the old régime may no longer be so in the new and hurt feelings and anger usually result. Even the factory with a tense and uncomfortable atmosphere has given satisfaction and power to some who will lose their authority when changes occur, and, of course, these changes in the balance of power are felt right down the line. Social change is, therefore, difficult, and never entirely popular at all levels.

It is in such matters as these that the large concern can, and does, do a great deal for industry as a whole. Many of these concerns, as we have seen, have made use of their secure position, goodwill, and money, to carry out research into the problems with which we have been concerned here. Group techniques are being worked out, welfare schemes (in both senses of the word) tried out, and new methods of selecting and training management and supervisors are utilized. In this way, pressure may be exerted on other firms to follow their lead; for, sooner or later, it will be discovered that the old methods are inefficient and that workers will not choose to work in firms which allow no participation and rely on ineffectual or authoritarian leadership. (It is only fair to say that many of the best firms in this country are quite small and yet have taken the lead in applying modern concepts of group organization.) But it seems likely that a considerable time will be required before the methods suggested here become generally applied in a majority of firms.

The large concerns, too, are in many cases dealing with the problem of over-centralization which is their main defect from the human point of view. Lewis Mumford has shown in his book *The Culture of Cities* that there is no longer any technical reason why huge factories should be located in limited areas close to the sources of coal, iron, or water-power. 'Under modern conditions an electric power plant may perhaps be gigantic in order to increase the operating efficiency or take advantage of a big head of water: but by means of long distance inter-connecting transmission systems or grids, the power itself may be produced in many centres and made available over a wide area, with a balanced load and little idle plant. No longer is the river, the coal bed, or the railroad line the sole effective power area. In other words, power production no longer demands local concentration, either within the plant or within the manufacturing area.' This fact has been understood by many large concerns in America and Britain which have utilized the principle described by Drucker as 'federalism' according to which, while the whole concern has a unified management in charge of basic functions, each unit firm is a business by itself with its own management which deals with all immediate and short-term local matters. There is some evidence, according to Gordon Rattray Taylor, that factories of 500 to 600 workers are about the optimum size, and, in this country, Unilever Ltd runs a large number of factories of about this size according to the federal principle. In the case of Unilever, which produces many products of a widely varied nature, the problem was relatively simple, but the Standard Oil Company of New Jersey, in which the difficulties would *a priori* seem to be far greater, has dealt with them by dividing the units up in terms of stages of production; exploration, crude oil production, refining, and sale – all the processes in the production of petroleum products – are carried out by separate units. As we have seen, it is most important that each unit should be small enough for the employee to be able to identify his own management and to be able to feel that he has the possibility of personal contact with the body which controls his fate, and this is an almost impossible condition in the very large firm. Although we are not here concerned with economics, it is worth while pointing out that the belief that size and efficiency are closely related, that small industrial units are necessarily inefficient, is incorrect. Colin Clark, in his *Conditions of Economic Progress*, has shown that there is no positive correlation between the size of firm and net output per worker, and that in certain industries large firms are technically more efficient than small while in others the reverse is the case.

But the changes suggested here go far beyond problems of industrial efficiency and production, since the social function of industry is no less important than its technical efficiency. Dr J. Koebakker of Holland, reporting on the findings of twenty-five groups throughout the world which had discussed industrial relations, had this to say at a Conference on Mental Hygiene in 1948: 'The industrial worker living in a democratic society where he has a responsible rôle in groups outside industry gets embarrassed about the situation in his plant where he has hardly any responsible rôle in the organization. Most students of the democracies complain of the poor sense of responsibility of the common man in his work, of his political apathy and the opiate nature of his leisure activities. The easiest way to initiate changes would be to give him an experience of democracy in his work, in that part of his life in which he spends half of his active hours.'

A genuine industrial democracy can only be based on the intelligent co-operation of primary working groups with responsibly-minded managements. It has nothing whatever in common with the propaganda, 'shock battalions', and pseudo-military formations of totalitarian states. But in order to bring about such a democracy it is not enough merely to put into practice the findings of the industrial psychologist with which we have been concerned in this book. It is necessary for the politician to bring about a state of affairs in which it is possible for the industrial worker to feel that his own interests and those of management coincide. How this should be done is not the concern of psychologists as such, but it is surely evident that no amount of enlightened management can satisfy the worker if he feels that the social system of which he is a member is in some respects unfair. The converse, of course, is also true – that no amount of political action can compensate for tyrannical, stupid, or incompetent management.

Paradoxically, while the large privately-owned concerns have in many cases concerned themselves with the problem of decentralization, the new nationalized industries seem to be tending towards greater centralization. Whatever may be said in favour of nationalization – and no doubt much may be said in its favour – the Labour Party appears to have a quite unjustified faith in its ability to solve the human problems of the worker. It is one thing to suppose, as one reasonably may, that in certain respects and in certain industries technical efficiency may be increased by such steps, or to believe that, for example, the nationalization of the coal industry removed certain barriers to co-operation on the part of the miners who disliked the old system and were glad to see it go, but it is quite another to suppose that this action, in itself, is capable of solving any of the problems discussed in this book. Ernest Watkins, whose book *The Cautious Revolution* is a sympathetic account of the work of the Labour Government during its last term of office, quoted the opinion of a miner on nationalization which there is every reason to suppose is an expression of a fairly general attitude: 'National Coal Board,' the miner says, and spits. 'The old faces at the top of a new suit of clothes. I am not taken in so easily as that, man.' F. Zweig in his *Men in the Pits* has a similar tale to tell: '"Before, we knew where we stood," a Derbyshire man told me. "When we had a grievance the manager could settle it in five minutes, if not on his own responsibility, after a short consultation on the telephone with the agent. Now we cannot settle anything with the manager. When we come to the manager, he always shifts everything on to the back of the N.C.B. 'I can't do anything without the N.C.B.,' he says. But we don't know the N.C.B."' There is no space here to discuss this problem, nor is the writer qualified to do so, but the reader will find a very full discussion in Hugh Clegg's *Industrial Democracy and Nationalization* and *Labour Relations in London Transport*. Mr Clegg comes to the conclusion that the public corporation has not, so far, achieved relations with its staff which are any improvement on those under good employers in other industries. This is not, of course, a criticism of nationalization as such, but it does indicate that the nationalized industry has to face psychological problems which in no essentials differ from those of the privately-owned firm.

A final problem which is of fundamental importance to good relations in industry is the attitude of the trade unions to the type of management policy described in this book. Many managers or industrial psychologists with progressive ideas have been surprised, perplexed, and finally resentful when they discover that the unions are not necessarily pleased when such policies are put into effect. For example, Gordon Rattray Taylor complains that the unions have a vested interest in maintaining a manager-worker conflict, because it is their function to organize such conflict. 'Thus,' he writes in his book *Are Workers Human?*, 'they [the unions] have urged progressive managements to join management organizations, even when this meant reducing the wages paid to their employees to conform with the organization's code, in order that they could negotiate with them more easily. They are opposed to managements who improve the situation of their employees freely, since they wish to represent all such improvements as due to their efforts, and seek in this way to prevent desirable changes until they can be won in conflict.' Mr Taylor goes so far as to suggest that in an industry run according to the principles described here there would be no function for the unions as they now exist (though they might, as in Russia, evolve into welfare organizations). This attitude seems, to the present writer, to be a most dangerous one. It is, of course, true that the trade unions, like all organizations, are not as good as they might be and have many serious defects. Many problems exist concerning the changing functions and status of the trade union in modern society, and these have been discussed by Professor Laski in his book *Trade Unions in the New Society* and elsewhere. But the student of human relations in industry who has directed his attention mainly to the study of small face-to-face groups in single industrial units, tends, precisely because of this, to neglect the importance of power relations within the state and, in particular, within industry. As Hugh Clegg has said, he tends to stress the importance of common endeavour to the exclusion of the need for independent checks to power. Democracy at the level of the national state is quite a different matter from the unity of the small informal group, and democracy as understood on this side of the Iron Curtain must always be based on the existence of an effective opposition. Progressive labour relations can only be created by managements which accept and are prepared to come to terms with trade unionism, for, as Mr Clegg rightly stresses, although without such a relationship between management and the unions it is possible to achieve a benevolent paternalism (or even a genuine democracy in miniature) under which the happiness and welfare of the workers is adequately cared for, there is in such a state of affairs no independent barrier against degeneration into autocracy. 'The more autocratic the employer, and the larger the group we consider, the more necessary it is to stress the element of opposition in democracy.' In the existing state of society there can be no doubt that industrial democracy cannot be brought about without fruitful conflict based on mutual acceptance between both sides of industry. For his part, the industrial psychologist has to learn that his own technique is not a cure-all and that it is dangerous to generalize from the behaviour of the small social grouping or the individual to that of the larger social aggregates. The problem of improving industrial conditions does not lie within the purview of any one type of specialist.

When the Middle Ages came to an end there was a long period of serious social disintegration when the old concepts no longer fitted the changing structure of society, but ultimately this was succeeded by the Renaissance when the new concepts of what we have described as the paleotechnic era were gaining general acceptance. There can be little doubt that we are now passing through a similar stage of disintegration as paleotechnic technology gives way to neotechnic. But, as we have seen, a new technological basis of society demands a new type of individual and a new type of social organization to work it. Exactly what this new individual and new social organization will be like we can only guess – but one thing is certain – that there can be no turning back. 'We are', writes Dr Rollo May in his book *Man's Search For Himself*, 'the generation which cannot turn back. We in the middle of the twentieth century are like pilots in the transatlantic flight who have passed the point of no return, who do not have fuel enough to go back but must push on regardless of storms or other dangers.' The ideology of the eotechnic period was a perfectly valid one for eotechnic society as was the theory of individual enterprise and *laissez-faire* for the paleotechnic; but neither of these is valid now and we must build our new society on other assumptions of man and his nature. In this book we have tried to suggest what some of these assumptions appear to be and for further information the reader must be referred to the short list of works in the Bibliography. Whether or not this reorganization of society will involve the end of 'Capitalism' depends, of course, upon how the word capitalism is defined – and here Sir George Schuster has some most interesting points to make in the book which we have elsewhere found reason to criticize. J. M. Keynes once defined capitalism as 'the astonishing belief that the nastiest motives of the nastiest men somehow or other work for the best results in the best of all possible worlds', and in this sense, at least, capitalism is dead, for the individual's striving for his own gain, without an equal emphasis on the welfare of others, no longer automatically brings good to the community. Reorganization must include, not only the field of industry, but every aspect of human life including that of religion, because as the great Catholic writer Charles Péguy has said: 'The Church will not reopen the door of the work-room and she will not be open once more to the people, unless she too, like the rest of the world, pays the price of an economic revolution. Such is, eternally, temporally, the mysterious subjection of the eternal itself to the temporal. Economic expenses, social expenses, industrial expenses, temporal expenses must be met. Nothing can evade it, not even the eternal, not even the spiritual, not even the inner life.'

It is wrong to say that moral standards are absolute and do not change – on the contrary, as we have seen, they are constantly changing. Certainly there are a few basic rules which are

305

'absolute' in the sense that they are tied up inevitably with the nature of society; for example, 'Love thy neighbour as thyself' is a basic rule precisely because society, by definition, is a state of affairs in which people are neighbourly (or are, for the most part, neighbourly). Outside such rules, however, standards can and must change, or, to put the matter in another way, loving your neighbour is an unconditional law which must be variously interpreted as the social context changes. *Laissez-faire* methods may well have been in the best interests of society as a whole in a developing economy, but they are neither good nor possible in the present circumstances when we have the choice between one world or none. The sex morality which is 'right' for one stage of development is not necessarily 'right' for another, and so on. In fact, this was precisely the meaning of the teaching of Jesus when he shifted the emphasis from the *external* rules of the Ten Commandments to *inward* motives. 'The ethical issues of life (Jesus), held, are not simply "thou shall not kill", but rather are inward attitudes towards other persons – anger, resentment, exploitative "lust in the heart", "railings", "jealousies", and so on. The wholeness of the man whose external actions are at one with his inner motives is what is meant by the expression in the beatitudes, the "pure in heart".' (Rollo May: *Man's Search for Himself.*) *Laissez-faire* economics are often confused with the concept of 'freedom' – another concept whose meaning is constantly changing, as it inevitably must. But freedom is not anarchy, because, just as competition can only rest and be parasitic upon a basic state of co-operation, so freedom cannot exist except in an ordered society against the background of which people are allowed to be, in certain sectors of behaviour, free. Twenty years ago I could have driven my car round Trafalgar Square and down any street I pleased. Now I cannot, because some of these streets are one-way only. Does this limit my freedom of self-expression? In a sense, of course, it does, but only in an abstract sense that is hardly worth considering; for if, with the present amount of traffic on the roads, everyone were free to behave as he might have done twenty years ago, there would be no freedom but complete chaos.

Of course, the words 'free enterprise' as used today are

merely a parrot-cry, because no such state of affairs exists to any significant extent in industrialized communities. With the exception of a few small shop-keepers, authors, and professional people who run their own businesses, 'free enterprise' came to an end many years ago, not because of the machinations of wicked socialists, but because businessmen could not tolerate the strain of unrestricted competition. Whatever else our new society becomes, it will not be based on free enterprise. It may be Communist, Fascist, or a Social Democracy, but it will not be anarchist, feudal, or (in the political sense) Liberal, since, for reasons already discussed, many theoretically possible choices are not open to us. It is up to us to decide whether the neotechnic phase develops within a framework of fascist barbarism, communist intolerance, or social democratic humanitarianism, whether government will be centralized or partially decentralized, bureaucratic or imaginative, and whether the people shall be civilized or uncivilized. The bricks and mortar of the new structure are already supplied and we cannot change them. But what sort of building we erect depends entirely upon ourselves.

BIBLIOGRAPHY

Of the works quoted in the text, the following are suggested for further reading:

HISTORICAL AND GENERAL

Religion and the Rise of Capitalism by R. H. Tawney. Pelican Books.

Religion and the Decline of Capitalism by V. A. Demant. Faber.

Technics and Civilization by Lewis Mumford. Secker and Warburg.

The Condition of Man by Lewis Mumford. Secker and Warburg.

The Human Problems of an Industrial Civilization by Elton Mayo. Macmillan.

The Social Problems of an Industrial Civilization by Elton Mayo. Routledge and Kegan Paul.

PSYCHOLOGICAL

Psychology and the Social Pattern by Julian Blackburn. Routledge and Kegan Paul.

Social Psychology by W. J. H. Sprott. Methuen.

Mirror for Man by Clyde Kluckhohn. Harrap.

INDUSTRIAL PSYCHOLOGY

An Introduction to Industrial Psychology by May Smith. Cassell.

Psychology in Industry by Norman Maier. Harrap.

Human Relations in Modern Industry by R. F. Tredgold. Duckworth.

INDEX

309

MORE ABOUT PENGUINS
AND PELICANS

Penguinews, which appears every month, contains details of all the new books issued by Penguins as they are published. From time to time it is supplemented by *Penguins in Print*, which is a complete list of all titles available. (There are some five thousand of these.)

A specimen copy of *Penguinews* will be sent to you free on request. For a year's issues (including the complete lists) please send 50p if you live in the British Isles, or 75p if you live elsewhere. Just write to Dept EP, Penguin Books Ltd, Harmondsworth, Middlesex, enclosing a cheque or postal order, and your name will be added to the mailing list.

In the U.S.A.: For a complete list of books available from Penguin in the United States write to Dept CS, Penguin Books Inc., 7110 Ambassador Road, Baltimore, Maryland 21207.

In Canada: For a complete list of books available from Penguin in Canada write to Penguin Books Canada Ltd, 41 Steelcase Road West, Markham, Ontario.

CONSUMER'S GUIDE TO THE BRITISH SOCIAL SERVICES

Phyllis Willmott

SECOND EDITION

Almost everyone has need of advice or help from a trustworthy source at some time. The social services exist to give us this aid: yet even experienced social workers get lost in the maze of complexities they present. The bewildering state of flux in the services calls for a realistic and up-to-date guide.

Phyllis Willmott, a writer and consultant on the social services, has prepared this comprehensive guide from the 'consumer's' point of view. Her book offers a practical directory, with explicit information about eligibility and difficulties likely to be encountered, to all government services open to the aged, the mentally sick, the delinquent, the widowed, the disabled ... the list could continue. Equally useful are the details about voluntary services she describes, for those needing all kinds of help – whether on homosexuality, alcoholism or muscular dystrophy.

For the public at large, as well as for doctors, teachers, clergymen and social workers, this guide has proved invaluable. In this fully revised edition, it not only gives a clear account of the services as they are now, but it foreshadows, with authority, many of the changes which are likely to be made in the near future.

'To all of us ... Mrs Willmott's book can be highly commended' – *The Times Literary Supplement*

A DICTIONARY OF PSYCHOLOGY

James Drever

The technical vocabulary of psychology is not in itself an unduly large one, but several other sciences border upon the psychological field and some knowledge of their terms is also necessary. The stimuli which act upon our sense organs are described in physical terms: what happens in the nervous system is relevant and has to be expressed in physiological terms; abnormal behaviour and the clinical description of it and its causes require medical terms. Thus the technical vocabulary actually used by psychologists tends to be rather extensive.

It is the aim of this dictionary to give some help, not merely to the layman, but also to the student, in what has now become an important branch of contemporary science.

'It is commended with confidence as a document relevant not merely to the experimental psychology of former days, but to recent developments in psychometrics, social psychology, psychopathology, and industrial psychology' – *Higher Education Journal*

MAN AND ENVIRONMENT

Crisis and the Strategy of Choice

Robert Arvill

What will the world look and be like tomorrow? Must the land-scape be an extension of today's? More air fouled by noise and poisonous fumes; more water polluted by chemicals and oil slicks; more land crushed under a sprawl of towns, motorways, airports, factories, pylons, opencast mines? Is man bound to build a steel-and-concrete hell for himself? Or can effective steps be taken now to preserve some of our countryside and sea-shore from technolog-ical clutter?

Man and Environment is the work of an expert who has had ex-perience both of planning and of nature conservation at the local, governmental and international levels. With special reference to Britain, where all problems are aggravated by the density of popula-tion, he outlines the policies and measures adopted by the official and voluntary bodies working in the field. And to ensure, at any rate for our children, healthy land, clean air, pure water, and adequate space, the book proposes a strategy and a set of standards to enable man to shape his environment according to a worthwhile design.

THE INTEGRITY OF THE PERSONALITY

Anthony Storr

'Self-realization is not an anti-social principle; it is firmly based on the fact that men need each other in order to be themselves.'

With this axiom of psychology Anthony Storr, at the outset of an excellent and simple study of human personality, counters the fear expressed by Bertrand Russell and others that analytical psychotherapy may tend to produce an anarchical race of Byrons or Hitlers.

Tolerant and impartial in tone, his book stands securely on the ground that is common to Freudian, Jungian, and other schools of psychology. Maintaining that many roads lead to self-realization, he discusses in successive chapters the mental mazes of identification, introjection, projection, and dissociation, through which the individual, sooner or later, must find his way on the path to maturity.

'The book is well-written, concise and clear, and is cordially recommended' – *Mental Health*

'He deals frankly, in comprehensible terms, with the hypotheses the therapist uses in treatment' – *British Medical Journal*

'His emphasis on the beliefs shared rather than the areas of controversy is right for a book intended for the lay public' – *Lancet*

THE PSYCHOLOGY OF THINKING

Robert Thomson

Ever since Aristotle defined man as a 'rational animal' psychologists have attempted to show how it is that men have a capacity, for thinking about themselves and their environment, which other animals have not managed to achieve. In recent years an increased interest has been shown by psychologists in the problem of describing and explaining the nature of thought. Indeed, one distinguished psychologist has said that the central problem for psychology today is the problem of thought. Not only does this book report some of the recent studies on thinking: it also attempts to evaluate the achievements and limitations of the work which has been carried out. It serves also as a general introduction to several branches of psychological inquiry: it discusses such varied topics as the intelligent behaviour of animals; the formation of a repertory of basic concepts by children; the direct experimental investigation of adult thought processes; the role of learning operations; and imaginative thinking in aesthetic and scientific work.

TECHNIQUES OF PERSUASION

J. A. C. Brown

Attempts to change the opinions of others are as old as human speech, but in recent years we have come to fear that our thoughts and feelings are open to manipulation by new methods and hidden techniques. To the pressures of the 'admen' are added a whole battery of *hsi nao* (literally 'wash brain') techniques.

Here is a timely and much needed survey of the whole area of persuasion. Dr Brown, the author of *Freud and the Post-Freudians*, ranges from political propaganda, religious conversion, and commercial advertising, through a detailed appraisal of the intentions and effects of the mass media, to a cool look at the spectacular case-histories of indoctrination and confession.

But *Techniques of Persuasion* is more than the only available review of the phenomena of persuasion: it also contains a lucid analysis of the concept of personality itself. Only if we understand first the development of the central personality can we understand and judge realistically the importance of attempts to change it.

FREUD AND THE POST-FREUDIANS

J. A. C. Brown

Freud and the Post-Freudians explains the main concepts of Freudian psychology and goes on to review the theories of Adler, Jung, Rank, and Stekel. Later developments in the orthodox Freudian school are also discussed, as are those of the American Neo-Freudians and Post-Freudians in England.

This is the first book published in Britain to bring together all these psychological and sociological schools and criticize them, both from the Freudian standpoint and that of the scientific psychologists.

SENSE AND NONSENSE IN PSYCHOLOGY

H. J. Eysenck

There are many topics in modern psychology about which speculation has been rife for hundreds of years. Much has been written (and some of it amusing) on the powers and dangers of the hypnotic trance, the wonders of telepathy and clairvoyance, the possibility of the interpretation of dreams, the nature and assessment of personality, and the psychology of beauty. In recent years, however, much experimental evidence has been collected regarding all these topics, and the author has attempted to give a reliable account of it in this book, frankly acknowledging ignorance where the facts are still in dispute, and boldly putting forward a definite point of view where the evidence appears to justify it. Throughout the book emphasis is laid particularly on the detailed discussion of the facts, leaving to the reader the decision as to whether the conclusions drawn are justified.

Also available:

USES AND ABUSES OF PSYCHOLOGY

KNOW YOUR OWN I.Q.

CHECK YOUR OWN I.Q.

FACT AND FICTION IN PSYCHOLOGY